INDIGENOUS KNOWLEDGES IN GLOBAL CONTEXʟᵤ.
MULTIPLE READINGS OF OUR WORLD

Edited by George J. Sefa Dei, Budd L. Hall, and Dorothy Goldin Rosenberg

Indigenous knowledges are understood as the commonsense ideas and cultural knowledges of local peoples concerning the everyday realities of living. They encompass the cultural traditions, values, belief systems, and world views that, in any indigenous society, are imparted to the younger generation by community elders. They also refer to world views that are products of a direct experience of nature and its relationship with the social world.

Bringing new and complex readings to the term 'indigenous,' this collection of essays from contributors from Canada and around the world discusses indigenous knowledges and their implication for academic decolonization. The book is divided into four sections: Situating Indigenous Knowledges: Definitions and Boundaries; Indigenous Knowledges: Resistance and Advocacy; Indigenous Knowledges and the Academy; and Indigenous Knowledges and Transforming Practices. Collectively the essays situate indigenous knowledges in relation to conventional knowledges, validate the existence of multiple sources of knowledge, and examine the varying strategies, projects, and theories that are currently being developed in support of indigenous knowledges.

The book draws attention to some of the nuances, contradictions, and contestations in affirming the place of indigenous knowledges in the academy, while maintaining that different bodies of knowledge continually influence each other.

George J. Sefa Dei is Professor, Department of Sociology in Education, Ontario Institute for Studies in Education/University of Toronto (OISE/UT).

Budd L. Hall is Professor, Department of Sociology in Education, OISE/UT.

Dorothy Goldin Rosenberg is Professor, Department of Sociology in Education, OISE/UT.

Indigenous Knowledges in Global Contexts

Multiple Readings of Our World

Edited by George J. Sefa Dei, Budd L. Hall,
and Dorothy Goldin Rosenberg

An OISE/UT book
published in association with
University of Toronto Press
Toronto Buffalo London

© University of Toronto Press Incorporated 2000
Toronto Buffalo London
Printed in Canada

ISBN 0-8020-4200-7 (cloth)
ISBN 0-8020-8059-6 (paper)

Printed on acid-free paper

Canadian Cataloguing in Publication Data

Main entry under title:

Indigenous knowledges in global contexts: multiple readings of our world

Includes bibliographical references.
ISBN 0-8020-4200-7 (bound.)
ISBN 0-8020-8059-6 (pbk.)

1. Ethnoscience.   I. Dei, George Jerry Sefa, 1954–   .   II. Hall,
Budd L.   III. Rosenberg, Dorothy Goldin.

GN476.I524 2000   306.4′2   C00-930345-6

University of Toronto Press acknowledges the financial assistance to its publishing program of the Canada Council for the Arts and the Ontario Arts Council.

University of Toronto Press acknowledges the financial support for its publishing
activities of the Government of Canada through the Book Publishing Industry
Development Program (BPIDP).

Contents

Foreword: Cultural Diversity and the Politics of Knowledge

DR VANDANA SHIVA

Colonialism has from the very beginning been a contest over the mind and the intellect. What will count as knowledge? And who will count as expert or as innovator? Such questions have been central to the project of colonizing diverse cultures and their knowledge systems. Indigenous knowledges have been systematically usurped and then destroyed in their own cultures by the colonizing West.

Diversity and pluralism are a characteristic of non-Western societies. We have a rich biodiversity of plants for food and medicine. Agricultural diversity and the diversity of medicinal plants have in turn given rise to a rich plurality of knowledge systems in agriculture and medicine.

However, under the colonial influence the biological and intellectual heritage of non-Western societies was devalued. The priorities of scientific development and R&D efforts, guided by a Western bias, transformed the plurality of knowledge systems into an *hierarchy* of knowledge systems. When knowledge plurality mutated into knowledge hierarchy, the horizontal ordering of diverse but equally valid systems was converted into a *vertical* ordering of *unequal* systems, and the epistemological foundations of Western knowledge were imposed on non-Western knowledge systems with the result that the latter were invalidated.

Western systems of knowledge in agriculture and medicine were defined as the *only* scientific systems. Indigenous systems of knowledge were defined as inferior, and in fact as unscientific. Thus, instead of strengthening research on safe and sustainable plant-based pesticides such as neem and pongamia, we focused exclusively on the development and promotion of hazardous and nonsustainable chemical pesticides such as DDT and Sevin. The use of DDT causes millions of deaths each year and has increased the occurrence of pests 12,000 fold. The manufacture of Sevin at the Union Carbide plant in Bhopal led to a disaster that killed thousands and that has disabled more than 400,000 people.

It is now recognized that the use of chemicals to control pests has been an ecological calamity, and as a result the use of plant-based pesticides is becoming popular in the industrialized world. Corporations that long promoted the use of chemicals are now looking for biological options. In their efforts to develop new markets and to control the production of biopesticides, transnational corporations (TNCs) such as W.R. Grace are claiming international patent rights on neem-based pesticides.

Research in the field of drugs and medicines has taken an identical path. Indigenous systems of medicine and the properties of medicinal plants were totally neglected in Western scientific research and health policy, which focused exclusively on the Western allopathic system and on 'exporting' technology from the Western pharmaceutical industry. Thus health and pharmaceutical budgets in the Third World were heavily weighted in favour of developing and disseminating the Western allopathic system. Indigenous medical systems have long been officially neglected in India, yet that nation's various systems of 'folk medicine' are based on over 7,000 species of medicinal plants and 15,000 herbal formulations. The Ayurvedic texts refer to 1,400 plants, Unani texts to 342, and the Siddha system to 328. Western homeopathy uses 570 plants, of which approximately 100 are native to India. The economic value of medicinal plants to 100 million rural Indian households is immeasurable.

Meantime, the Western public is growing increasingly aware of the side effects of hazardous drugs, and of the rise of strains resistant to antibiotics; and as a result, the Western pharmaceuticals industry is turning more and more to the plant-based systems of Indian and Chinese medicine. Drugs derived from indigenous medicinal systems are now being patented at an exponential rate. The current value of the world market for medicines derived from indigenous and local knowledges is estimated to be $43 billion. The use of traditional knowledge has increased the efficiency of screening plants for medical properties by more than 400 per cent.

It is now generally recognized that the chemical route to strengthening agriculture and health care has failed, and must be abandoned. This provides us with an opportunity to re-evaluate indigenous knowledge systems and to move away from the false hierarchy of knowledge systems back toward a plurality. The pluralistic approach to knowledge systems requires us to respect different such systems – to embrace their own logic and their own epistemological foundations. It also requires us to accept that *one* system (i.e., the Western system) need not and must not serve as the scientific benchmark for all systems, and that diverse systems need not be reduced to the language and logic of Western knowledge systems. The integrity of our biological intellectual heritage can be protected only after we embrace the pluralistic perspective. A hierarchical perspective will continue to project the Western paradigm as scientifically superior in spite of its now proven failure to keep people healthy and to safeguard their food supplies. As well, the assumption that a hierarchy exists, and *should* exist, is the underlying basis for legitimizing piracy as invention.

The phenomena of 'biopiracy' and 'intellectual piracy,' whereby Western commercial interests claim products and innovations derived from indigenous traditions as their 'intellectual property' (through protections such as patents), have emerged because indigenous knowledge systems have been devalued and (it follows) have not been afforded protection. This lack of protection reflects the reductionist approach that the West imposes on indigenous knowledge systems. Also, Western-style IPR systems are biased toward Western knowledge systems, which reduce biodiversity to its chemical or genetic structures; thus, indigenous systems get no protection, yet the theft of these systems *is* protected. As long as Western-style IPR regimes continue to gain influence, such intellectual and biological piracy will continue to grow until a system for protecting biodiversity and indigenous knowledge systems is established.

Protecting this planet's biological and intellectual heritage in the age of biopiracy will require that we recognize and rejuvenate this heritage, and develop legal systems for guarding it in the context of emerging IPR regimes.

Indigenous knowledge is thus at the heart of the global issues of our times. The future of indigenous knowledges will not simply determine whether the diverse cultures of the world evolve in freedom or are colonized; it will also determine whether humanity and diverse species survive. The theft of indigenous knowledges by the West will not offer protection to the world's indigenous communities or to the diverse species with which they have coevolved.

Knowledge of other species – of biodiversity – has been central to the survival of indigenous peoples. It is also at the heart of the global economic enterprise. There are two paradigms of biodiversity conservation. The first involves local communities, which sustain themselves by utilizing and conserving biodiversity. The second involves commercial interests, which make their profits harvesting this planet's biodiversity and feeding that harvest into industrial systems of production. For indigenous communities, conserving biodiversity means conserving the integrity of ecosystems and species, safeguarding their rights to these resources, and maintaining their production systems, which are based on long awareness of biodiversity. For them, biodiversity has intrinsic value as well as high use value. For commercial interests, biodiversity itself has no value; it is merely 'raw material' for producing commodities and maximizing profits.

In ecologically diverse and technologically pluralistic societies such as ours, legal systems can no longer content themselves with protecting the interests of TNCs or of practitioners of Western science and technology. Rather, they must broaden their objectives sufficiently to protect diverse economic organizations and diverse knowledge systems.

Indigenous knowledge systems aimed at local self-reliance in nutrition and health care need criteria for protection that are different from Western models, which are based mainly on patents. Such protection must be based not on individual rights but on community rights and collective innovation – that is, on the concepts of 'heritage' and of innovation over time.

Indigenous knowledge producers innovate collectively. Also, their innovations are accretional and informal and take place over time. Indigenous knowledge evolves by modifying, adapting, and building on existing knowledge. 'Innovation' must therefore be redefined so as to reflect all of this. The current definition is based on the erroneous idea that innovation is an individual, 'one-shot' process. Neither in traditional indigenous systems, nor in the Western scientific tradition, is innovation an isolated activity in the temporal or social context.

The survival of indigenous knowledges is thus tightly connected to whether biodiversity is viewed as kin to the human species or as industrial raw material, and to whether the integrity of the community will be recognized and not merely the rights of individuals.

These fundamental questions of our time gain vital insights from the contributors to *Indigenous Knowledges in Global Contexts: Multiple Readings of Our World.*

Preface

As editors of this book, we would like to begin with some comments about our personal/subjective locations, about how individually and collectively we have come to the topic of 'indigenous knowledges,' and about the need to disrupt mainstream/standard academic knowledge.

George J. Sefa Dei

I am an African-Canadian male teaching in a Canadian institution of higher learning. I come to this topic of indigenous knowledges well aware that practice and experience constitute an important contextual basis for exploring and producing knowledge. Elsewhere (Dei, 1996), I have discussed some of the frustrations I felt with aspects of my education as a young person in Ghana. I was deeply disappointed – not so much, however, with what colonial education taught me, as with what it did *not* teach me. For example, I have wondered in later years why my lived experiences in Ghana were not contextualized as part of the education I received there. During my Ghanaian school days I learned much about Western societies and their histories but very little about the history, culture, and geography of my birthplace. While I was pursuing postgraduate studies in Canada, new and related questions were emerging around the issue of how important it is for educators to provide *all* students with a fuller history of the ideas and events that shape human growth and development. In my time teaching in the Canadian education system, these questions have grown even more important, particularly in the context of interrogating critically those educational processes encountered in the North American milieu. I hear my students – especially though not exclusively those from minoritized groups – ask me why certain experiences and histories count more than others when 'valid' academic knowledge is being produced and validated. I hear students lament the effort it is taking for educators to recognize the powerful linkages between identity, schooling, and knowledge production. But more importantly, I hear my students worry about how indigenous knowledges are being marginalized in the academy, and about the impact that the 'ranking' of knowledges may well have on the prospects for educational transformation and social change. Indeed, this reminds me of a tale I was told as a young boy in my village in Ghana. Three tailors set up their shops on the same street corner in a small town. One tailor put up a sign in front of his shop that read THE BEST TAILOR IN THE WHOLE WORLD. The second tailor, a few metres away, and obviously in total disagreement, put up a sign that read THE BEST TAILOR IN THIS VILLAGE. Then, in a move calculated to undo his competitors, the third tailor put up a sign that read THE BEST TAILOR ON THIS STREET CORNER.

I offer three of the possible interpretations of this story as a means of highlighting the personal politics that I bring to this book. *First*, the story conjures up concerns about why we engage in and even yearn for a competitive system that is based on the establishment of hierarchies. *Second* and perhaps more importantly, the story speaks to the fact that hierarchies can be overturned: What appears at first sight to be the smallest boast ends up superseding the bombastic, universal boast. This points out the power of human agency, thought, and resistance. *Third*, it could be argued that these tailors were challenging that approach to knowledge which designates a particular social reality as the only reality worth talking about. As Hunter long ago noted, 'the idea that one's view of reality is the only reality is the most dangerous of all delusions' (1983: 243).

Budd Hall

I am a middle-aged white heterosexual male. I am currently a professor at the Ontario Institute for Studies in Education at the University of Toronto in the Department of Adult Education and Community Development. I am also associated with OISE's Indigenous Education Network and the Transformative Learning Centre. I think of myself as a social movement educator and have been engaged in activist community, international, and scholarly work since 1964. My earliest and most powerful intellectual influences came from Africa. In the summer of 1964, as a young student of political science, I was studying at the University of Nsukka in Nigeria. There, my Nigerian professors confronted me with the idea that there is an 'African' perspective on history and political science and indeed on all forms of social science. The idea that knowledge could be approached from different points of view, and could be constructed differently according to differences in race, history, culture, class, gender, and so forth, shook me up. Until then, I really had not thought about how knowledge was constructed or about who participated in that construction, or about the conditions under which knowledge was disseminated. The confusion and doubt that Professors Ndem and Njokwu instilled in me in those few months are with me even now.

The second most profound intellectual influence on me was Julius K. Nyerere. Between 1970 and 1975, I headed the Research Department of the Institute of Adult Education at the University of Dar es Salaam in Tanzania. Mwalimu Julius K. Nyerere was president of the United Republic of Tanzania and a towering anticolonial intellectual. His writings, speeches, and policies in the areas of education, health, development, and agriculture reinforced ideas that had been planted in me as an undergraduate in Nigeria. In Nyerere I encountered someone who was articulating the links between knowledge production and the colonial relations of power. He noted that if education had been used by the colonial powers to enslave peoples, then it could also be used by anticolonial powers to liberate peoples. All peoples had the capacity to produce knowledge: Not only the political leaders of the newly independent African nation, but *all* women and men in rural Africa, had the power to create knowledge about their lives and aspirations.

In this atmosphere, I began to have profound doubts about the orthodox approaches to research that I had been trained in and had been training others in. I began to question whether university professors or university researchers have any right to monopolize the knowledge production process. Together with others, I began to formulate ideas about a research process that would explicitly recognize community knowledge. In this approach, the researcher participates actively in a particular community's activities while listening critically, from his or her own political, economic, cultural, and social perspective, to the other participants. This process involves the community differently than does conventional research, in which participants merely respond to the researcher's agenda. In participatory research, all members of the community support one another in an ongoing manner to actively inform the purpose, context, methodology, and emerging data of the work. For example, a researcher who wishes to involve rural Tanzanian women in participatory research, not only will listen to and learn from the voices of the women themselves, but also will invite the women to become equal partners, participant observers, and co-researchers with the voice and agency to engage in the ongoing negotiation and construction of knowledge and knowing. The term 'participatory research' has come to be associated with this kind of research (Maguire, 1991; Fals-Borda, 1980).

I continue to work from an intellectual stance that seeks to open up organizational and academic spaces for 'majority world' forms of knowledge to be heard, seen, and acted upon. As a white settler in an aboriginal land (Canada), I accept complicity in the injustices that were perpetrated in earlier times and that continue today. I have benefited from being born into the dominant culture of Canada and of the wider world. I cannot change my race or gender, but I *am* able to shape my approach to my work. Privilege offers me some choice in what I assign my students to read, what kinds of research I support, and what kinds of writing projects I undertake. Working with George Dei and Dorothy Goldin Rosenberg on this project has allowed me to learn from the two of them and from our authors.

Dorothy Goldin Rosenberg

I write as a Jewish-Canadian mother, grandmother, feminist educator, and activist of over three decades in the areas of peace, equality, ecology, health, and social and economic justice. The Holocaust in Germany, which was supported and perpetuated by many other countries of the world, was my earliest exposure to anti-Semitism, the destruction of cultural heritage, and genocide. It was but the first of my lessons in abusive systemic power, in domination and oppression, and in environmental and miliary racism, as well as in the incredible resistance and bravery of those faced with despicable evil. Unfortunately, the world has learned little from the Holocaust about curbing racism, militarism, greed, violence, patriarchal power, and the destruction of ecosystems. In recent years all of these things have been perpetuated in North, South, and Central America, in the Gulf War, Bosnia, and Rwanda, and in South Africa during the decades of Apartheid, to name but a few examples. In addition, as a health professional I became aware of how medical tragedies can arise from mistakes of science and technology. Examples: thalidomide, tainted blood, DES, and cancers induced by X-rays. These experiences are integral to my long-standing commitment to education for peace, social justice, equality, health, and the environment. I seek a better understanding of how knowledge can be enhanced in both formal and nonformal settings, of how consciousness can be changed, and of how analysis and advocacy can be integrated in society with the goal of defeating corporate/military/toxic ideologies and cultural pathologies. All of this involves understanding and reversing frameworks of patriarchal power and domination in all societies in order to halt inequality, militarism, and ecological destruction, and in order to develop a more just, healthy, peaceful, and ecologically safe world. It involves moving toward 'wholeness' in the sense of those principles of ecological integrity which this planet's indigenous peoples have been enunciating clearly for centuries: that the health of the planet is the primary context for the health of all life on it, and that what we do to the planet we do to ourselves. Social movements in both the South and the North are beginning to produce new political cultures that are departures from existing dominant political and patriarchal modes, and that are bringing these struggles to the world-historical stage. Parallel to and often integrated with these social movements are cross-cultural and inter-faith reclamations of ancient spiritual treasures long marginalized by modern culture – treasures that can offer a paradigm of resistance, creativity, and renewal for our time. For all the obstacles, there is growing evidence of a renewal of indigenous knowledges and practices; of a commitment to empowering women in the search for equity, justice, and peace between and among the peoples of the Earth; and of a new balance between all biological species and the ecosystems that sustain them.

We are compiling this book deeply informed by the limits of academic knowledge and by the ways in which these limitations can be overcome through the pursuit of indigenous knowledges. For us, a project to interrogate both 'valid' (i.e., global) knowledge and the processes of disseminating such knowledge locally and globally is both academic and political. In an intellectual and political exercise such as this, there are dangers and challenges, as well as pleasures and desires. In pursuing this project, we have challenged ourselves to rethink how other alternative (and sometimes oppositional) knowledge forms are, and ought to be, produced and legitimated. In the process we have been aware that we are opening ourselves to critique, assault, and misinterpretation. Yet in working on this project, we have found pleasure in contributing to the reformulation of what constitutes 'knowledge.' There is pleasure in knowing that we are not alone in our desire to interrogate what has come to be perceived as 'valid' knowledge in the academies. In fact, we join a very long tradition of exploring diverse and multiple forms of knowledge. The diversity of authorship and the range of subjects broached under the rubric of indigenous knowledges have made it easier for us to move between theory, case study, and practice. The study of indigenous knowledges in multiple educational and social institutional settings has helped us locate means by which to change the course and direction of both educational processes and social practices. By 'education' we refer to the options, strategies, processes, and structures through which individuals and communities/groups come to know and understand the world and act within it.

Our goal is not simply to incorporate indigenous knowledges into conventional knowledge forms, but as well to transform how people produce, interrogate, value, apply, and disseminate different forms of information. Our objective is to bring indigenous knowledges into the present as a contemporary means of constructing 'valid' knowledge about ourselves. Indigenous knowledges are used by marginalized peoples to make sense of and live in today's world.

Our academic and political interests lie in developing multiple knowledge centres through shifts in knowledge production and use. We approach marginalized groups in the context of their own experiences and histories, with the goal of centring them as sources of knowledge rather than as sources of mere data.

REFERENCES

Dei, George J.S. 1996. *Anti-Racism Education: Theory and Practice*. Halifax, N.S.: Fernwood.
Fals-Borda, O. 1986. Investigación participativa. Montevideo: Instituto del Hombre, Ediciones de la Banda Oriental.
Hunter, Deborah A. 1983. The Rhetorical Challenge of Afro-Centricity. *Western Journal of Black Studies* 7(4): 239–43.
Maguire, P. 1987. Doing Participatory Research: A Feminist Approach. Amherst, Mass.: Center for International Education, School of Education, University of Massachusetts.

INDIGENOUS KNOWLEDGES IN GLOBAL CONTEXTS: MULTIPLE READINGS OF OUR WORLD

Introduction

GEORGE J. SEFA DEI, BUDD L. HALL, DOROTHY GOLDIN ROSENBERG

Increasingly within communities, refreshing critical voices are emerging to question the processes of knowing and validating knowledge and disseminating it across national and global spaces. Because of their complexity, lived realities require multiple readings, social representations, and understandings. Knowledge is produced and acquired through collaborative processes. No individual, group, community, or nation can justifiably claim ownership of all knowledge. What constitutes valid knowledge, and how such knowledge should be produced and shared internally and globally, is still a subject of intense debate. It is important that there be no academic closure on this subject. Unfortunately, far too many educators privilege certain ways of knowing and interpreting the world over other ways.

In Euro-American circles, academic and political projects are seeking to rupture and/or deconstruct hegemonic social science paradigms. In doing so, they are encouraging marginalized and minoritized communities to demand that academic knowledge respond to their most pressing concerns – the rise of new forms of colonialism, imperialism, domination, and social oppression. Critical voices both in the academy and in local communities are drawing attention to the situation that subordinated peoples' knowledges, histories, and experiences have been left out of academic texts, discourses, and classroom pedagogies, or have been erased from them. These hitherto silent and silenced voices are no longer willing to accept the status quo and are urging that the problems associated with the systematization and commodification of knowledge be addressed.

To a great extent, we are witnessing a 'crisis of knowledge.' In large part this crisis can be attributed to globalization, which has intensified the processes of commodifying knowledge. As pointed out elsewhere (Dei, 1996), this 'crisis' is manifested in the contradictions and tensions of a competitive knowledge economy, the internationalization of labour, and the concomitant struggles over power sharing among social groups and among women and men. Globalization has accelerated the flow of cultures across geographical, political, and cultural borders; it has also transformed knowledge into a commodity to which the most powerful in society usually lay unjustifiable claim. For indigenous peoples, the 'crisis of knowledge' can be seen in, or has resulted in, the following: fragmentation of traditional values and beliefs; erosion of spirituality; distortions in local, regional, and national ecosystems and economies; and tensions related to cultural revitalization and reclamation.

All knowledges exist in relation to specific times and places. Consequently, indigenous knowledges speak to questions about location, politics, identity, and culture, and about the history of peoples and their lands. The process of teaching (and learning about) their histories and cultures is, for many indigenous peoples, an act of political resistance to colonialized and imposed ways of knowing.

Indigenous knowledges cannot be dismissed as mere localized phenomena. Such knowledges extend across cultures, histories, and geographical spaces, as well as across time. At different times many educators, community workers, and social activists have expressed their frustrations with the patriarchal colonizing practices of educational institutions. In our work we have often been confronted with questions about the absence and/or devaluation of certain knowledge forms. The negation, devaluation, and denial of indigenous knowledges, particularly those of women, is the result of deliberate practices of establishing hierarchies of knowledge. This problem of knowledge hierarchies in homes, families, schools, and workplaces cannot be dismissed lightly; after all, such knowledge hierarchies have always shaped schools, communities, and political lives. Institutions are not unmarked spaces of thought and action. Knowledge forms are usually privileged to construct dominance, and can be 'fetishizhed' so as to produce and sustain power inequities. Fetishized knowledges are assigned or come to acquire an objectified, normal status, *the status of truth.* Thus they become embedded in social practices and identities, as well as in institutional structures, policies, and relationships.

In working to dismantle stratified constructions of knowledge forms, we must bear in mind that knowledges cannot be examined as fixed categories experiences and social practices. Similarly, while stressing those qualities which are shared by all indigenous knowledges, we must remember how complex such knowledge forms are, and the implications of this complexity for rethinking 'indigenous knowledges' as a whole. This book is not intended to create a false dichotomy of 'conventional/colonial/external' knowledge as bad, and 'indigenous/marginalized/non-Western' knowledge as good. Our objective is to rupture the present relationship between 'valid' knowledge and 'not valid' knowledge, and to introduce 'indigenous knowledges' as legitimate ways of knowing that are both dynamic and continuous. In so doing we interrogate aspects of Western science that have had destructive effects on indigenous communities. We are careful not to treat indigenous knowledges as static, or to romanticize the past of indigenous peoples. We are well aware of how complex indigenous knowledge forms are, and we are proposing a multiplicity of centres through shifts in knowledge production.

After the Berlin Wall fell, many in the West – particularly in the United States – assumed that democratic liberalism had triumphed globally and would be taken up by all nations, along with free market economics. It hasn't turned out that way. For example, at the Earth Summit of 1992 in Rio de Janeiro, indigenous peoples from all continents, *who are responsible for most of the world's cultural and biological diversity*, gathered to consolidate concepts, strategies, and approaches to assist governments, agencies, NGOs, and other groups to work more effectively with them to attain sustainability with justice (IUCN, 1997: 178–216). Since then, indigenous peoples have attended similar gatherings to the same purpose. It is true that a world élite – heads of state, senior politicians, heads of TNCs, and leaders of the World Bank, the International Monetary Fund (IMF), the Asian Pacific Development Bank, and the like – controls virtually all international financial institutions. (It is these people who are most visible at each year's World Economic Forum in Davos, Switzerland.) But outside of Europe and North America, few people share this culture and perspective; Huntington estimates them at 1 per cent of the world's population. Arguably, there are powerful movements of indigenization and resistance at work even in places such as Asia – places that have seemingly adapted to Western market norms. In most of the world's nations the dominant attitude toward unfettered free markets and individualism is one of scepticism or even intense opposition. Nowadays many Asian economists attribute the dramatic changes in their region to adherence to traditional and even indigenous values and cultures. Indigenous knowledges, which have existed apart from colonial or imperial formations, are found at the very heart of the profound transformation of the world that is presently underway.

What Are Indigenous Knowledges, and Why Do We Need Them at This Time?

A study of indigenous knowledges brings a complex array of theoretical and methodological issues to the table. There is the problem of defining 'indigenous knowledges' and establishing workable boundaries for studying them. Also, there are issues relating to measurement (i.e., What units do we use for our analysis?), locations of data collection, methods of analysis, and how indigenous knowledges are to be disseminated and used. This book does not claim to have answers to all the issues and questions. In fact, a number of key questions have not yet been answered: How do we make sense of cognitive processes/ categories of local people? How do we deal with questions of access, control, and ownership of knowledge? How do we protect local indigenous knowledges from systematization and commodification, and from being swallowed up by corporate material interests? How do we preserve indigenous knowledges? And in particular, women's indigenous knowledges? And to what ends for what peoples? How do we deal with the tensions regarding 'whose' culture[s], traditions, norms, and social values are to be conveyed in indigenous knowledge systems? The answers to all these questions aren't yet clear.

We conceptualize an 'indigenous knowledge' as a body of knowledge associated with the long-term occupancy of a certain place. This knowledge refers to traditional norms and social values, as well as to mental constructs that guide, organize, and regulate the people's way of living and making sense of their world. It is the sum of the experience and knowledge of a given social group, and forms the basis of decision making in the face of challenges both familiar and unfamiliar. For millennia, many indigenous cultures were guided by a world view based on the following: seeing the individual as part of nature; respecting and reviving the wisdom of elders; giving consideration to the living, the dead, and future generations; sharing responsibility, wealth, and resources within the community; and embracing spiritual values, traditions, and practices reflecting connections to a higher order, to the culture, and to the earth. In her essay in this book, Njoki Nathani-Wane notes that this form of knowledge, accrued over time, is a critical aspect of any culture. It is accumulated by the social group through both historical and current experience. Through the process of learning the old, new knowledge is discovered; this is what makes indigenous knowledges dynamic rather than static.

This body of knowledge is diverse and complex given the histories, cultures, and lived realities of peoples. In considering why we need indigenous knowledges, it is important to reiterate some basic facts. While indigenous knowledges are characterized by the absence of colonial and imperial imposition, such knowledges emerge in the contemporary sense partly in response to colonial and 'postcolonial' intrusions. In other words, indigenous knowledges are emerging again in the present day as a response to the growing awareness that the world's subordinated peoples and their values have been marginalized – *that their past and present experiences have been flooded out* by the rise in influence of Western industrial capital.

This book has an anticolonial rather than a postcolonial discursive framework. Issues of cultural representation, history, and social identity, all of these so crucial to indigenous knowledge forms, are discussed in terms of the narrative accounts and discursive practices of peoples. The anticolonial discourse emphasizes the power held by local/social practice to survive the colonial and colonized encounters. It argues that power and discourse are not possessed solely by the 'colonizer.' Discursive agency and the power of resistance reside in and among colonized and marginalized groups. For example, subordinated/colonized populations had a [theoretical and practical] conception of the colonizer that functioned as a platform for engaging in social and political practice and relations. The notion of 'colonial' is rooted in imposed relations and power inequities engendered by history, tradition, culture, and contact. Anticolonial theorizing rises out of alternative, oppositional paradigms, which are in turn based on indigenous concepts and analytical systems and cultural frames of reference. All knowledges and discourses are heavily coloured by situations and relations of power, but every knowledge form is constructed differently. Therefore, the reader must be aware of the specific historical and gendered origins that produce theory and text.

Deeply embedded in all writing about indigenous knowledges are implied lessons for teaching and learning. Indigenous knowledges are largely oral, passed on through the generations by women and men who have the trust of the elders or the community. Indigenous knowledges are not learned in formal educational settings, nor are they learned in isolation from the Earth or from other people. As Lawlor has noted about Aboriginal education in Australia, 'the goal is the extending, relating, and expanding of being, forming of kinship through the ritual enforcement of the universal law of reciprocity' (1991: 154).

For those of us who wish to work with, learn from, and interact with indigenous knowledges while based in dominant institutions, this makes our work more complex and challenging. It is not enough simply to add a set of readings on 'indigenous knowledges' to our reading lists. As several of the essays in this book point out, we must transform our way of understanding knowledge, learning, and teaching.

An important position taken in this book is that indigenous knowledges differ from conventional knowledges because of an absence of colonial and imperial imposition. As Dei argues in his article, the notion of 'indigenousness' is central to the power relationships and dynamics embedded in the production, interrogation, validation, and dissemination of global knowledge about social development. Indigenous knowledges recognize the multiple and collective origins of knowledge as well as its collaborative dimensions. Indigenous knowledges affirm that the interpretation and analysis of social reality is subject to different and sometimes oppositional perspectives. It is also acknowledged that indigenous knowledge systems and traditions often contain sites and sources of cultural disempowerment for some groups, particularly women and ethnic/ cultural minorities.

The diverse readings we offer in this book amount to a disruption of the prevailing ideas about what constitutes 'knowledge.' All of the readings highlight the rich sources of indigenous knowledge, as well as its intellectual complexities. Our intention is to interrogate these forms of knowledge rather than to romanticize them.

This collection of essays challenges the continuing absence, erasure, and subordination of local people's knowledge, history, and experience from academic texts, discourses, and material social and political practices, particularly in Northern societies. To a disturbing extent, patriarchal Eurocentrism continues to masquerade as universalism. In many academic circles, projects that seek to break the silence around the knowledge held by minoritized and subordinate groups are fiercely discredited. Patriarchal Western science is presented as the only valid knowledge. Indigenous knowledges challenge Western science's commodification of values in the 'consumer cultural paradigm.' The theoretical conceptions of 'indigenous knowledges' that the authors of this book bring to the current discussion problematize the idea that unlimited human and material progress is possible through science, technology, and competition. As many critiques have noted, Western science views the universe as a mechanical system and defines the 'essence' of society as a competitive struggle for existence. Western science enthuses over the dualistic/binary mode of thought and the hierarchical ordering of knowledge. It overglorifies 'quantification' and is sceptical of anything that cannot be quantified. Positivist thinking and the traditions of 'rationality,' 'objectification,' 'reason,' 'progress,' and the certainty of knowledge are the hallmarks of Western scientific knowing. Social phenomena are often presented in structural forms that downplay the human element and the dimensions of emotion and intuition.

Indigenous Knowledges: Challenging Colonialism, Modernity, and Patriarchal Corporate Globalization

We start from a philosophical, theoretical, and practical position that perceives a powerful link between indigenous knowledges and what has constituted 'social development' for many peoples. As a result of colonial, patriarchal, corporate, exploitative, and often ecologically destructive development models, indigenous knowledges have been underestimated and undervalued. Knowledge production has been socially constructed so as to become a near monopoly from which most ordinary people are excluded. With the globalization of Western development, most indigenous cultures are being forced into programs of modernization that tend to regard the acquisition of material goods as the central purpose of life.

As Paul Wangoola reveals in his essay, poverty is perceived to be the central enemy, for which 'development' is the antidote. What has been institutionalized as development has come at a high cost in human, ecological, health, economic, political, and social terms. Economic gains have largely benefited a small group of corporate élites (mostly male), while often reducing the majority to poverty, malnutrition, and debt. Accompanying all of this is political and economic disintegration in the face of global financial capital.

We contend that it is reprehensible to allow this 'maldevelopment' agenda to continue – to the benefit of transnational corporate interests – while the basic needs of people remain unmet. The policies of the World Bank, the IMF, and the World Trade Organization (WTO) have resulted in well-described hardships. They have also created a crisis of knowledge about society – a commodification of knowledge across space and time – and led to what has been described in the South as insidious attempts at cultural, economic, and political recolonization.

Development failures are not confined to Africa, Asia, and Latin America – they are also prevalent in European and North American contexts. An important source of learning for North Americans is the Third World *inside* North America: the places where the aboriginal peoples of Canada and the United States live, the rural and urban ghettos of hardcore poverty that trap racial and ethnic minorities, female heads of households, and poor whites. For example, in recent decades in many parts of the world, indigenous knowledges of aboriginal peoples have begun to be heard. Native peoples' knowledges in North America are based on a philosophy of native science that has a sacral basis and whose teachings are grounded in the natural world. Seeking truth and coming to knowledge necessitates studying the cycles, relationships, and connections between things.

Interest in indigenous knowledges is growing quickly, as manifested in recent academic and cultural projects (see, for example, Stephen, 1996; Warren, 1991; Fast, 1994; Sadler and Boothroyd, 1994; Schoenhoff, 1993; Warren, Slikkerveer, and Brokensha, 1995). Of more direct relevance to our current work is Shiva (1989), who writes that the Age of Enlightenment, and the theory of progress to which it gave rise, was centred on the sacredness of two categories: modern scientific knowledge and economic development. Along the way the unbridled pursuit of 'progress' began to destroy life without any assessment having been made of how much and how fast the diversity of life on this planet – our life support system – was disappearing. The notion of living and celebrating and conserving life in all its diversity seems to have been sacrificed to progress; the sanctity of life, of people and nature, has given way to the sanctity of science and development. Shiva argues that throughout the world a new questioning is growing, rooted in the experiences of those for whom the spread of the Enlightenment has been the spread of darkness, of the extinction of life and life-enhancing processes. There is an expanding awareness that those things which are presently called 'progress' are merely, in fact, the special projects of modern Western patriarchy.

Shiva points to the exploitative nature of the global economy and calls for 'development' to be given a new definition, one that is not based on the ethnocentric categorizations of nature and women as passive, worthless, and ultimately dispensable. There have been two central shifts in thinking: the first relates to concepts of knowledge and to the identities of the knowers and producers of intellectual value; the second relates to concepts of wealth and to the identities of the producers of economic value. We agree with Shiva that the production of sustenance is basic to survival and cannot be expunged from economic calculations, but that we should also see knowledge and human survival as inextricably linked. The intellectual heritage for ecological survival lies with those who have the knowledge and experience to extricate us from the dead end in which we now find ourselves. While women and the marginalized peoples of the South have survival expertise, their knowledge is inclusive, not exclusive, and the categories with which they think and act are categories for liberation for men as well as for women, for the West as well as for the 'non-West,' and for humans as well as for nonhumans on the Earth.

Shiva presents a feminist ecological analysis of patriarchal power and domination. Other studies focus on the marginalization of indigenous knowledges and the need to build bridges between the old and the new. For example, Kinker and Gieryn (1995) examine the use of composting in the history of agriculture in twentieth-century India and describe how as a British colony and as an independent state, India's land and people were the intended benefactors of successive schemes to uplift rural farming. In the 1920s, primacy in such schemes was accorded to the age-old system of composting. Western science legitimated composting as a solution to India's ills; thus, the practices of Indian and Chinese native farmers were brought within the Western scientific discourse, which uses experiment, statistics, and plant biochemistry as means to verify indigenous knowledges. However, by the middle of the century modern corporate science had lined up against indigenous knowledges and practices, and chemical fertilizers, herbicides, and pesticides had taken the lead role in scientifically reorganizing many Indian farms.

Composting played only a small part in the Green Revolution of the 1950s and 1960s; indigenous cultivators were treated as subjects for technological intervention rather than as 'knowers' in their own right. Later still, various supporters and agencies came to configure composting as an agent of scientific advance. Debates about the viability of organic farming are coloured heavily by political and economic factors. Indian farmers are at present redefining composting, history, and nature in light of the current situation (see Kinker and Gieryn, 1995). Rajesekaran and colleagues (1991) examine the consequences of the disappearance of indigenous knowledge systems (IKs) for natural resource management, such as in agroforestry and herd management. They have found that indigenous natural resource management systems are underutilized by national planners owing to a lack of documentation and to a preference for transferable agricultural technologies. The consequences of the disappearance of IKs include drought, flooding, erosion, loss of soil nutrients, loss of genetic diversity, and in many cases, the total loss of indigenous knowledges.

Posey (1990) addresses questions of intellectual property rights and just compensation for indigenous knowledges in recognizing that agriculture, ranching, mineral exploitation, and timber extraction – all of which require the destruction of forests – are currently the principle options for reaping economic benefits from tropical ecosystems. Entire tropical forests are being destroyed in order to exploit less than 3 per cent of their species. In contrast, indigenous peoples know, classify, and utilize over 99 per cent of the rich diversity of tropical flora and fauna. Indigenous knowledges have long been a source of new ideas for natural resource management; they have also provided innumerable new products, including foods, medicines, natural insecticides and fertilizers, and natural colourings and dyes. A proper exploitation of tropical species might well give economic value to the living while taking development pressure off virgin forest areas. Here some difficult problems arise. For example, how can indigenous peoples be compensated for their traditional knowledge, which is the key to this more sensitive utilization? And how can consumer capitalism be controlled so as not to overstimulate the demand for natural products, which would in turn lead to overexploitation of tropical ecosystems? Other important questions relate to the settling of Aboriginal land claims and decision-making control.

Going Beyond Critique to Reclamation

We need to create bridges between academia and the wider community. We need to understand and move beyond the often genocidal effects of decades of colonialism and maldevelopment practices; we need to offer a critique of both Western capitalist and (former) Eastern communist economic growth and development models. We need to call for locally defined models of sustainability in which will prevail the lived realities of local peoples, with all their social, cultural, political, spiritual, moral, and ecological goals and aspirations.

The essays in this book provide genuine alternatives to existing discourses on development, development education, health knowledge, and adult learning. Many of the contributors apply both theory and practice in examining the major concepts in the social sciences, the humanities, and the arts for their applicability to groups outside the mainstream.

In the politics of knowledge production, certain key questions have guided this work. For example, how can we, as knowledge producers and consumers, bring the 'periphery' to the 'centre' and thereby develop a 'multiplicity of centres'? And how do we search for alternative visions that will remove the scepticism of indigenous and marginalized peoples? And how can we assist in the decolonization of social investigations about the 'other' in such a way as to ensure that the reality of the 'other' is not constructed in terms of patriarchal Western/Euro-American hegemony and ideology? And what are the consequences for the 'other' of the current global processes of knowledge production and dissemination? And how do we create a climate in which intellectual discursive practices are sensitized to the socio-environmental demands and needs of peoples? Clearly, there is a need to develop critical, integrative indigenous knowledges as a basis for social, political, and educational praxis.

All the essays in this book illustrate the emergence of critical, integrative indigenous knowledges – knowledges exemplified by the people themselves in various locations, as they reclaim and utilize their cultures with the goal of social transformation. This book also suggests how we can understand and alleviate contemporary economic, health, and ecological hardships as well as alleviate the social, cultural, gendered impacts of maldevelopment. Indigenous knowledges can assist us greatly in understanding and resolving many dilemmas. There is no shortage of suggestions, proposals, and living examples of such reclamation, as this collection will reveal. In fact, every day in many parts of the world, colonized cultures are being reconstructed and oral traditions are being recovered. Approaches to development can reclaim diverse local peoples' world views – and must do so if we are to identify, generate, and articulate new visions of social transformation. To this end, an understanding of local experiences is invaluable in providing the building blocks for social and economic change (see Boulding, 1983).

This collection of essays argues that we must understand and move beyond the often tragic effects of decades of colonialism and maldevelopment, and offers both a critique of these things and a direction forward.

We begin with Section I: 'Situating Indigenous Knowledges: Definitions and Boundaries.' In the first essay, Marlene Brant Castellano emphasizes the dynamic nature of aboriginal knowledge and suggests that traditional knowledge will assume new forms of expression as it is applied to contemporary social and environmental challenges. She draws on documents of the Royal Commission on Aboriginal Peoples, current literature, and personal experience to review the emerging consensus about the knowledge systems that Canada's native people are engaged in revitalizing.

Leilani Holmes's essay describes the strong commitment felt by Hawaiians to revitalize their culture and control their own destiny in the face of the environmental degradation of their ancestral lands – lands from which they were dispossessed as a result of colonialism and its aftermath. Central to this surge of political and cultural activity are the stories, reminiscences, and lessons voiced by and attributed to Hawaiian elders.

Njoki Nathani Wane's chapter explores lessons from elders in one particular community in Kenya. She shows how elderly women have become custodians of traditional knowledge about culture and language. She pieces together a body of thought that women possess about everyday practice. Her work provides a healthy understanding of Kenyan rural women's knowledge systems.

George J. Sefa Dei's chapter explores the relevance of 'indigenous knowledge' and 'development.' He introduces the concept of indigenousness to examine the implications of local understandings of nature, society, and culture for the development process. The work emphasizes traditional world views and how the projects and objectives of development can tap into local knowledge systems to enhance daily survival. The chapter uses a Ghanian case study to show how local people use their own creativity and resourcefulness to respond to national economic contraction.

In the opening essay of Section II: 'Resistance and Advocacy,' Elizabeth McIsaac examines the objective position of the people in relation to the powers of Canadian colonialism and the subjective experiences and interpretations of the community elders, and argues that the knowledge which emerges from the narratives cannot be contained in an academic framework that does not originate from indigenous knowledges and experiences.

In an African setting, Patience Elabor Idemudia examines how indigenous knowledges, as embodied in folkways or sayings of the wise, contribute to the formation of identities. She postulates that for people from cultures where folkways are still valued, identities formed in this manner assist people in developing a cultural basis for resisting and challenging assimilation to imposed ways of knowing.

Sandra Awang describes the harm to indigenous peoples being inflicted by the workings of the Human Genome Diversity Project (HGDP), which is collecting and patenting genetic materials from indigenous peoples around the world. The multibillion-dollar, fifteen-year Human Genome Initiative, which began in 1991, has as its goal to map and sequence all human genes. The consortium engaged in this project includes the U.S. National Institutes of Health, the U.S. military, and universities and transnational pharmaceutical corporations. The HGDP is an excellent example of the relationship between science, capitalist patriarchy, and the resources of indigenous nations. In this 'biocolonialism,' the weapon of intellectual property rights is being applied against communities in the South (as well as in the South of the North), to allow for the privatization of life itself and the patenting of traditional medicines.

Continuing the theme of biomedical/technological corporate control, Dorothy Goldin Rosenberg critiques the West's largely curative approach to health and shows how it serves the medical/industrial complex, and marginalizes and largely suffocates indigenous knowledges, which emphasize preventive approaches. She describes the ecological/health crisis as a crisis of cultural pathology precipitated by the thought processes and institutions that shape modern life, and how feminist ecological praxis is challenging Western power structures, which too often disregard (and or attempt to cover up) the environmental and health consequences of their actions.

In Section III: 'Indigenous Knowledges and the Academy,' Joseph Couture places Native Studies programs in the context of Canadian aboriginal history and present conditions. He posits that aboriginal ways of knowing encompass mastery, which is deemed central to defining native culture, values, and relationships to the land.

Roxana Ng describes traditional Chinese medicine (TCM) as a system of healing developed and refined in China over 5,000 years ago. With the onset of European imperialism and the rise of Western biomedicine, this art was demoted to a superstitious, prescientific belief. She juxtaposes TCM and biomedicine as two contrasting ways of looking at health, illness, and the body. In the process, she reclaims her cultural heritage and challenges malestream and hegemonic science from a feminist, antiracist perspective.

Handel Wright argues that certain African advances in development studies, reappraisals of indigenous African education, and literature studies reconceptualized as cultural studies, together can create a discursive environment in which literature studies may contribute significantly to the discourse and praxis of development in Africa. While 'development' began as a purely economistic field, today virtually every contemporary school of thought on the matter would incorporate education as an integral tool for development. Unfortunately, education in development discourse is almost always synonymous with Western formal schooling.

Budd L. Hall describes and explores an important resource for learning: the CD-ROM version of the Royal Commission on Aboriginal Peoples final report to the government of Canada. This CD-ROM provides the report, transcripts of the extensive public hearings, and previously published reports, papers, and studies prepared for the commission. As such, it has remarkable potential as a resource for educators and learners everywhere.

In Section IV: 'Indigenous Knowledges and Transforming Practices,' Farah Shroff discusses the history and fundamental aspects of the ancient and modern system of indigenous knowledge, Ayuveda. Ayuvedic theory, which emanates from Hindu texts, is considered the mother of holistic health care and has parallels in Chinese, Tibetan, and First Nations medicine. Despite British colonialism, it continues to be used by 70 per cent of the Indian population; it is now also being recognized outside India.

Susanne Dudziak discusses how since 1985, the Ontario government has favoured varying forms and degrees of aboriginal inclusion in the design, development, and implementation of policies that directly affect them. She describes 'joint policy development' as part of a new emerging paradigm in the federal government's relations with aboriginal peoples. She outlines a comprehensive strategy for dealing with family violence (healing) and an aboriginal-specific health policy (wellness). She then describes how knowledge was created and shared among partners and how aboriginal concepts and values were highlighted – findings that raise implications for future policy development in this era of negotiation.

Thomas Turay presents a conceptual framework of the role of peace research and practice in sustaining African development, focusing on African-centred knowledge and initiatives. He examines indigenous alternatives to living peace in contemporary Africa and their implications for social transformation. He argues that peace and social justice are fundamental to sustaining African communities and calls for a rediscovery of nonviolent indigenous alternatives to conflict prevention, resolution, and management on that continent.

Finally, Paul Wangoola introduces a new institution, Mpambo, the African Multivarsity, which is guided by a philosophy for rekindling the African spirit of the millennia when African communities were guided by a world view at the centre of which was a closely intertwined trinity of values – Spirituality, Development, and Politics – with Spirituality as the predominant element. This changed with the introduction of the modern development paradigm, in which collective identities, collective self-reliance, and humanity were diminished, and in which leadership fell into the hands of deculturalized Africans supervised by experts from the North. In the mid-1980s a group of African NGOs and Civil Society leaders examined post–Cold War opportunities for change and resolved that their way forward must involve popular self-reliance from bottom-up initiatives to create a new economy centred around the community.

The goal of this collection of essays is to begin a dialogue for bringing local/ indigenous knowledges within the orbit of Western scientific knowledge. Our primary argument in this book is that there are other valid ways of 'seeing' and understanding the world besides those of the dominant West. The task of social and educational change requires a recognition that indigenous peoples have knowledge systems for theorizing and conceptualizing their social and natural worlds. Local communities are not simply the source of raw data for academic theorizing elsewhere. Local peoples must be seen as key players in the construction of knowledge about their societies.

REFERENCES

Boulding, E. 1983. Reflections on Fundamental Problems and Challenges for the Social Sciences. UNESCO Symposium on the Fundamental Problems and Challenges for Volume on Social Sciences in North America. Symposium, Mont. St-Marie, Quebec (referred to in P. Colorado, 1988. Bridging Native and Western Science. *Convergence* 21(2/3): 49–72).

Dei, G.J.S. 1996. *Anti-Racism Education: Theory and Practice.* Halifax: Fernwood Publishing.

Fast, H.B. 1994. *Natural Land Use: Traditional Knowledge and Subsistence Economy in the Hudson Bay Bioregion.*

Hunter, A. 1983. The Rhetorical Challenge of Afro-Centricity. *Western Journal of Black Studies* 7(4): 239–43.

Huntington, S. 1997. Westernization of the World. *Resurgence* no. 182 (May/June): 14–15.

IUCN Inter-Commission Task Force on Indigenous Peoples. 1997. *Indigenous Peoples and Sustainability: Cases and Actions.* IUCN Indigenous Peoples and Conservation Initiative. Utrecht: International Books.

Kinker, A., and T. Gieryn. 1995. Cultivating Progress: How Science Saved Compost and Compost Saved Science in Indian Agriculture. Presented at the American Sociological Association Annual Meeting, August, Washington, D.C.

La Duke, W. Impact of Northern Development on Indigenous Communities and Women. *Second World Women's Congress for a Healthy Planet.* Beijing. 1995.

Lawlor, R. 1991. *Voices of the First Day: Awakening in the Aboriginal Dreamtime.* Rochester: Inner Traditions.

Posey, D. 1990. Intellectual Property Rights and Just Compensation for Indigenous Knowledge. *Anthropology Today* 6(4): 13–16.

Rajesekaran, B., Denni M. Warren, and S.C. Babu. 1991. Indigenous Natural Resource Management Systems for Sustainable Agricultural Development: A Global Perspective. *Journal of International Development* 3(4) (July): 387–401.

Sadler, B., and P. Boothroyd. 1994. *Traditional Ecological Knowledge and Environmental Assessment*. Vancouver: UBC Centre for Human Settlements.

Schoenhoff, D.M. 1993. *The Barefoot Expert: The Interface of Computerized Knowledge Systems and Indigenous Knowledge Systems*. Westport, Conn.: Greenwood Press.

Shiva, V. 1989. *Staying Alive: Women, Ecology, and Development*. London: Zed Books.

Spretnak, C. 1991. *States of Grace: The Recovery of Meaning in the Postmodern Age*. New York: HarperCollins.

Stephen, S. 1996. *Valuing Local Knowledge: Indigenous People and Intellectual Property Rights*. Washington, D.C.: Island Press.

Warren, D.M. 1991. *Using Indigenous Knowledge in Agricultural Development*. Washington, D.C.: International Bank for Construction and Development, World Bank.

Warren, D.M., L.J. Slikkerveer, and D. Brokensha (eds.). 1995. *Indigenous Knowledge Systems: The Cultural Dimension of Development*. Exeter: Intermediate Technology Publications.

PART I

Situating Indigenous Knowledges: Definitions and Boundaries

Indigenous knowledges are unique to given cultures, localities, and societies. As pointed out, indigenous knowledges are those acquired by local peoples through daily experience. They deal with the experiential reality of the world. They are forms of knowledge that reflect the capabilities, priorities, and value systems of local peoples and communities. An important dimension of indigenous knowledge relates to how traditional forms continue to emerge and coexist in diverse situations and settings as part of a local people's response to colonial and imperial intrusions. This interrogation helps offer appropriate definitions and/or conceptualizations of the bodies of knowledge that constitute 'indigenous' and 'traditional,' and how they coexist with multiple knowledge forms. In responding to the current global challenges of social development, indigenous peoples rely on oral traditions, on historical/ancestral knowledges, and on their cultural resource bases to make sense of events around them in ways that are continuous and consistent with their traditional world views and cosmologies. It follows that the importance of understanding (a) the complex and diverse needs and responsibilities of indigenous knowledges, and (b) the nature of local struggles of retrieving and affirming marginalized knowledge forms for social development in modern contexts, cannot be overemphasized. As colonized and marginalized peoples respond to the challenges of global development, there is a strategic recourse to cultural resource knowledges. This recourse marks a sustaining of the traditional knowledge base and the maintenance of viable social institutional networks with a view to providing indigenous/authentic solutions to urgent human and planetary problems.

By situating the processes of indigenous knowledge creation in local systems of thought, in human feelings and actions, in institutional practices, and in narrative and discursive accounts, we signify the power of both individual and collective agency for change. The search for definitions and boundaries of indigenous knowledges reveals that these forms of knowledge are connected to the axes of social difference (e.g., these knowledge forms are gendered) and are also linked to human understandings of both the social and the natural environment.

1

Updating Aboriginal Traditions of Knowledge

MARLENE BRANT CASTELLANO

Establishing a Focus

When I was invited to contribute to this collection of papers on indigenous knowledges, I thought at first of bringing together lectures I had given on teaching and learning as they are talked about among First Nations people in Canada. However, the experience of five intensive years with the Royal Commission on Aboriginal Peoples, as co-director of research, would not be denied.[1] Articulation of the features of aboriginal knowledge, supplemented by the writings of colleagues, seemed insufficient.

The search for words that have immediacy and relevance resulted in this essay, in which I begin by placing the discussion of aboriginal knowledge within a historical process of change, and reinforce my points by referring to the Royal Commission report, which explicitly identifies the affirmation of aboriginal knowledge as an essential goal of aboriginal policy.

Next, I review what I consider to be the sources and characteristics of aboriginal knowledge, with appreciative reference to the work of colleagues. Then I raise questions about the process of validating aboriginal knowledge and about the role of written commentaries. Finally, I sketch some opportunities and challenges for applying and adapting aboriginal knowledge in the context of fundamental change in aboriginal/nonaboriginal relations in Canada and the physical and social environment in which aboriginal people now find themselves.

A Turning Point in Aboriginal/Nonaboriginal Relations

The aboriginal peoples of Canada have diverse histories and identities, ranging from the Cree hunters and gatherers of the eastern woodlands and the Iroquoian agriculturalists of the Great Lakes, to the buffalo hunters of the western plains and the ocean-going nations of the Pacific coast. Different again are the Inuit, who live in the treeless expanses of the north, and the Métis, who emerged historically from the encounter of European and aboriginal peoples.

The many nations who used to be called 'Indians' prefer to use their tribal names such as Mi'kmaq, Mohawk, and Dene. Generically they call themselves 'First Nations.' Along with the Inuit and the Métis, First Nations peoples enjoy protection under Canada's Constitution Act for their aboriginal and treaty rights, which are still in the process of being articulated and defined within the boundaries of Canadian law and government.

Although the right of aboriginal peoples to maintain their identity within Canada has been recognized in the highest law of the land, their means to exercise that right are severely constrained by the antiquated laws embodied in the Indian Act; by restricted access to land and resources, which impoverishes them and relegates them to the margins of Canadian life; and by lack of respect for their distinct cultures, languages, and ways of relating to the world, both in popular discourse and in public institutions.

The Royal Commission on Aboriginal Peoples was established by the federal government in 1991 to carry out an independent inquiry into the troubled relationship between aboriginal peoples, the Canadian government, and Canadian society as a whole. It was given a broad mandate and asked to propose specific solutions to the problems that confront aboriginal people and plague intercultural relations.

The commission submitted its five-volume report in November 1996. Central to its recommendations for establishing more harmonious relations, and for ensuring the equitable participation of aboriginal people in Canadian life, were its endorsement of principles of respect for cultural differences and recognition of the moral, historical, and legal right of aboriginal peoples to govern their collective lives in ways they freely determine.

Fundamental changes in political relations between aboriginal nations and the Canadian state, in the distribution of lands and resources and in the economic outlook of revitalized communities, will take time to achieve. However, the multitude of changes required to improve life for aboriginal individuals, families, and communities need not wait upon these structural changes: they can and should begin now.

In the commission's analysis and recommendations, the participation of aboriginal people, applying indigenous knowledge and incorporating tradition to the extent they deem appropriate, is proposed as the basis for devising policy in political relations and governance, land use and economic development, family rehabilitation and community development, and health and education.

The commission's report charts paths by which education under aboriginal control can break through current barriers to learning and achievement encountered by children, youth, and adults. For aboriginal people the challenge is to translate the well-honed critique of colonial institutions into initiatives that go beyond deconstruction of oppressive ideologies and practices to give expression to aboriginal philosophies, world views, and social relations. For nonaboriginal people the challenge is to open up space for aboriginal initiative in schools and colleges, work sites, and organizations so that indigenous ways of knowing can flourish and intercultural sharing can be practised in a spirit of coexistence and mutual respect.

Sources of Knowledge

The knowledge valued in aboriginal societies derives from multiple sources, including traditional teachings, empirical observation, and revelation. These categories overlap and interact with one another, but they are useful for examining the contours of aboriginal knowledge.

Traditional knowledge has been handed down more or less intact from previous generations. With variations from nation to nation, it tells of the creation of the world and the origin of clans in encounters between ancestors and spirits in the form of animals; it records genealogies and ancestral rights to territory; and it memorializes battles, boundaries, and treaties and instils attitudes of wariness or trust toward neighbouring nations. Through heroic and cautionary tales, it reinforces values and beliefs; these in turn provide the substructure for civil society. In some of its forms, it passes on technologies refined over generations.

In most aboriginal societies the wisdom of elder generations is highly regarded and elders are assigned major responsibility for teaching the young. This makes for a conservative attitude toward change, which Waldram (1986) argues is inherently compatible with the normally slow pace of change in the surrounding natural environment.

Empirical knowledge is gained through careful observation. With reference to knowledge of ecosystems, Waldram describes how knowledge is created from observations by many persons over extended time periods: 'This information processing forms a constant loop in which new information is interpreted in the context of existing information, and revisions to the state of knowledge concerning a particular phenomenon are made when necessary.'

He illustrates his concept of 'indigenous science' with three examples in which the assessments of professionals in the Western academic tradition were contradicted by the judgment of aboriginal people, and the conclusions based on aboriginal knowledge turned out to have greater validity. He notes, however, that the inferences or theories developed in the aboriginal context were not based on quantitative analysis of repeated observations in a controlled setting. Rather, they represented a convergence of perspectives from different vantage points, accumulated over time.

Revealed knowledge is acquired through dreams, visions, and intuitions that are understood to be spiritual in origin.

In times past, youths of many nations undertook vision quests during which they made the transition to adult roles and responsibilities. In contemporary times it is often adults of mature years – many of them in troubled circumstances – who seek out the help of elders to discover their identity and purpose through fasting and ceremonies.

Knowledge gained through spiritual means can serve economic as well as psychological needs. In *Maps and Dreams*, Hugh Brody (1983) describes the power of dreaming as well remembered and still accessible to a select few of the Beaver people of northeastern British Columbia, among whom hpatriarchal e was doing fieldwork:

> Some old-timers, men who became famous for their powers and skills, had been great dreamers. Hunters and dreamers. They did not hunt as most people now do. They did not seek uncertainly for the trails of animals whose movements we can only guess at. No, they located their prey in dreams, found their trails, and made dream-kills. Then, the next day, or a few days later, whenever it seemed auspicious to do so, they could go out, find the trail, re-encounter the animal, and collect the kill. (44)

Sometimes knowledge is received as a gift at a moment of need; sometimes it manifests itself as a sense that 'the time is right' to hunt or counsel or to make a decisive turn in one's life path.

In current discourse about their knowledge, aboriginal people often emphasize the timeless value of their teachings. One hears about instructions given at the creation of the world on how to maintain harmony in relationships among human beings and with the natural world. However, in these accounts it is not always made clear that culture is dynamic, and adjusts to changing conditions, and that a particular practice that embodies a timeless truth may need to be adapted if it is to remain effective. Constant testing of knowledge in the context of current reality creates the applications that make timeless truths relevant to each generation. This is the work of aboriginal adults, who are fully engaged in the economic, social, and political life of their communities.

Aboriginal knowledge has been under assault for many years. In residential schools and other educational institutions, in the workplace, in social relations, and in political forums, aboriginal people have been bombarded with the message that what they know from their culture is of no value. Intergenerational transmission of ancient knowledge has been disrupted, and the damage has not been limited to the loss of what once was known: the process of knowledge creation – that is, the use of cultural resources to refine knowledge in the laboratory of daily living – has also been disrupted. As aboriginal people reassert their right to practise their cultures in a somewhat more hospitable social environment, they will have to decide how to adapt their traditions to a contemporary environment.

Sacred knowledge, enduring knowledge, is often described using fire as a metaphor. Art Solomon, an Anishnabe (Ojibway) elder from Ontario, speaks of sifting through the ashes to discover the embers from the sacred fire, which when it is rekindled brings the people back to their true purpose.[2] It is the nature of fire that it is ever-changing and has to be fueled by the materials at hand here and now.

Characteristics of Aboriginal Knowledge

Among the small corps of people writing about aboriginal knowledge in the Canadian context there is a measure of consensus on its characteristic content and mode of transmission. Aboriginal knowledge is said to be personal, oral, experiential, holistic, and conveyed in narrative or metaphorical language. This list is not exhaustive.

Personal Knowledge

Illustrating the personal nature of aboriginal knowledge, there is a story that has been repeated often enough to have acquired a place in contemporary oral culture. At the hearings considering an injunction to stop the first James Bay hydro-electric power development in northern Quebec, an elder from one of the northern Cree communities that might be affected by the development was brought in to testify about Cree lifeways and the environment. When asked to swear that he would tell the truth, he asked the translator for an explanation of the word. However truth was translated for him, as something that holds for all people, or something that is valid regardless of the rapporteur, the elder responded: 'I can't promise to tell you the truth; I can only tell you what I know.'

Aboriginal knowledge is rooted in personal experience and lays no claim to universality. The degree to which you can trust what is being said is tied up with the integrity and perceptiveness of the speaker. If Joseph X reports that he saw signs of moose in a given direction, the information will be weighed in light of what is known of Joseph X, how often in the past his observations have proven accurate, what is known about this part of the territory, and the habits of moose. His observations would not necessarily be accepted uncritically, nor would they be contradicted or dismissed. Rather, they would be put in context.

The personal nature of knowledge means that disparate and even contradictory perceptions can be accepted as valid because they are unique to the person. In a council or talking circle of elders you will not find arguments as to whose perception is more valid and therefore whose judgment should prevail. In other words, people do not contest with one another to establish who is correct – who has the 'truth.' Aboriginal societies make a distinction between perceptions, which are personal, and wisdom, which has social validity and can serve as a basis for common action. Knowledge is validated through collective analysis and consensus building.

Some of my nonaboriginal friends have described their initiation into the decision-making process of northern aboriginal communities. In what seemed like endless village meetings, issues affecting the common well-being of the community were discussed. Gradually comments or experiences with a particular bent were heard reinforcing one another; and at a certain point, everyone would get up and leave. A perceptive observer might be able to see the exchange of looks or nods between certain elders, signalling the emergence of consensus; but such consensus would not normally be confirmed in a vote. Collective wisdom is arrived at by a process of 'putting our minds together.'

Oral Transmission

Oral cultures are often described as 'preliterate,' as if literacy were a form of communication more advanced on an evolutionary scale. Elders who are asked to have their words recorded in print or on videotape often decline because they insist that what they have to say must be communicated in person.

Aboriginal people know that knowledge is power and that power can be used for good or for evil. In passing on knowledge the teacher has an obligation to consider whether the learner is ready to use knowledge responsibly. In recent years there has been a great increase in the number of young aboriginal people seeking out elders to acquire knowledge, including knowledge about ceremonials and medicine – the use of spiritual power. While much of what is taught focuses on personal transformation and self-discipline, the possibility exists that even this knowledge can be used for self-serving ends. One hears cautionary tales of novices in medicine ways who failed to demonstrate proper respect for the knowledge that had been entrusted to them, and who came to a bad end, usually through accidents.

This is the reasoning behind the refusal of many elders to allow their presentations to be taped, and their resistance to having their traditional teachings transcribed so that they can be disseminated in print form. Teachers who allow these things relinquish the possibility of adjusting their teaching to the maturity of the learner and thereby influencing the ethical use of knowledge.

Oral teachings are necessarily passed on in the context of a relationship – or they were before the arrival of electronic media in aboriginal communities. The teaching encompassed not only intellectual content but also the emotional quality of the relationship. It drew on the shared experience of a common environment and, in all likelihood, on a history stretching back over generations. It was essentially nonprescriptive, respecting norms of noninterference in social relations (Brant, 1990).

Rupert Ross in *Dancing with a Ghost* (1992) describes the noninterfering behavioural norms that govern communications among many aboriginal people – norms that often puzzle nonaboriginal people who attempt to interact with them. Ross recounts his travels with an Ojibway justice of the peace who calmly allowed him to make particular gross mistakes of interpersonal etiquette repeatedly without correcting him. Eventually Ross learned that the lack of response or cooperation from the people with whom he was interacting was a signal that another perception of the situation was operating and that there were effective and ineffective ways of exploring those alternative perceptions. One of the most effective ways of learning was to listen to the stories of personal experience that were told – stories that inevitably had some oblique instruction to set him straight.

That may sound like a very inefficient way of communicating, and so it may be in terms of transmitting information from person A to person B as quickly as possible. However, if the objective is understood to be maintaining a relationship between A and B so that the channel of communication remains open and the flow of information is undistorted, it makes *more* sense.

Experiential Knowledge

In papers exploring the nature of aboriginal knowledge, Colorado and Couture each write of the subjective, qualitative character of aboriginal knowing. Colorado writes:

> The Basis, the Medium, the Message, the Understanding – the nature of Native science is that it is qualitative and subjective rather than quantitative and objec-

tive ... *Skanagoa*, literally interpreted as 'great peace,' is the term used to describe the still, electrifying awareness one experiences in the deep woods. This feeling or state of balance is at the heart of the universe and is the spirit of Native science.

Couture (1991) makes reference to the congruence between inner and outer reality:

> Reality is experienced by entering deeply into the inner being of the mind, and not by attempting to break through the outer world to a beyond. This positions the Native person in 'communion' with the living reality of all things. His 'communion' is his experience of the ideas within, concentric with reality without. Thus, to 'know,' to cognize, is experiential, direct knowing. (61)

In an exploration of the fundamentals of aboriginal knowledge, Ermine (1995) proposes:

> Individuals and society can be transformed by identifying and reaffirming learning processes based on subjective experiences and introspection ... Those people who seek knowledge on the physical plane objectively find their answers through exploration of the outer space, solely on the corporeal level. Those who seek to understand the reality of existence and harmony with the environment by turning inward have a different, incorporeal knowledge paradigm that might be termed Aboriginal epistemology.

Ermine explains that inquisitiveness about mystery and continued exploration of the inner space is a legacy we must promote in our own time (102, 103, 105). He goes on to articulate the dynamic relationship between the acquisition of inner knowledge and the application of that knowledge in the outer world to foster continued learning:

> Ancestral explorers of the inner space encoded their findings in community praxis as a way of synthesizing knowledge derived from introspection. The Old Ones had experienced totality, a wholeness, in inwardness and effectively created a physical manifestation of the life force by creating community ... Each part of the community became an integral part of the whole flowing movement and was modelled on the inward wholeness and harmony ... The accumulation and synthesis of insights and tribal understandings acquired through inwardness, and the juxtaposition of knowledge on the physical plane as culture and community, is the task for contemporary Aboriginal education. (104–5)

Knowledge of the physical world, which forms an essential part of the praxis of inner and outer learning, does not flow exclusively or primarily through the intellect, as Matthew Coon-Come, a Cree leader from northern Quebec, learned. After spending years in residential school and university, Matthew asked his father to teach him about the land of his ancestors. He arrived in the bush with a topographical map of the territory they were about to explore: 'The first thing my Dad did was to tear that map into tiny little pieces. He said I was committing the white man's mistake, making plans for the land without ever setting foot on it, without ever getting a feel for it' (Came 1995, 16). The Royal Commission report comments thus on this anecdote:

> The need to walk on the land in order to know it is a different approach to knowledge than the one-dimensional, literate approach to knowing. Persons schooled in a literate culture are accustomed to having all the context they need to understand a communication embedded in the text before them ... Persons taught to use all their senses – to absorb every clue to interpreting a complex, dynamic reality – may well smile at the illusion that words alone, stripped of complementary sound and colour and texture, can convey meaning adequately. (Canada 1996, 1: 622–3)

Holistic Knowledge

All of the senses, coupled with openness to intuitive or spiritual insights, are required in order to plumb the depths of aboriginal knowledge. Dumont (1976) calls this sensitivity 'three hundred and sixty degree vision.' Ceremonies are the primary means of instilling the attitude of expectant stillness that opens the door to full awareness (Cardinal, 1990).

Couture (1991) quotes an anonymous mentor as saying, 'There are only two things you have to remember about being Indian. One is that everything is alive, and the second is that we are all related' (61).

Hampton (1995) quotes two widely used prayer formulas: 'Have mercy on me that my people may live' and 'Pity me ... for all my relatives.' He then describes how his awareness of the deep meaning of these words expanded while he fasted for a vision:

> On the second day of the fast, as I prayed I began to ask myself, 'Who are my people?' Over the following days my identity expanded from my own skin outwards to family, friends, relatives, Indian people, other humans, animals, growing things, to finally reach the earth itself and everything that is. I came away from the fast with a deep awareness of feeling at home, related to all that is. (19–20)

The medicine wheel is one of the most powerful instruments currently used to convey the holistic character of aboriginal knowledge and experience. The circle, representing the circle of life, contains all experience, everything in the biosphere – animal, vegetable, mineral, human, spirit – past, present and future. Two lines mark the quadrants of the circle. The point in the centre where they intersect symbolizes a balance point. Traditionally, the medicine wheel was part of the culture of nations of the plains – Dakota, Blackfoot, and Cree. When I first learned about the medicine wheel I found it easy to see how the life stages of human beings corresponded to the quadrants – child, youth, adult, and elder. I found it more difficult to accept that the diverse colours of humankind belonged in the quadrants as well. The wheel seemed to be saying that red people have a gift for relating to the natural world and animals, white people are inclined to movement and intellectual activity, black people have the gift of vision, and yellow people have the gift of time or patience. To me, this was contributing to stereotypes.

Gradually I became aware that my resistance to the symbolic representation arose in part from my awareness that if people were divided up according to their gifts, I would probably be placed in the white quadrant because I work so easily with words and concepts. Aboriginal teaching that threatened to alienate me from my roots and my community was not welcomed! At some point an elder elaborated on the flags at the ends of the intersecting lines. They signify the winds that blow and move the wheel, reminding us that nothing is fixed and stagnant, and that change is a natural condition of life. I remembered that learning and growth in each of the quadrants had taken precedence in various stages of my life.

It dawned on me then that the medicine wheel is not a model of rigid categorization or racial division; rather, it is a model of balance. Some of us find ourselves predominantly in one quadrant of the wheel, with gifts that by themselves are insufficient for a full life. The medicine wheel teaches us to seek ways of incorporating the gifts of the other quadrants. It encourages us to bring more balance to our own lives or and to form relationships and work in teams. So the model of the world is not of people separated in quadrants, but rather of people united in a circle. Through the sharing of diverse gifts, balance is created in individual lives and in society as a whole.

The holistic quality of knowledge implies that isolating pieces of experience and trying to make sense of them apart from the environment that gave rise to them flies in the face of reality and is bound to lead to frustration. This does not mean that analysis of parts of the circle of life is to be dismissed; it simply means that analysis must be balanced with synthesis – placing the part that we have come to know by close analysis in the context of all its relations, which will continually impact on that which we thought we knew, and thereby transform it.

Narrative and metaphor

Traditionally, stories were the primary medium used to convey aboriginal knowledge. Stories inform and entertain; they hold up models of behaviour; and they sound warnings. Recounted in ceremonial settings and confirmed through many repetitions, they record the history of a people. They teach without being intrusive, because the listener can ignore the oblique instruction or apply it to the degree he or she is ready to accept, without offence. Stories of personal experience can be understood either as reminiscences or as metaphors to guide moral choice and self-examination.

Issues of Authenticity and Authority

It will be evident by now to the reader that although this essay talks about aboriginal knowledge, it conforms to almost none of the defining characteristics put forward. It would be reasonable to suggest these questions: Can the integrity of aboriginal knowledge survive the transition to a literate form? And what are the tests of authenticity? Who has the authority to represent aboriginal knowledge?

Most aboriginal people who write about aboriginal knowledge have spent a good deal of their lives interacting with mainstream society and see a need to make explicit those elements of their culture which are at risk of being lost. Most nonaboriginal people who write on the subject have worked closely with aboriginal people and feel moved to advocate among their peers for a greater understanding and respect for aboriginal knowledge. Both types of writers may be motivated as well by a sense that the philosophies of aboriginal people belong to the store of knowledge that ought to be accessible to all peoples. What aboriginal and nonaboriginal writers have in common is a degree of distance from the everyday practices of an oral culture.

They are also insulated from the discipline imposed on purveyors of knowledge in an oral culture – that is, from the collective analysis and judgment of a community, each of whose members shares equal authority to interpret reality. Immunity from corrective influence renders suspect any outsider interpreting insider knowledge and, indeed, any writer whether a member of the community or not. Writing things up gives authority to a particular view and a particular writer.

In a paper prepared for the Royal Commission on Aboriginal Peoples, Julie Cruikshank (1997) points to experience in Uganda, where a surge of interest in oral history resulted in the recording of certain clan histories. This record gradually assumed the status of official history, even though it marginalized other, less powerful clans. Those who were excluded never accepted the legitimacy of the written accounts, because in their eyes authentic information about their lives is active – debated, discussed, and revised in daily activities. Some participants in that process are recognized as being more knowledgeable than others, but this does not close off circulation of knowledge through the whole community, nor does it undermine the authority of the hearers to validate the knowledge being voiced. This example illustrates the effects of extracting a portion of an oral tradition and translating it into a medium that carries with it an aura of power.

The dilemma for aboriginal educators is that while they recognize the limitations of texts, the traditional media for transmitting aboriginal knowledge have become largely unavailable to many aboriginal people, especially the young. The young people no longer have daily access to experiential learning on the land; they have decreasing levels of fluency in aboriginal languages that would keep them in communication with elders; and they spend much of their time in educational institutions that socialize them into dependence on the written word. There is a real danger that the elders who still retain traditional and spiritual knowledge, and who know the context in which empirical observations must be evaluated, will join their ancestors without passing on what they know.

In answer to the challenge that I have implicitly presented to my own authority to teach about these things, my first response is that my words represent aboriginal knowledge only in the sense that they emerge from the consciousness of an aboriginal woman fully engaged with the aboriginal community as a family and clan member and as an educator. I acknowledge that my understanding has been shaped by intercultural experience, and my communication by the semantics of the English language. I have told my story with as much honesty as I can muster, but it represents only one view of reality, a perspective that needs to be evaluated in the context of other stories by other members of the community.

In briefs and oral presentations to the royal commission, aboriginal women in particular cautioned against accepting at face value claims to authority asserted on the basis of tradition. Examples:

Tradition is invoked by most politicians in defence of certain choices. Women must always ask – Whose tradition? Is 'tradition' beyond critique? How often is tradition cited to advance or deny our women's positions? (Women of the Métis Nation, 1993: 25, 27)

We have also come across many self-proclaimed healers who have abused and exploited traditional spirituality in their own Aboriginal people. (Sanderson, 1993)

Women making submissions to the Royal Commission emphasized that readiness to challenge abuses of power does not in any way imply a lack of respect for tradition. Rather, it is necessary to preserve the integrity of traditional knowledge.[3]

To the anxiety (which I share) that the modes of representing aboriginal knowledge are changing so rapidly that perhaps that knowledge is losing its soul, I respond that aboriginal culture has always been adaptive. In earlier times, when the climate was warmer, the Inuit hunted whales in large skin boats called umiaks. When the climate cooled, inlets became ice-bound and the whales disappeared. The Inuit developed kayaks, one-man boats that were much more efficient for hunting in the changed environment, and the technology of building umiaks fell into disuse. That is how the people survived.

Elders are coming together in gatherings such as the annual elders' conference at Birch Island, Ontario, to talk about how to be an elder in a changing environment, and how to adapt old forms of sharing knowledge to ensure that the next generation benefits from the wisdom of our ancestors.

Educators writing about aboriginal knowledge and elders talking about how to communicate with young people enamoured with Walkman radios and Nintendo games are part of the process of cultural adaptation. Each of us knows that traditional knowledge of how to maintain balance in our lives, how to relate to other human beings, and how to practise respect for the Earth which supports us, is desperately needed – and not only by aboriginal people. We need to devise appropriate means to navigate in a radically changed environment.

The ultimate test of the validity of knowledge is whether it enhances the capacity of people to live well. Jake Thomas, an Iroquois hereditary chief and ceremonialist, speaking about the Great Law of Peace which is at the heart of Iroquois philosophy and government, told members of the Royal Commission: 'That Peace is supposed to work. It's the power of the words of the Creator [from whom] they came, of unity, being of one mind, a good mind' (1993).

The validity of new formulations of old wisdom can best be tested in the crucible of everyday life.

Putting Knowledge into Practice

The confidence of aboriginal people in what they know from experience, and their trust in knowledge that has been handed down to them, suffered as the quality of their lives deteriorated historically under the control of external governments and institutions. With the political accommodations that have occurred over the past twenty years and the possibility now that the Royal Commmission's report will accelerate fundamental change in relations between aboriginal people and Canadian society, many aboriginal people anticipate that aboriginal knowledge will resume its place as the basis of decision making and social order in their communities.

The imposition of assimilative education, economic dislocation, and government control from an external culture interrupted for generations the transmission of knowledge from grandparents to children and youth. It also disrupted the normal work of adults applying traditional knowledge to the demands of daily living and adapting that knowledge to evolving conditions.

Self-government and economic renewal as proposed by the Royal Commission and pursued by aboriginal people and their organizations will open the way for aboriginal adults to become fully involved, as they were traditionally, in shaping the economic, social, and political life of their communities and nations. However, they will still be confronted with externally generated problems of huge proportions – the contamination of the food supply in polluted ecosystems and the marginalization of rural peoples in a competitive world economy, to name but two examples.

The knowledge that will support their survival in the future will not be an artifact from the past. It will be a living fire, rekindled from surviving embers and fuelled with the materials of the twenty-first century.

NOTES

1 Many of the formulations and quotations in this essay echo the language of the commission's reports and public hearings. For help in shaping my own perceptions, I am indebted to the hundreds of Aboriginal people who shared their experience at hearings and round tables; to colleagues at the commission, who shared my quest for knowledge; and to the commissioners, who maintained an unfaltering commitment to finding ways to communicate the depths of cultural awareness that they had gained.

2 The reference refers to presentations over the years at elders' conferences at Trent University. For further exploration of this elder's teachings, see Solomon, 1990, especially p. 117.

3 For further discussion of aboriginal women's views on these and related subjects, see Canada, 1996, Volume 4, Chapter 2, 'Women's Perspectives.'

REFERENCES

Brant, Clare C. 1990. Native Ethics and Rules of Behaviour. *Canadian Journal of Psychiatry* 35, August, pp. 534–9.

Brody, Hugh. 1983. *Maps and Dreams*. Markham, Ont.: Penguin Books.

Came, Barry. 1995. 'Fighting for the Land.' *Maclean's* 108/9 (27 February), 16.

Canada. 1996. *Royal Commission on Aboriginal Peoples: Report of the Royal Commission on Aboriginal Peoples*, Volume 1, *Looking Forward, Looking Back*; Volume 2, *Restructuring the Relationship*; Volume 3, *Gathering Strength*; Volume 4, *Perspectives and Realities*; and Volume 5, *Renewal: A Twenty-Year Commitment*. Ottawa: Canada Communications Group. (Also available with related documentation on CD-ROM under the title *For Seven Generations: An Information Legacy of the Royal Commission on Aboriginal Peoples*. Ottawa, Libraxus, 1997.)

Cardinal, Douglas. 1990. Interview: 'Dancing with Chaos.' *Intervox* 8. Quoted at length in Dennis H. McPherson and J. Douglas Rabb, *Indian from the Inside: A Study in Ethno-Metaphysics*. Thunder Bay: Lakehead University Centre for Northern Studies, Occasional Paper 14, 1993.

Colorado, Pam. Bridging Native and Western Science. *Convergence* 21 (2/3): 49–68.

Couture, Joseph E. 1991. 'Explorations in Native Knowing.' In John W. Friesen (ed.), *The Cultural Maze: Complex Questions on Native Destiny in Western Canada*. Calgary: Detselig, 53–73.

Cruikshank, Julie. 1997. Claiming Legitimacy: Oral Tradition and Oral History. A discussion paper prepared for the Royal Commission on Aboriginal Peoples, published in the CD. *For Seven Generations: An Information Legacy of the Royal Commission on Aboriginal Peoples*. Ottawa: Libraxus, 1997.

Dumont, James. 1976. Journey to Daylight Land: Through Ojibway Eyes. *Laurentian University Review* 8/2.

Ermine, Willie. 1995. 'Aboriginal Epistemology.' In *First Nations Education in Canada: The Circle Unfolds*. Ed. Marie Battiste and Jean Barman. Vancouver: UBC Press, 101–12.

Hampton, Eber. 1995. 'Towards a Redefinition of Indian Education.' In *First Nations Education in Canada: The Circle Unfolds*. Ed. Marie Battiste and Jean Barman. Vancouver: UBC Press, 5–46.

Ross, Rupert. 1992. *Dancing with a Ghost: Exploring Indian Reality*. Markham: Reed Books.

Sanderson, Lillian. 1993. Aboriginal Women's Council, RCAP Public Hearings. Saskatoon, Sask., 13 May. Published in the CD *For Seven Generations: An Information Legacy of the Royal Commission on Aboriginal Peoples*. Ottawa: Libraxus, 1997.

Solomon, Arthur. 1990. *Songs for the People: Teachings on the Natural Way*. Toronto: NC Press.

Thomas, Chief Jacob (Jake). 1993. RCAP Public Hearings, Akwesasne, Ontario, 3 May. Published in the CD *For Seven Generations: An Information Legacy of the the Royal Commission on Aboriginal Peoples*. Ottawa: Libraxus, 1997.

Waldram, James B. 1997. Traditional Knowledge Systems: The Recognition of Indigenous History and Science. *Saskatchewan Indian Federated College Journal* 2(2): 115–24.

Women of the Métis Nation. 1993. Women Who Own Themselves: The Final Report of the Conference on Métis Women and Governance. Brief submitted to the Royal Commission on Aboriginal Peoples. Available in the RCAP files, National Archives, Ottawa.

2

Heart Knowledge, Blood Memory, and the Voice of the Land: Implications of Research among Hawaiian Elders

LEILANI HOLMES

Ancestry and Experience

I am interested in the words of Hawaiian *kupuna* (elders) and in the ways they pass down knowledge. I am also interested in the relationship between the knowledge making of the *kupuna* and scholarly knowledge making. As a student of *hula kahiko* (ancient Hawaiian dance), I found that our stories, *hulas* (dances), and chants often constructed histories different from those written by non-Hawaiians. Much knowledge making goes on in the Hawaiian community; at the same time, knowledge making *about* Hawaiians goes on in scholarly communities. Scholars tend to approach data collection with theoretical frameworks that lie outside the lives of the people whose voices are being used as data. Practitioners of Hawaiian culture consult, critique, and create scholarly texts, and their conclusions circulate back into the academic realm. For this reason, when we consider indigenous knowledge we also need to consider scholarly claims about indigenous knowledge.

There exists a great body of oral and written literature by Hawaiians, which I refer to as the 'Hawaiian corpus.' *The Kumulipo* (Lili'uokalani, 1978); *Ka Po'e Kahiko*: 'The People of Old' (Kamakau, 1964a), *Na Hana a ka Po'e Kahiko*: 'The Works of the People of Old' (Kamakau, 1964b), and *Fragments of Hawaiian History* (Ii, 1983) are works in this Hawaiian corpus; all four provide a Hawaiian philosophy of knowledge as well as a theoretical framework. In this grounded epistemology, knowledge comes first from the family (i.e., from those in one's lineage). Ways of knowing are not based on the limits of one's own physical senses and may include prayer, prescience, dreams, and messages from the dead. The ties of humans to the cosmos are familial and hierarchical. Knowledge is intended to incite humans to act in such ways as to ensure the protection and reproduction of *all* creatures in the universe. Political and social history does not exist in a different realm from indigenous cosmology; rather, it *intersects* with that cosmology.

Scholarly frameworks and debates (or systemic conventional knowledge) and the Hawaiian corpus are alternative discourses; each offers insights into the voices of the *kupuna*. Both sorts of knowledge make claims about Hawaiians as indigenous people. In this article I will give a brief outline of Hawaii's history and then discuss *kupuna* at length, emphasizing those points at which their words seem to echo the corpus. I will briefly note and take a limited stand on a scholarly debate about Hawaiian cultural production, discussing what it tells us about indigenous and academic knowledge making. Finally, I will discuss how the *kupuna* speak of the earth/human relationship and how we may speak about their voices.

Historical Background

In 1895 Queen Lili'uokalani was imprisoned at Iolani Place, having been overthrown by American sugar planters, and was pleading for the restoration of her rule. She was also translating *The Kumulipo*, a creation chant that related the origins of the Hawaiian people to Haloa, the younger sibling of Kalo (the taro plant), and to the mating of earth (Papa) and sky (Wakea). It traced the genealogical roots of all Hawaiians back to the creation of the cosmos. The Queen completed her translation while in exile.

Prior to 1778, Hawaiian government was grounded on two things: moral/religious practices, which were largely controlled by the *ali'i*; and a system of communal land use. *'Aina* (land) was considered sacred and alive. Chant and *hula* told stories about creation, history, genealogy, and the movement of deities on the land, constructing a deep relationship to the cosmos. After 'discovery' in 1778, Hawai'i became a trading site. Calvinist missionaries furthered assimilation, and their progeny advanced the interests of capital. By 1890 the Hawaiians had suffered a population collapse and a foreign-dominated political economy had caused many Hawaiians to become dispossessed.

In 1898, following the overthrow of Lili'uokalani, Hawai'i was annexed to the United States. After statehood in 1959, tourism tied Hawai'i to global corporate structures; Hawaiian culture was commodified and Westernized in the public view, while privately sustained in families and communities. By the 1960s Hawai'i's economy depended heavily on the American military and on tourism, whose projects further endangered Hawaiian practices and land holdings. In the 1970s Hawaiians began to resist development, speaking about the sacred nature of the land, the importance of communal ways of life, and Hawaiian self-determination. Various sovereignty groups coalesced around the goal of reclaiming a land base, and a 'Hawaiian Renaissance' or cultural revitalization took place.

By the 1990s, pro-sovereignty organizations were debating the form that self-determination should take and the means for achieving it, asserting the Hawaiian ethics of *aloha 'aina* (love of the land) and *malama 'aina* (protection of the land) in opposition to the idea that land was private property (Weinberg, 1996). In 1994, Hawaiians initiated a debate-filled process leading to self-determination. In 1996 the majority of Hawaiian voters (73.3 percent) responded 'ae' (yes) to the ballot query, 'Shall the Hawaiian people elect delegates to propose a Native Hawaiian government?' (Ward, 1996).

Political and economic forces have shaped social change in Hawai'i; at the same time, everyday talk creates and sustains Hawaiian formulations of land, identity, and the universe story (cosmology). People act on these formulations, transforming the social structure and producing social change. Central to this surge of political and cultural activity are the stories, reminiscences, and lessons voiced by elders (*kupuna*). To understand present-day Hawaiian social action, we need to listen to the voices of the *kupuna*.

The Voices of the *Kupuna*

In order to listen to these voices I first interviewed Kalo, who is *makua* generation – that is, one generation below *kupuna*. Kalo is a school administrator and community activist in her forties. In turn, she interviewed her *kupuna* while I tape-recorded their talk. As the *kupuna* shared their knowledge with Kalo, I did not interrupt; thus, the interviews adapted to the rhythm of talk to which Kalo and her *kupuna* were accustomed.

I approached the interviews with themes from interpretive inquiry and ethnomethology; these themes represented not organizing theoretical frameworks, but rather ways of understanding subjectivity in research. The process of interpretive inquiry enabled me to treat myself as a 'subject' as I analyzed the Hawaiian corpus and engaged in field work. It involved divulging and interrogating my responses to text or experiences, thereby revealing the non-neutral and limited nature of my own language and perspectives. The ways that the corpus and the field work experience transported me beyond my limited ways of knowing pointed to important dimensions of the Hawaiian corpus and field work.[1]

Following are excerpts from my interview with Kalo and from her interviews with two of her *kupuna*, Tutu (grandmother) Ohi'a and Aunty Lau. Tutu Ohi'a is a retired schoolteacher and active community leader in her nineties. Aunty Lau, an accomplished *lauhala* (pandanus) weaver, teaches Hawaiian culture in the schools, and is in her eighties.

As I listened to the *kupuna,* it seemed as if through them, knowledge lodged in the heart of the listener, memory flowed through blood lines, and the land was given voice and agency. Thus, the words of the *kupuna* arrive here in three sections: heart knowledge, blood memory, and the voice of the land – categories that I will explain further.

Heart Knowledge

For Tutu Ohi'a, knowledge is not a personal achievement; rather it is conferred 'by God,' is related to others unseen, and exists beyond the earthly human experience. Here, Tutu Ohi'a discusses her grandmother: 'And she'd say, "We're going over there, to that house, to see that *kupuna*. She's not well." And I said, "How do you know?" And she'd say, "Because I had a dream last night." So sure enough, when we get to that place, this *kupuna* is in bed.'

Another of Tutu Ohi'a's stories features her as a child, taught through schooling that the *kahuna* (healers, priests) and Hawaiian healing practices were bad: 'I would say to my grandmother. "I don't like what you're doing ... they're going to call you a *kahuna!*" We never knew much about the good *kahuna*. And she said: "No, I had to go because that is *my* job. It was given to me to go and help. And that's why we go."'

In Tutu Ohi'a's story, knowledge is a gift from a higher power, revealed and contextualized through relationships. During the interviews both Tutu Ohi'a and Aunty Lau anchored Kalo as part of their *'ohana* (family) before they told stories passed down to them through their families. Kalo received not only personal directives from the interviews but also a sense that each interview was, in fact, *for* her, and given in the context of a relationship.

In answer to a question about the future, Aunty Lau spoke of humility: 'If we are more humble people, our future will be beautiful. But if ... our Hawaiians think that they're better than the next person instead of learning from one another ... our future [is] going to be the same way, same way from one generation to the next. That's the way I feel.'

For Aunty Lau, stasis is a consequence of not learning from one another. Kalo also links knowledge to connection:

Everything we do now ... is in preparation for our youngsters, or people who come after us ... whether it be the environment, or whether it be our Hawaiian values and concepts that we pass on to the next generation and a positive wellness, wholeness, of who we are as Hawaiians ... a legacy ... of strength, of courage, of energy ... the Hawaiian values that are being passed down to us, through our *kupuna* [grandparent generation]. And then through us as *makua* [parent generation], and then to the next *'opio* [youngster] generation. 'Cause Hawaiians ... don't separate themselves from the environment. We are one, one and the same, and we need each other, and depend on each other, and have this interrelationship with our environment.

Kalo constructs knowledge as an almost tangible force flowing through the bodies of successive generations. In this sense, the continuum of time is collapsed into and manifests out from the bodies of humans. Kalo uses the term 'our youngsters,' constructing the younger generation as existing relationally rather than in the abstract. She transforms the idea of knowledge, or legacy, into a claim about human relatedness to the environment, and thus links knowledge with cosmology.

Tutu Ohi'a focuses on knowledge rather than on external material conditions:

I always say, we are poor people, but we can be rich in whatever we do. Respect for the land, respect for our families and us for them, we'll be there. We'll be there, you see. So ... it's a hard thing for me to know. How they would fare in the future. If they listen. They are full of the teachings. If they would only listen. Because in this ear coming out the other one doesn't do any good!

For Tutu Ohi'a, the future exists as a manifestation of knowledge through humans. As in the Hawaiian corpus, the *kupuna* include prescience, dreams, and messages from the dead as ways of knowing. Knowledge is given through relationships and for the purpose of furthering relationships. It surpasses the intellectual realm, and lodges itself in the emotional realm, so I have called it 'heart knowledge.'

Blood Memory

Kalo speaks of the importance of blood (although not blood quantum)[2] and then of family, or genealogy, as connecting Hawaiians to one another:

It doesn't matter where Hawaiians live. They can live all over the world ... when you say that you are Hawaiian, we never say ... 'how much Hawaiian do you have?' Which is a total ... *alien* concept, but the fact that you *are* Hawaiian and you *are* *'ohana* [family] and that we eat out of the same *poi* [a food made from taro] bowl ... And that we come from the same roots. And that's the connectedness that ... brings all Hawaiians together, no matter how much Hawaiian they have by blood quantum. Wherever they live, if you are Hawaiian, you are Hawaiian. You are accepted into the *'ohana* [family]. Unconditionally. There are no ... restrictions, no limitations, no obstacles, no barriers. And that is very important. That's why our genealogy is so important and that genealogy connection ... to our *ali'i*, and then of course because [of] the *ali'i* [our connection] to the gods themselves ... and again, back to the land, so ... it's a *circle*, it's a circle of love.

For Kalo the circular connection between the people, the *ali'i*, the gods, and the land is forged not by information but by blood and 'roots.' Central to this idea of blood and roots is the notion that experience is crucial to knowledge. If one does not have the experience, knowledge must come through the experiences of the *kupuna*. Tutu Ohi'a describes how *malama 'aina* (protecting the land) is not part of the experience of present-day Hawaiians: 'Because they don't understand, because they have not had it ... they didn't have that feeling, that there is this thing that God has given us, for us to use, but at the same time take care of it.'

Tutu Ohi'a later completes this idea by saying that 'it's up to us to tell them.' The implication is that through the *kupuna*, Hawaiians who have no experience of living on the land will learn *malama 'aina*, by receiving the memories and admonitions of their *kupuna*. The *kupuna* are conceptualized as containers of memory. Aunty describes how she used to argue with her aunt: 'I used to argue back to her. I said, "How do you know?" She said, "My *kupuna* told me, and I'm telling you." And ... you know, this is only what I believe, you know, because that was handed down.' As these words are passed from her aunty (and her aunty's *kupuna*) to her, so Aunty Lau passes them to us. For Aunty Lau, ties forged through blood and connection (or roots) are the source of living memory. She vividly remembers a conversation she had with her aunty decades ago: 'And you know, I *sat*, I *looked* at her, and, you know, she's old, but my mother's last sister. And she put her head down, she said, "I'm telling you that." She told me, "You teach your children that. So they know what love is."'

The notion that through families different knowledges emerge via the *kupuna* surfaces in several of Aunty Lau's stories. In these stories knowledge is validated not through the notion of 'truth value' but rather through connection. The memories passed down through connection are inviolable. Aunty Lau describes how she spoke to another *kupuna* in Hawaiian about how their families had similar beliefs concerning the *ali'i*: 'And [she] and I were sitting outside and we were talking in Hawaiian. And I said, "Oh, we believe the same way too." And we cannot [speak of this] to some others ... because they think different ... We don't want to hurt anybody. This is the way ... we believe. So anyway, that's what I believe ... and I tell my grandchildren about it.'

Aunty Lau moved from this story to a story about her grandson:

I would share with him, so one evening he said he had an argument with his girlfriend's grandmother ... telling her what he believed in. And ... she argued back with him ... she asked him, 'Who did you hear it from?' He said, 'My grandma.' She said, 'Oh well, your grandma didn't learn it right.' So he brought ... [a] book and showed her. And she said she really didn't know it was like that. So I said, 'You know ... don't argue. Just say, "This is the way I was taught, and this is the way I have to go research on it."' I said, 'And if they argue, don't argue. If they think differently, then you respect what they say.' Yeah ... I said, 'You don't argue with older people especially ...' He said, 'But, Grandma, I had to show them that ... I may be younger than them, but I knew what I was talking about.' He said, 'Because Grandma, when you told me, I took it up to Kamehameha [school], to our Hawaiian teacher.'

In this story, Aunty Lau's grandson uses a book and a teacher at school as verifiers for his genealogical source, Aunty Lau. Aunty Lau's wish is not that her grandson validate her teachings, but that he practise respect for the words of other *kupuna* who are now (through his girlfriend) connected to him. In her mind, these two strands of knowledge, flowing through the generations of two different families, can *both* flourish. In another story told by Aunty Lau, an older *kupuna* does not respect the words of a *kupuna* who is younger in years. Aunty Lau feels that the younger *kupuna* learned from *his kupuna*, who learned from their *kupuna* and from generations of experience living on the land. Therefore his knowledge, intact as passed down, must be respected: 'So you see sometimes we have to listen to the young generation too. And that's what's wrong with us. You know, there are some that say, "We were taught this way." No ... Listen to other people too, 'cause they learned their way too.'

In the stories of the *kupuna*, historic acts have present-day consequences, whether or not we are conscious of them. When Kalo asks Aunty Lau about 'our strong points,' Aunty Lau proceeds to 'fix' Kalo in relationship with Aunty Lau's mother. She then tells a powerful story about how Hawaiians mistreated others in the distant past, and suggests that Hawaiians examine and undo their own bad practices. This cycle of atonement spans generations of Hawaiians via blood lines:

OK ... let me share something with you. And I told you, Kalo, way back, I think you're related to my mom, them. So let me share something with you, from what my *kupuna* had shared with me. [Aunty Lau describes how ancient Hawaiians mistreated others.] [My] *kupuna* said, 'Until they undo what they did to these people ... they [the Hawaiians] will never be happy.' She said, 'You see how they *hukihuki* [pull in different directions]?' She *told* me, 'You teach your children that. So they know what love is.'

Aunty Lau also asserts that humility and Hawaiian practices and values will lead toward collective responsibility and self-determination. She suggests (as does Tutu Ohi'a) that inner spiritual integrity and ethical actions are essential to social change: 'So until they learn how to love [Hawaiians won't get self-determination], and I think that's what's wrong with our Hawaiian people. Ah, a lot of it is jealousy too. Yeah. Instead of helping, yeah? Coming together. Like they say, *lokahi* [come together]. Be together, all in one. They're not doing it. They're talking about it. But they're not practising it.'

The Voice of the Land

In answer to a question about the strengths of Hawaiians, Tutu Ohi'a poetically recalls abundance and living on the land:

My grandmother and grandfather always had everything ... and we lived the Hawaiian way. We ... cooked outside, you know ... but in spite of that, the food was good, and simple food, like ... taro tops, taro stalks, the taro in the *poi* [gets louder, more emphasis], the sugar cane for us to chew, and ... *every mahealani, mahealani* is the full moon ... we'd all plant. Yeah. Our bananas.

In answer to a question about spirituality, Tutu Ohi'a refers to *malama 'aina* and her vivid memories of living on the land:

You see the early days, when people had big tracts of land, they took care of their land. They took care of the water! Everything came that way because that's the way we did. We had the land, and we had the water. Nobody went into the pool where the water was because our water came from the river ... and when summer came and we had a long drying, dry period ... that's when Grandma would clean *all* of that pool, leaves and rocks and things that have come from *mauka* [the mountains]. And so we all had clean water. And people would come to our *'ohana* [family] that way. OK. Today, when we say, 'Take care of the land,' I don't think many Hawaiians have that ... cause they live in cities, towns, and they live ... in apartments ... The only way they can get it is by us. Us telling them. Take care. Take care of the land. You know the land feeds us. And the rivers give us water.

Tutu Ohi'a ties abundance to a particular way of caring for the land and the water, which resulted in people connecting to her *'ohana*. She uses the English translation of *malama 'aina*: 'Take care of the land.' She then says that *kupuna* who lived on the land must teach modern-day Hawaiians the value of *malama 'aina*. Importantly, Tutu Ohi'a describes land and rivers as subjects who act to 'feed us' and 'give us water.' Aunty Lau also articulates her belief about the land, which she learned by listening to her *kupuna*: 'Actually nobody *owns* the land. God owns the land ... and you know ... when I was a child, because I was able to understand Hawaiian I used to *hear* the old folks talk about that.'

Tutu Ohi'a told of an incident when she took a plant without asking for it:

> I got out of my car and hurried, went in, pulled the thing, and you know, I felt as though somebody [had] taken me and threw me down. And my arm began to hurt. So I came home driving. I was all alone with [the plant] and when I got home I said to my husband, 'Take me to the doctor, I think I broke my arm.' He said, 'How?' I said, 'I felt I was thrown down on these rocks. I was pulling [the plant].' He said, 'You didn't ask for it. You just took it. You had no business to just take it without asking for it ...' You see. So we believe that things don't belong to us. They belong to God. But if you want to use it, ask. And then they [her *kupuna*] respected that. They respected so much. They respected land, respected the trees. They respected the air ... Water. Everything that gave life to them. And to me, I lived that life as a child. [Voice shakes.] And I didn't appreciate it. Because I was aiming to be ... American. And to, you know, to do things like an American. Because we were going to school then. You see, and it took many, many years for me to realize that I had the *best* ... of the culture.

Notable in this story are the consciousness and apparent intent of an unseen entity or entities whose behaviour is related to the heedless taking of the plant. Tutu Ohi'a feels as if 'somebody' has taken her and thrown her down. She also describes being 'all alone with this plant.' Tutu Ohi'a's phrase may subtly imply that the plant has consciousness and is another *being*. In her phrase, 'You see. So we believe ...' Tutu Ohi'a constructs the instructional nature of her story. Knowledge flows from the story, not as an abstract 'moral' but rather as knowledge conveyed to her through her experience with the plant. Trees, air, water, and everything that 'gives life' are again described as subjects who must be approached in the right way, who must be 'asked,' and who must be respected. This knowledge exists in opposition to schooling, which involves alienation from Hawaiian culture.

Kalo connects land and humans using the story of Haloa and Kalo, and reflects on ancient cosmology as constructed in *The Kumulipo*:

> And that's why the land is so important ... because without the land there would be no life. If we reflect on the story of Haloa and Kalo ... the story of how ... the Hawaiians got Kalo, which is taro, which is the Hawaiian staple, from which we make *poi*, and which is at every ... Hawaiian meal, the story of Haloa teaches us

that ... you need ... Kalo first in order to *feed* your people, and that's why *poi* is so important. If you make that kind of ... connection with the earth, and with God, in ... *one* being. That Hawaiians ... are so connected to the heavens ... to the earth, to themselves.

In this story we see the fixed and timeless genealogical link between land and humans, as symbolized by taro and as enacted in the eating of *poi*.

In their stories, Kalo and her *kupuna* discuss land and a host of entities who are related to humans. As in the Hawaiian corpus, the relationship of humans to the cosmos is familial and hierarchical. The practices and consequences of *aloha 'aina* (love of the land) and *malama 'aina* (taking care of the land) are detailed in their talk. Those who abdicate their relationship to the land suffer dire consequences. As in the Hawaiian corpus, the purpose of knowledge is to incite humans to ensure that *all* creatures in the universe are protected. Political/social history does not exist in a different realm from indigenous cosmology; rather, it intersects with that cosmology. Land and one's relationship to the land are not just 'talked about'; rather, the *actions* of the land and the *actions* of beings who are other than human are described. The *kupuna* describe earth as a presence and as a subject; it has agency. Through Kalo's talk and that of her *kupuna,* the voice of the land is articulated.

An Ancestry of Experience

For Kalo, Tutu Ohi'a, and Aunty Lau, knowledge is passed to others in the context of relationships and deep feelings of connection. I have described this as heart knowledge. Knowledge also passes through the generations; thus, Hawaiians are united with the *kupuna* of generations past. I have called this knowledge blood memory. Knowledge is also embedded in a grounded cosmology; it exists not for its own sake but rather as a continuing reminder of the subjectivity of *'aina*. As the *kupuna* share knowledge, they articulate the voice of the land.

Like many *kupuna,* Tutu Ohi'a often said, 'My *kupuna* told me, and now I'm telling you.' Within the experiences and memories of Kalo's *kupuna,* the experiences of their own *kupuna* live. In this way heart knowledge, blood memory, and the voice of the land constitute an *ancestry of experience* that shapes dreams, desires, intentions, and purposeful activity.

Feelings of connectedness entering the talk of the *kupuna* may make this knowledge more memorable than 'book learning.' In their associations, sequences, and patterns, Tutu Ohi'a and Aunty Lau present a grounded philosophy of knowledge and a deeply layered cosmology wherein the knowledge of their own *kupuna* lives. They, like many *kupuna*, are the last in their families to have grown up 'on the land.' A sense of responsibility pervades their talk. As with *The Kumulipo* and other works in the Hawaiian corpus, the talk of the *kupuna* links learning, lineage, living memory, and, most importantly, land.

The words of the *kupuna* and of indigenous elders worldwide should play a central role when we consider indigenous struggles toward self-determination, and recuperation of the land. Aunty Lau connects Hawaiian loss of land to Hawaiian loss of values and to inhumanity to others in the past; atonement will lead to social change. Tutu Ohi'a asserts that having recovered humility and Hawaiian practices and values, Hawaiians will move toward collective responsibility to one another and toward self-determination. The *kupuna* describe cultural practices, values, and conventions as *continuous* within their families – as having been passed down through the generations. Memories centre on the land as the basis for communal existence and translate into ethical imperatives. This lends Hawaiians an incredible amount of agency; it is not external power relations that bring about self-determination, but rather right action and inner integrity on the part of Hawaiians themselves. According to the *kupuna*, self-determination is tied to the notions of *lokahi* (together as one), *aloha 'aina* (love of the land), and *malama 'aina* (protection of the land).

At many junctures the words of the *kupuna* echo ideas found in the Hawaiian corpus, which can therefore be seen as providing an indigenous theoretical framework for understanding the talk of the *kupuna*. I will now discuss scholarly frameworks and claims about Hawaiians as indigenous people, focusing on a debate about Hawaiian cultural production. I will take a limited stand in this debate, and briefly discuss what it uncovers about indigenous as compared to academic knowledge making. Finally, I will discuss how the *kupuna* speak of the earth/human relationship, and how we may speak about their knowledge.

Alternative Discourses: Conflicts and Possibilities

Historical materialism (political economy) is a framework that has influenced anthropological work in Hawai'i; for that reason, it deserves to be compared briefly with the Hawaiian corpus. In the Hawaiian corpus, knowledge emanates from forces that lie outside human agency to generate social change. In contrast, Marx and Engels perceived social change as generated solely through human agency. In the Hawaiian corpus, political/social history has spiritual dimensions that collapse into cosmology. For Marx and Engels, cosmology and political/social history emanate from economic relations of production; the spiritual dimension proceeds from the material dimension. Matter guides, transforms, and generates spirit.

In the Hawaiian corpus, emotion, intent, and purpose manifest themselves in every creature and feature in the cosmos. In the literature of political economy, these same things are manifested only by humans in praxis (productive action), as they use technology to control nature. In the Hawaiian corpus, beings in the cosmos exist in familial, hierarchical, and protective relationships to one another. In terms of destiny or social change, the future depends on maintaining protective relationships between humans and other beings. For Marx and Engels, such relationships exist only in precapitalist societies and are destined to disappear. From the vantage point of the Hawaiian corpus, the notion of social change in historical materialism seems anthropocentric. The Hawaiian corpus substantiates the voices of the *kupuna,* providing a closely fitting theoretical framework; whereas the literature of historical materialism represents an inversion of both the Hawaiian corpus and the voices of the *kupuna.*[3]

Is it possible to fully engage Hawaiian cultural production using a framework centring on the notion of political economy? A critical anthropology of colonialism and political economy would consider the effects of colonialism on Hawaiians and the role Hawaiians played in negotiating this process.[4] In the 1970s anthropologists shifted their gaze to indigenous movements in the Pacific, and work on the 'invention of tradition' proliferated. Some writers have claimed that contemporary discourses of cultural identity (sovereignty and cultural revival movements) are derived from Western discourses and are embedded in urban mainland traditions. They have claimed that Hawaiians are reappropriating culture in selective or inauthentic ways as a political tool. According to this view, present-day Hawaiian cultural identity and such notions as *aloha 'aina* and *malama 'aina* are a consequence of the colonial encounter.[5]

In contrast, others have asserted that values such as *aloha 'aina,* and *malama 'aina* have continuity and are being reproduced in the lived experience of Hawaiians as part of a sustained rather than an invented discourse. These writers discuss discursive authority, noting that anthropologists' writings about Hawaiians may be politically influential and may be limiting the right of Hawaiians to define their own past, present, and future. They have suggested that this work may be trivializing the idea of cultural continuity and thus shortening the roots of Oceanic culture.[6] Tobin (1994: 125) states that Hawaiians have access to 'members' resources' that anthropologists do not have,' yet Hawaiian voices are invariably shut out.[7] Sahlins questions whether it is valid to use the framework of political economy when discussing the cultures of indigenous peoples.[8] He notes that this perspective constitutes 'an attack on the cultural integrity and historical agency of indigenous peoples' (1994: 380). Lindstrom and White note that this debate indexes 'anthropology's own crisis of identity in the late twentieth century' (1995: 201).

The 'invention of tradition' debate has become a debate about the nature of evidence, indigenous subjectivity, the politics of discursive authority, and insiders' versus outsiders' knowledge. It is an argument about the conflicting identities of 'anthropologist' and 'Hawaiian' and about the repercussions for people who hold either identity (or both). As a debate it has not centred around findings from present-day studies of everyday talk and action on the part of Hawaiian people (Lindstrom and White, 1995: 209).

How do the words of the *kupuna*, which articulate a grounded epistemology and deeply layered cosmology, exist in relation to this debate? These voices suggest that just because terms such as *malama 'aina* and *aloha 'aina* are deployed in political ways, it does not necessarily follow that the notions underlying them are discontinuous, borrowed, or 'invented.' In the case of Hawai'i, living memory may be inherently political; not because living memory is a political invention, but because political action sometimes rises from the ground of living memory. Based on the voices of the *kupuna*, I lean toward those writers who speak to a continuous culture that happens to be political.

Here we must acknowledge the limitations inherent in using the words of the *kupuna* to further a position in an academic debate. While the tensions in this debate are interesting, the words of the *kupuna* seem more compelling. The debate does not open many spaces for further research on the words of the *kupuna* or Hawaiian (indigenous) cultural production. The importance of the debate lies in our acknowledgment that it is an alternative discourse informed by a particular theoretical framework, which should not be the defining grid for looking at the words and cultural work of the *kupuna*.

Current scholarly work on living memory and the body may point to more meaningful research when it comes to studying Hawaiian (and indigenous) cultural production. Using the words of the *kupuna*, we can approach living memory as a form of pedagogy and gauge the impact of living memories on people's lives. The stories of the *kupuna* contain historic discourses about knowledge, memory, land, and social change. It would be useful to ask how living memory and the stories of indigenous elders may eclipse histories taught through schooling and offer indigenous peoples a way to envision and enact social change. These stories may embody what Simon calls a 'pedagogy of possibility,' that acknowledges 'the spiritual desire to understand our presence in both historic and cosmic time' (1993: 151).

As we note the words of the *kupuna*, we can also address how Hawaiians view themselves both as bodies and as part of the cosmic body. The *kupuna* conceptualize the body as a container for memory. As I watched and listened to the *kupuna*, it seemed to me that our senses were engaged as memories, stories, and ethical imperatives were invoked. In my meetings with the *kupuna*, touch, gesture, embrace, expression, and the sharing of food were all involved. Is the idea of the body as a container for memory merely conceptualized, or is it also enacted? That is, through such practices as touch, gesture, embrace, expression, and the sharing of food do we ready the body to contain memory? I suspect that as students or instructors in the academy, our bodies are engaged in contrasting ways. How does indigenous history come to be contained in bodies and in lived spaces, or (in contrast) in academic journals and institutional spaces?

The Voice of the Land: Finding Our Voices

Larger issues than how current academics make sense of indigenous knowledges come to mind in relation to the voices of the *kupuna*. How do Hawaiian *kupuna* speak of the Earth/human relationship, and how should we take up what they say?

Nonindigenous ways of understanding our relationship with the Earth are implicated in global ecological devastation. In the Hawaiian context, the *kupuna* speak of this planet in a way that is recuperative of our present relationship with Earth. Indigenous relationships to the land play a part in the discourse on international development and 'progress.'[9] Berry and Clarke (1992), Dei (1993), and Roszak (1992) discuss how indigenous knowledge *maps* the Earth/ human relationship. Many *kupuna* represent the last living generation of 'Earth competents' – the last generation to live in a particular way in relation to the Earth. In their talk, the *kupuna* structure communion between humans and humans, and humans and the Earth. The Earth arrives to us as a presence and as a voice in relation to humans, who are constructed as listeners to this voice. In the coming years we will all need to listen to indigenous elders, and through them, hear the voice of the land.

How may indigenous people, who are increasingly part of the academy, speak about the voices of elders in our own communities and about the knowledge that is our own ancestry of experience? We may know how to speak as indigenous people, and we may be all too aware of how people establish (or refute) the authority to speak in the academy. Some of us will need to find a 'space in between' where both the knowledge of our elders and the knowledge of our colleagues or professors may enter, live, and be voiced. It will be difficult to establish a language that has integrity. For as Kalo has said, 'It's not just for us that we speak.' We must find ways to take responsibility for these stories our *kupuna,* our elders, *carry down to us.* For many of us as indigenous peoples, these are stories about our people and about our *'aina,* our land. We must listen to these stories and tell and retell them as we live out our own ancestry of experience.

NOTES

1 For instance, my desire to skim passages detailing various species, and my disinterest in their relationships to one another, betrayed that I was reading *The Kumulipo* as an anthropocentric practice.
2 Blood quantum has been used by the U.S. government to determine whether people are 'Native Hawaiian' and thus eligible for certain 'benefits.' See Laenui (1993: 133).
3 Robillard suggests that indigenous analyses of social change be privileged (1992: 1–2).
4 See Dening, 1988; Linnekin, 1990; Obeyesekere, 1992; and Sahlins, 1981.
5 For core arguments, see Handler and Linnekin (1984); Keesing (1989, 1991); Linnekin (1983, 1991a, 1991b); and Linnekin and Poyer (1990).
6 For core arguments, see Friedman (1992a, 1992b); Hau'ofa (1994); Tobin (1994); and Trask (1991, 1993).
7 Tobin says of the Trask–Linnekin debate: 'Their exchange casts doubt on whether the subjects of anthropological inquiry can retain their subjectivity in relation to Anthropologists' (1994: 123).
8 Sahlins earlier posits that 'everything in capitalism conspires to conceal the symbolic ordering of the system, especially those academic theories of praxis by which we conceive ourselves and the rest of the world' (1976: 220).
9 For indigenous responsibility to the Earth as related to development and self-determination, see Brascoupé (1992); and the Traditional Circle of Indian Elders and Youth (1992).

REFERENCES

Berry, T., and Clarke, T. 1992. *Befriending the Earth: A Theology of Reconciliation between Humans and the Earth.* Mystic: Twenty-Third Publications.
Brascoupé, S. 1992. Indigenous Perspectives on International Development. *Akwe:kon Journal* 9(2): 6–17.
Dei, G. 1993. Indigenous African Knowledge Systems: Local Traditions of Sustainable Forestry. *Singapore Journal of Tropical Geography* 4(1): 28–41.
Dening, G. 1988. *History's Anthropology: The Death of William Gooch.* Washington, D.C.: University Press of America.
Friedman, J. 1992a. Myth, History, and Political Identity. *Cultural Anthropology* 7(2): 194–210.
– 1992b. The Past in the Future: History and the Politics of Identity. *American Anthropologist* 94(4): 837–59.

Handler, R., and Linnekin, J. 1984. Tradition, Genuine or Spurious. *Journal of American Folklore* 97: 273–90.

Hau'ofa, E. 1994. Pasts to Remember. Paper delivered as an Oceania Lecture at the University of the South Pacific. October.

Ii, J.P. 1983. *Fragments of Hawaiian History*. Trans. M.K. Pukui. Rev. ed. Honolulu: Bishop Museum Press.

Kamakau, S.M. 1964a. *Ka po'e Kahiko*: 'The People of Old.' Trans. M.K. Pukui. Ed. D.B. Barrére. Honolulu: Bernice Pauahi Bishop Museum (Special Publication 51).

– 1964b: *Na Hana a ka Po'e Kahiko*: 'The Works of the People of Old.' Trans. M.K. Pukui. Ed. D.B. Barrére. Honolulu: Bernice Pauahi Bishop Museum (Special Publication 61).

Keesing, R.M. 1989. Creating the Past: Custom and Identity in the Contemporary Pacific. *Contemporary Pacific* 1(12): 19–42.

– 1991. Reply to Trask. *Contemporary Pacific* 3: 168–71.

Laenui, P. 1993. 'Hawaiian Dialogue.' In *He Alo A He Alo Face to Face*. Honolulu: American Friends Service Committee.

Lili'uokalani, L.K. 1978. *The Kumulipo: An Hawaiian Creation Myth*. Kentfield: Pueo Press.

Lindstrom, L., and G. White 1995. Anthropology's New Cargo: Future Horizons. *Ethnology* 34(3): 201–29.

Linnekin, J. 1983. Defining Tradition: Variations on the Hawaiian Identity. *American Ethnologist* 10: 241–52.

– 1991a. Cultural Invention and the Dilemma of Authenticity. *American Anthropologist* 93: 446–8.

– 1991b. Text Bites and the R-Word: The Politics of Representing Scholarship. *Contemporary Pacific* 2: 171–7.

Linnekin, J., and L. Poyer (eds.). 1990. *Cultural Identity and Ethnicity in the Pacific:* Honolulu: University of Hawai'i Press.

Obeyesekere, G. 1992. *The Apotheosis of Captain Cook: European Mythmaking in the Pacific*. Honolulu: Bishop Museum Press.

Robilliard, A.B. 1992. Introduction: Social Change as the Projection of Discourse. Pp.1–33 in A.B. Robilliard (ed.), *Social Change in the Pacific Islands*. London: Kegan Paul International.

Roszak, T. 1992. *The Voice of the Earth: An Exploration of Ecopsychology.* New York: Touchstone.

Sahlins, M. 1976. *Culture and Practical Reason*. Chicago: University of Chicago Press.

– 1981. *Historical Metaphors and Mythical Realities: Structure in the Early History of the Sandwich Islands Kingdom*. Ann Arbor: University of Michigan Press.

– 1994. 'Goodbye to Tristes Tropes: Ethnography in the Context of Modern World

History.' Pp. 377–94 in R. Borofsky (ed.), *Assessing Cultural Anthropology*. New York: McGraw–Hill.

Simon, R. 1993. 'Remembrance as a Source of Radical Renewal.' Pp. 137–56 in *Teaching against the Grain*. Toronto: OISE Press.

Tobin, J. 1994. Cultural Construction and Native Nationalism: Report from the Hawaiian Front. *Boundary* 2, 21(1): 111–33.

Traditional Circle of Indian Elders and Youth, Onondaga Nation via Nedrow, New York. 1992. Communiqué 13. *Akwe:kon Journal* 9(2): 106–7.

Trask, H. 1991: Natives and Anthropologists: The Colonial Struggle. *Contemporary Pacific* 3(1): 159–67.

– 1993. *From a Native Daughter: Colonialism and Sovereignty in Hawai'i*. Monroe: Common Courage Press.

Ward, D.L. 1996. Native Hawaiian Vote. *Ka Wai Ola O OHA*: 'The Living Water of OHA.' October.

Weinberg, B. 1996. Land and Sovereignty in Hawai'i. *Native Americas: Akwe:kon's Journal of Indigenous Issues* 13(2): 30–41.

3

Indigenous Knowledge: Lessons from the Elders – A Kenyan Case Study

NJOKI NATHANI WANE

What could you learn from me, an old woman like me with no education? I cannot speak English ... What do I know except to hold my hoe? ... I am sure you have not come all this way to learn about that.

These words, from an old Kenyan rural woman I was interviewing as part of research carried out in Embu District, Kenya, illustrate clearly the widely held belief that knowledge comes from formal schooling. There was a time when Africans knew that wisdom and knowledge come with age, but this woman obviously no longer feels this way. This explained in part her reluctance to answer my questions and share with me her everyday experiences. Eventually I was able to convince her of my sincere interest and desire to learn from her, but only after what I call the 'threshold crossing ritual,' whereby I was able to demonstrate that we share a common lineage and legacy. I managed to persuade this woman to accept me into her intimacy and to share details about her experience that she normally would not divulge to outsiders.

This paper is based on information I obtained from the elder quoted above and from other women who live in Embu, Kenya. I intend to explore indigenous knowledge and the role women play in its production. I contend that indigenous knowledge has been relegated to the periphery and that, as a result, its custodians are reluctant to discuss it, especially with people who have acquired formal (i.e., Western-style) education (Kipusi, 1991). I firmly believe that knowledge production is not merely an exercise for the academy but is also for lay people, since knowledge is acquired through our everyday experiences.

My awareness of the importance of indigenous knowledge is something that grew over time. As a Kenyan woman educated first in Kenya, then later in Canada, I grew up being taught that the most important and useful knowledge came from books and the formal school system. My parents stressed the importance of getting an education; but by education they meant earning diplomas and degrees awarded by the formal school system. Like most Kenyans, I was not taught about my culture or about the things my parents learned from their parents in school; yet I *was* taught about the American Revolution, Niagara Falls, and the Second World War. As a graduate student in Canada, I realized that my formal education had somehow divorced me from my roots, and that what I had was a partial education. Hence my desire to learn more about my own culture, and to give voice to and legitimize the knowledge of people we do not hear most of the time: rural women.

In my study I wanted to explore the central role that Kenyan rural women play in knowledge production. To this end, I used food processing as an entry point into women's lives in all their complexity. During my research work among the Embu women, I sought to understand and document the vital role they played in knowledge production. My aim was not to end the struggles, or to resolve the problems of rural women; rather, it was to shed light on the rich indigenous knowledge they hold and to show how they have used it to survive.[1]

Methodology

I adopted historical as well as dialectical approaches, so as to place my analysis in the broader political and economic context in which my research occurred. I used feminism as my theoretical framework and perspective, as it does not imply a narrow focus on women's lives; rather, it places women in the centre and allows the researcher to begin a systematic inquiry into where women are located socially, politically, and economically. When this approach is used, women's experiences are placed in a broad social context, and not only can gender relations issues be dealt with, but also issues of class, race, ethnicity, and other social categories, all of which contribute to defining women's conditions of existence (Charlton, 1984; Harding, 1987; Okeke, 1994). An important aspect of this approach is that it provides space for the 'other' who has been excluded in the knowledge production process.

This providing of space is important because knowledge is socially constructed, and as Smith states, 'its production is nearly a monopolized industry and ordinary people are excluded from it' (1987a: 2). Smith further argues that a privileged few, whom she refers to as a 'circle of men,' have for centuries been writing and talking to one another about issues that are of significance to them. She goes on to add that women have been excluded from these circles in which society's meanings are constructed. According to her, the outcome of this exclusion has been that women have been deprived of the opportunity to define or raise to social consciousness the problems that concern them (Maguire, 1987: 83; Smith, 1987b: 2).

Because anyone can drop in at a home at any time without prior arrangement, and because I carried out most of my interviews in the open, it was not unusual for passers-by to drop in and participate in our conversation; thus one-person interviews often ended up as group interviews. For many respondents, this was an opportunity to talk, to look back nostalgically on their past, to educate and be educated. There were some times when I spent a whole day at one homestead, just 'conversing' with a group of women. During the interviews the respondents were always busy doing something. The passers-by, if they were not carrying their weaving baskets, would always ask the hostess for something to do, or join the hostess in the activity she was engaged in. Usually I would also help. It is important to note that despite their show of acceptance, these women were still reluctant to talk about their traditional way of life. I believe this reluctance was due to their uncertainty as to how an 'educated' person such as myself would judge their knowledge.

Knowledge Acquisition

It is easy to listen to the stories of other people; it is not always simple to make sense out of them. From the older women, I heard about their fading past; the younger women spoke about their frustration at being at a crossroads. I listened to the older women with wonder at the amount of knowledge they held on traditional healing methods and on the social, political, and economic practices that kept the traditional structures together. I learned about these women's intricate relationship with nature. From the young women I learned how to combine several chores and carry out each efficiently. As it is not possible here to describe in full all aspects of their indigenous knowledge, I will concentrate on some aspects, such as language, lineage and legacy, education, land, and food as an aspect of social relations. Under education, I will deal with such issues as circumcision, discipline, health and healing, and food.

Language

The proper use of language, verbal and nonverbal, was central to the interview process. The women used proverbs, idioms, songs, wise sayings, events, and incidents as their mode of communication. To indicate that I was actively participating and listening, I had to keep saying, 'uhmu.'

Again, as a sign of respect, all older women were referred to as grandmothers, while others were addressed as mama, aunt, or 'mama so-and-so' (the mother of so-and-so). It was considered disrespectful to ask an old woman how old she was. I still recall how furious a woman was when I asked her how old she was: 'Didn't your mother tell you that it was not appropriate to ask people their age?'

To determine the ages of the women, I would ask them to recall any important events that had taken place in their lives, hence the theme of connection between the personal and the social. The women's use of historical events such as the coming of Europeans, the First World War, famines, droughts, and circumcision enabled me to estimate their ages. Through this procedure, I also learned about most aspects of their communities' lives. For example, to estimate Cucu's[2] age, I used the earliest remembered occurrence in her life:

> I can still remember when these Wazungu [white people] came. When they saw Kirinyaga [Mt Kenya] they were taken aback by the mountain with a white top, but they could not pronounce its name and called it Kii-nyaa. My child, everybody was fascinated by these people, their feet had no toes, they ate fire and they wore clothes that were not like ours. It was soon after this that I got circumcised.

With most of the older women, I often used such connections to events as a method of information retrieval. Language was an important aspect of the community's history, especially when the women made reference to the past. For instance, when they spoke of a number of moons, this meant a number of seasons. Also, the sun was an important element in women's lives. They would always look up to check the position of the sun in order to know what time it was and how much more daylight they had to complete their daily chores. The importance of language became quite clear when it came to the issue of legacy and lineage as discussed below.

Legacy and Lineage

Knowing the name of one's tribe or clan was not enough as far as these women were concerned. One had to know several generations of one's family tree. This allowed lineage to be established, and since this was a small community, I usually learned that all of us were connected at some point in the family tree. After lineage was established, the women felt more comfortable talking to me. I would be asked questions such as, 'Whose daughter did you say you are? What is your clan? What about your mother's clan? Do you know your aunties and uncles?' It was during my interviewing that I found out who my great-great-grandparents were and where they had come from. Once that bond was established, I knew the women could question my opinion and understanding on any issue. I had become their grandchild or daughter. For instance, Cucu knew I was in the middle of the various cosmologies. I was at a crossroads, trying to carry out an academic exercise and, at the same time, to re-establish my identity. She saw clearly that I was in the middle of various discourses and that everything was gravitating toward the centre, where I stood overwhelmed by the knowledge coming from her. My sincerity, and my patience in going through the ritual of crossing the threshold, earned me the trust that was necessary before the women would agree to treat me as a pupil.

Education

The purpose of the educational process for children is to expand their minds. In traditional societies, learning embraces every aspect of life, including socio-economic realities. With traditional societies, it is important to place the learning process in context. For instance, the memorization of idioms and proverbs and the telling of stories protect the knowledge necessary for the society's survival. Unfortunately, the use of oral history has been subjected to a great deal of criticism (Holmes, 1996). Some facets of the learning process among the Embu are those relating to traditional education (inculcation of social skills), discipline, health and healing, and circumcision.

Every society, whatever its level of development, has some form of purpose-ful education. In its broadest sense, education can be defined as a conscious attempt to help people live in their society and participate fully and effectively in its organization in order to ensure a continued existence (Sifuna, 1990). The Embu community has been exposed to both indigenous and formal education. Within Embu traditional society, the purpose of indigenous education was to train young people for adulthood. Children were taught their social, economic, and political roles as well as their rights and obligations. The instructional 'tools' included oral narratives, myths, fables, legends, riddles, and proverbs, as well as processes of observation and participation (Kenyatta, 1965).

The various rites of passage marked the final stages of children's education. For both boys and girls, ear-piercing marked the passage from childhood to girl/ boyhood. Before that rite was performed, both boys and girls were under the mother's care. Afterwards, the boys were placed under the guidance of their fathers, while the girls were left with their mothers to learn through role-playing, imitation, and observation. For more details, see the studies of Kenyatta (1965), Sifuna (1990), Wamahiu (1984), and Njoki Nathani (1996).

Mothers used lullabies as a method of instruction. According to Kenyatta, the entire history and tradition of the family and clan were embodied in these lullabies, and by hearing them daily, children were able to assimilate this early teaching without strain (Kenyatta, 1965: 83–4). During my fieldwork, I noticed that the singing of lullabies to babies was not common, especially among the young women. The older women sang to their grandchildren, but not on a daily basis. This in itself signified a loss of an important mode of instruction for the children. To try to make sense of some of the traditional modes of teaching, I will examine the following: circumcision, discipline, health and healing, and food.

Circumcision

Circumcision was considered important by all the women in their fifties whom I interviewed. Every woman I talked to recalled her circumcision ceremony and the name given to her group of initiates. The name depicted the current situation in the community. If a group of children was circumcised during an exceptionally heavy rainfall that caused flooding, or during an outbreak of an epidemic such as smallpox, the age group was given a name that described the particular situation. It is interesting that among the older women, these names were still in use. This system ensured that important historical events were remembered and passed down from generation to generation. Out of the names, it is possible to reconstruct the history of a people. Once circumcision became illegal, a gap was created in information transmission.

According to Kenyatta (1965), circumcision as a rite of passage cannot be discussed intelligently unless we understand the emotional attitudes of those for and against this practice. He contends that the real issue does not lie in the rite itself; rather, it revolves around the fact that the rite has enormous educational, social, moral, and religious implications that are quite far removed from the operation itself. Wachiuma stressed this point:

It was not so much the operation, but the significance of it ... during the healing we learnt how to care for a family, about sex ... For instance we were told ... if we had sex, we had to tie a knot on a string from the first day until the day we had our monthly period ... The knots represented the days ... If the knots became too many, then you knew you were pregnant ... This was a learning period for us.

The disappointment that these rites had been discontinued could be felt in the voices of the older women. Cucu commented:

These days I see girls piercing their own ears with the help of their older sisters or cousins ... I see mothers making secret arrangements to have their daughters circumcised ... They forget it is not just the cutting of the flesh, it's the significance ... These days children are born and given names, there are no naming or dedication ceremonies ... Is it any wonder then that your generation has lost its sense of direction?

According to Cucu, the rites of passage created bonds not only between individuals who shared the experience, but also within the community as a whole. These same lamentations were expressed by Rwamba, Wachiuma, and Mama, some of the other women I interviewed. According to Wachiuma, much had changed: 'When a girl or a boy doesn't get circumcised, they can never grow up, they remain children all their lives.' Circumcision for girls has been depicted merely as a bodily mutilation, but many of the critics of this rite seem to forget that the whole process was for purposes of learning. The institution helped ensure that children in the same age group would be taught together; this promoted uniformity in the knowledge passed from generation to generation. The bonding that was created by the rite was quite evident among the older women. As one of them commented:

> All those who got circumcised with me experienced pain together, we shed blood and became women on the same day on the same spot ... we learnt together ... and as a result no matter what happens, have always stood by each other ... We cry together and laugh together ... We have always celebrated together the birth of our children, their circumcision and their marriage ... The whole experience gave us a lifetime bonding.

It is important to note that in today's social setting in Kenya, weddings, pre-weddings, naming ceremonies, or circumcisions of boys are no longer community events, but family affairs.

In traditional society, the significant stages in one's life were marked by special ceremonies referred to as *mambura*. The most celebrated stages were the naming of a newborn baby, the piercing of ears (for girls), circumcision (for both girls and boys), and marriage rites. Each of these was marked by the coming together of the community and the organization of a ceremony. There would be drinking, eating, dancing, rejoicing, and teaching.

Unfortunately, when I was carrying out my research most of the above rites were no longer being practised, either because they had been outlawed, or because economic hardships did not permit the lavish and expensive ceremonial celebrations, or because the rites had lost their significance. Quite clearly, there had been a breakdown in the traditional social structure. The older women complained that the younger generation had lost respect for their elders and that there was no longer strict segregation between sexes and age groups. According to Cucu, 'these days, circumcised, uncircumcised, boys and girls, mix, play, and even marry.'

Circumcision as a rite of passage had been declared illegal by the colonial government in the early 1940s at the instigation of the church, the schools, women's and human rights groups, and modern medicine. According to Kenyatta, 'the custom of clitoridectomy of girls [was] the center of controversy as early as 1920 ... The custom was referred to as barbaric in a conference held at the United Nations in Geneva in 1931' (1965: 130). The delegates to the conference advocating the abolition of this custom ignored the fact that no girl could be married without going through this rite of passage; also, they failed to consider that it was taboo for a man or woman to have sexual relations with an uncircumcised person. Despite the government restrictions, most families continued to circumcise their children well into the 1970s, even though they risked prosecution by doing so.

Discipline

Disciplining was part of the learning process, and the way it was carried out depended on the age and sex of the children. Before the children were circumcised, both parents could discipline them, but the responsibility was left more to the women of the homestead than to the men. In other words, it was the duty of the 'mothers,' aunties, and grandmothers to correct and give the young spankings, regardless of whether they were the biological parents. After puberty or circumcision, the boys became the men's responsibility while the girls remained the responsibility of the women.

This pattern has changed. Neither the grandparents nor the aunties or uncles have any hold on the children. This has resulted in a breakdown in communication and has created resentment among the elders and resistance among the youth. There is dislocation – a gap between the young and the old, with each viewing the other as ignorant. There is a rupture between the traditional and modern social structures. The older women resent that they have no say in shaping the lives of the next generations. They can feel the resistance when they try to talk to younger people and give them advice. In most instances they are ignored and labelled ignorant and backward.

Health and Healing

Although my study did not specifically address health systems, it is important to mention the state of health care facilities in the country, especially in rural areas. In the 1970s, two-thirds of Kenya's health budget went into curative care in the form of building, running, and maintaining large medical facilities (Republic of Kenya: Development Plan 1984–88). In 1980, 70 per cent of all deaths were found to have resulted from preventable diseases. In the same year, malnutrition was found to have been a contributing factor in 33 per cent of children's deaths (UNICEF/Kenya Central Bureau of Statistics, 1984).

Despite the increase in the number of medical facilities and personnel, Kenya's health care system is of limited effectiveness. Because of the shortage of facilities and services, much of the population, especially in rural areas, continues to rely on indigenous medical practices. About 51.4 per cent of the women who were interviewed used traditional herbs to treat ailments, while 34.5 per cent combined modern medicine with traditional herbs. Only 2.8 per cent did not use any of the traditional herbs to treat their own or their family's ailments.

The older women's knowledge of health and healing reinforced my determination to foster greater awareness of indigenous knowledge among rural women. The women lamented that due to modern farming practices, most of the medicinal plants had disappeared. The challenge faced by development advocates is to 'save' the few plants that are still available. Kenya has many modern hospitals, and big hospitals such as the Kenyatta General Hospital cater to people from all over East and Central Africa. However, due to budgetary constraints and conditions imposed by the World Bank and the International Monetary Fund (Dei, 1992), the health care system is highly inadequate. Most patients have to wait months for surgery, as most of the operating theatres have been closed because of lack of supplies. Given the harsh economic conditions, many women have returned to traditional healing practices, which are within 'easy' reach and 'free,' and which provide an alternative to the modern health services.

The elders spoke proudly of how they used traditional herbs to cure ailments, or simply as drinks. Their knowledge about the herbs they had at their disposal was impressive. Lemon leaves, grass, and sugar were good for colds, coughs, headaches, and so on; other herbs could be used to cleanse the blood, cure stomach ailments and backaches, and give strength to women who had just given birth. The herbs are usually boiled alone or with bones to give the drink some taste. The women have always known how to use their resources for both their own and their families' survival.

The treatment provided would depend on the type and seriousness of the illness. The women had herbs for malaria, headaches, relaxation, spacing of children, and stomach aches; for increasing a woman's milk; for removing the placenta; and for cleansing the uterus after childbirth. They knew the exact quantities to be prepared and given to a patient. For those women who could not practise abstinence as a birth control method, there was a special plant that could be tied around the waist that was believed to prevent pregnancy. Ciarunji revealed how she had to deal with health problems in her family as circumstances made it necessary to rely on indigenous forms of knowledge:

> What do you do when you have a sick child or sick person in the house? You cannot sit and watch them die. If we cannot afford the medical fee, I do not hesitate to go to the bushes, collect a few herbs and prepare a drink for the sick person. For instance, if one of us has malaria, I collect *Muvangi* [marigold], boil it and dip a cloth in hot water and massage the sick person, then cover the person over the steaming water and let them inhale. If you repeat this twice, the person gets cured. We had cures for all ailments, but the introduction of the 'modern' medicine made us forget all that we knew. Now that times are hard, we have no alternative but to go back to our roots.

Social Relations and Food

Food plays a central role in many family occasions and is important to the social reproduction of the family in both nuclear and extended families. Present research reveals that food items can be seen as symbolizing important social relations of power and subordination within the family (Cashman, 1991). Within the family, food functions to maintain and reproduce a specific aspect of social order as well as the age and gender divisions that characterize it (Charles & Kerr, 1988). The central role of women in food preparation is not only universal but also a major component of female identity and an important source of women's links to other family members. It follows that through food, women indirectly exercise a certain degree of power and authority. This power is accrued not through force or the ability to deny, but rather through giving and the obligations created in that process. However, with their limited resources and diminishing control over food, women are losing this power and with it a part of their source of identity.

In Kenyan traditional societies, food preparation and consumption are differentiated along age and gender lines. Food reflects and symbolizes social relations as well as social status. It also carries its own special values. For instance, among the Turkana and Rendille ethnic groups, when women ask their neighbours for milk this is considered a begging act; yet it is not considered begging when the men do the same regarding livestock (Kettel, 1990). Why should one practice be viewed as different from the other? Begging is associated with poverty and is a practice for the underprivileged, while getting a loan is perceived as a matter of dealing with equals. Kettel's study reveals that

Turkana and Rendille women could only share cooked food, or give out grains if they were assisted during harvesting. It is frustrating to know how limited their powers are over an item they have laboured over for months.

Food-processing practices help maintain and reinforce a coherent ideology of the family throughout the social structure. It is during the harvest period that women's and men's skills complement each other. Men make the indigenous technology, and women put it to practical use. During the harvesting season, women's organizational and managerial skills are quite evident: it is they who take charge of the food-processing activities. Women who have no men on their homestead ask their neighbours' men to make the tools for them. This service is free and can only be rewarded with a bowl of food or porridge – never cash. The women test the tools, and if these tools are not appropriate (they could be too heavy, too light, too short, or too long) and may return them for modification.

At this particular time of the year, women's knowledge of food processing is highly valued; the success of the harvest depends on their skill and their leadership qualities. They know when all the grains have been thrashed from the stalks, and which members of the family are skilled enough to take part in the food-processing activities, and when there is enough wind that the chaff can be removed through winnowing, and whether the thrashing ground is ready or needs repair. And once the grains have been cleaned, it is the women who decide how to store them. To gauge the dryness of the grain, the women sift it through their hands, using their skin as a thermometer. The use of hands is a common practice among the shea butter (similar to cocoa butter) extractors.

In food-processing activities, the women's knowledge of the environment and the weather places them in a crucial position. For example, without listening to any radio forecast they can tell whether the day will be appropriate for harvesting, thrashing, or winnowing the grains. However, all this women's knowledge and work has been undervalued. Despite their vital contribution to the process, once all the food has been safely stored it becomes the property of men. Hence women's subordination continues, as they have to repeatedly ask their men for permission to sell the grain in case of need.

Land

The women's knowledge of and connectedness to the land was rooted in their many years of experience. No amount of reading could have provided me with the information I was able to gather from their stories. Most of the women I interviewed, especially the older ones, lamented the above changes that had taken place, particularly the destruction of the environment. During our sessions, Cucu often turned to me now and then and said: 'Gaka [grandchild], so much has changed ... so much has been destroyed and there is so much that is foreign, that you should be the one telling me why we never get enough rains, and if we do, so much of it pours that it takes away the little that was left ... You are the one who has gone to school, how can you explain all this?' Cucu knew I was the learner and that she was my instructor. I knew she did not expect me to answer. Cucu's question was not directed at me in particular but at my generation. It was meant for those who had taken as their responsibility the development of the world, the production of legitimate knowledge, and the protection of the environment.

Questions of trust resonated within me when she posed her question. Did I have the capacity and the stamina to absorb all the dimensions of Cucu's world? The dimensions of love, learning, culture, tradition, sharing, and language? How was I going to bring together all this information about knowledge production? Could Cucu sense my doubts that I would be able to articulate appropriately the knowledge she was passing to me?

Cucu had not heard about the depletion of the ozone layer, and had not read about chemical fertilizers and how they interfered with soil composition and structure; yet she was able to read the signs and intuit the reasons for the various changes. Her question to me was a test of whether the knowledge acquired through formal education could explain the current situation facing her rural community. I pleaded ignorance by keeping silent, as I wanted to learn of the various changes that had distorted not only Cucu's world but the world at large. Cucu had witnessed the destruction of the virgin forests, and the interference, not only with what was on the surface, but also with what was underneath. Projects had been constructed on top of graveyards, and sacred trees had been cut down, destroying ceremonial grounds. For Cucu these were signs of disrespect, not only for the community but also for Mother Earth.

Cucu's synthesis of the various changes may not make a lot of sense to the advocates of development, even though she based her analysis on deep-rooted knowledge that she had acquired during her (approximately) 100 years of living in the same place. Some may argue that women like her are resisting change, but how can they embrace change that is destroying their world? The arguments of the older women illustrate that those without formal education are capable of looking at issues logically and philosophically. They recognize the losses when a forest is destroyed to build a road, when lands are cleared for plantations, when a hydro station is built to provide electricity for urban populations, and when poor families are displaced to make way for a manufacturing plant or an office building. They see how the clearing of forests and scrublands interferes not only with rainfall patterns, but also with the life cycles and support systems on which plants, insects, animals, and people depend. Our present generation believes in controlling nature rather than living in harmony with it. Cucu concluded with the following statement:

> By the time you are my age the world will be completely destroyed ... Look around you, where are the thick forests that we used to have? ... Kirimiri [name of a forest] was thick and the canopy created by the trees would not allow the rays of the sun through ... These days, people have cultivated up to the top of the mountain ... Man's greed has chased the spirits of our ancestors that used to live there ... For us this was a sacred mountain ... But its sacredness has been destroyed ... Gaka ... your generation needs to halt or ... slow down the pace of destruction.

The significance of this narrative is to show women's knowledge of and connection with nature – a connection now being severed by forces beyond their control. The destruction of the Earth has been an intricate phenomenon. For instance, why have nation-states institute laws that are contrary to the laws of nature? Why do 'Third World' states allow multinationals to clear virgin forests and plant cash crops? Why do nation-states allow advanced states to dump nuclear waste on their land in exchange for food or aid, when they know the consequences? It is not because both parties are ignorant of the global consequences of the environmental abuse, and of the interconnections between development and environment. Governments around the world have acknowledged the need to change those production and consumption patterns, which have contributed greatly to the destruction of the environment.

Cucu should have been one of the participants at UNCED, the Rio Earth Summit of 1992. Her analysis of environmental degradation and of the severed relationships between people and nature emphasizes the consequences of destroying the Earth under the guise of development.

The social fabric that enables Embu people to care for nature and respect it is made up of customs and beliefs. The breakdown of these beliefs and customs has resulted in the clearing of virgin forests, the cutting down of fig trees, and the drying up of rivers. The reproductive cycle of the universe has been interfered with. The women can no longer depend on the environment for their survival, and perceive that the creator has stopped listening to their pleas. We need to acknowledge the destructive side of human nature if we are to reconstruct a world that is meaningful and habitable. The ongoing destruction of the environment is a reflection of destructive processes going on within ourselves. In the eyes of the women, desertification, degradation, and the thinning of the ozone layer represent the various stages of human self-destruction.

When Cucu looked at me and asked why the social, economic, and political world around her was disintegrating, and I did not answer, I should have known the answer was within me. Her ending note – 'You have all the education ... You are supposed to know all this' – was a reminder that there is a crisis in the modern paradigms of development, education, and technology, and therefore a need to redefine our models of development on the basis of her assessment of the present-day world. I am not advocating a recreation and reconstruction of Cucu's world; as she put it, 'It would not be easy to find the spirituality, the purity and sincerity that existed during our time.' Cucu's pessimism should not stop us from making a concerted effort to rescue and protect our planet. This responsibility must not be left solely to the ecologists, the environmentalists, or the women; it must be everybody's concern.

There is a mistaken notion that rural women are resisting change, but that is not the case. The women I interviewed made it quite clear that they were not against what the modern world has to offer; however, they *were* troubled by the destructive element embedded in the development paradigm. The commitment to embrace some forms of modern technology was reaffirmed by Rwamba: 'I am not against modern technology or modern foods, or the new learning ... What I am opposed to is the total rejection of the past without understanding what the past has to offer your generation ... We should learn from you and you should also be ready to listen to us.'

Conclusion

My study showed that women's local knowledge is important. Despite its importance, development experts, national governments, and local authorities have not given this knowledge due recognition (Carr, 1987; Stamp, 1992). The women's acceptance of their subordinate position has had a toll on their self-esteem, to the point where they think the knowledge they possess can be of no value to others, especially the educated. These women can and *do* make a great contribution to the progress of their community. Their accumulated knowledge and experience can be incorporated in designing food-processing technologies, alternative healing practices, and new ways of disciplining and educating youth. The questions to ask ourselves are these: How will this be done when traditional knowledge and modern knowledge seem to diverge instead of converge? And is it possible to establish a common ground? I hope to have contributed to the debate around these important issues.

ғ

NOTES

1 In my study, 200 questionnaires were distributed; 14 in-depth interviews and 3 histories were selected for this project.
2 All names used are pseudonyms for confidentiality. Cucu represents several

generations. Her interpretation of various ideologies such as indigenous knowledges and colonization enabled me to think through my collected data. She spoke for and on behalf of several generations, hence her central place in my analysis.

3 Nathani, Njoki. 1966. *Sustainable Development: Indigenous Forms of Food Processing Technologies. A Kenyan Case study*. Unpublished PhD dissertation, University of Toronto.

REFERENCES

Amadiume, I. 1987. *Male Daughters, Female Husbands: Gender and Sex in an African Society*. London: Zed Books.

Carr, M.R. Sandhu. 1987. *Women, Technology and Rural Productivity: An Analysis of . Impact of Time and Energy-Saving Technologies on Women*. Rugby: Intermediate Technology Consultants.

Cashman, K. 1991. Systems of Knowledge as Systems of Domination: The Limitations of Established Meaning. *Agriculture and Human Values* 8 (1, 2): 49–58.

Charles, N., and M. Kerr. 1988. *Women, Food, and Families*. Manchester: Manchester University Press.

Charlton, S.E. 1984. *Women in Third World Development*. Boulder, CO: Westview Press.

Collins, P. 1991. *Black Feminist Thought: Knowledge, Consciousness, and the Politics of Empowerment*. Boston: Unwin Hyman.

Dei, G.J.S. 1992. *Hardships and Survival in Rural West Africa: A Case Study of a Ghanaian Community*. Dakar: CODESRIA.

Harding, Sandra. 1987. Is There a Feminist Method? Pp. 1–14 in *Feminism and Methodology*. Indianapolis: Indiana University Press.

Holmes, L. 1996. Elders' Knowledge and the Ancestry of Experience in Hawai'i. Unpublished doctoral dissertation, University of Toronto.

Kenyatta, Jomo. 1965. *Facing Mount Kenya: The Traditional Life of the Gikuyu*. London: Biddles.

Kettel, Bonnie. 1986. Women in Kenya at the End of the UN Decade. *Canadian Woman Studies*.

Kipusi, C.N. 1991. Empowerment of Women through Mutual Groups. Paper presented at the Women in Development Conference, Washington, D.C., November.

Maguire, P. 1987. *Doing Participatory Research: A Feminist Approach*. Boston: Center for International Education.

Maina, N., and E.C. Murray. 1993. Women's Knowledge about Foods: A Kenyan Case Study. Paper presented to the Canadian Association of African Studies Conference, May 12–15, University of Toronto.

Mulikita, N. 1985. The Ongoing Food Crisis in Africa and the Rights of Female Farmers. *Canadian Woman Studies* 7(1).

Okeke, P. E. 1994. Patriarchal Continuities and Contradictions in Africa Women's Education and Socio-Economic Status: An Ethnographic Study of Currently Employed University Educated Igbo Women in Nigeria. PhD thesis, Dalhousie University, Halifax.

Sifuna, D. 1990. *Development of Education in Africa: The Kenyan Experience.* Nairobi: Initiative.

Smith, Dorothy. 1987a. *The Everyday World as Problematic: A Feminist Sociology.* Toronto: University of Toronto Press.

– 1987b. Women's Perspective as a Radical Critique of Sociology. Pp. 84–96 in *Feminism and Methodology.* Indiana: Indiana University Press.

Stamp, Patricia. 1992. *Technology, Gender, and Power in Africa.* Ottawa: IDRC.

Wamahiu, Sheila P. 1984. Women and Basic Education. Basic Education Resource Centre, E.A. Kenyatta College, Nairobi, Kenya.

4

African Development: The Relevance and Implications of 'Indigenousness'

GEORGE J. SEFA DEI

Educators, like all other social actors, increasingly are having to confront some basic but critical questions about their work in the academy. For example, how do we ensure that learners are informed by the complete history of ideas and events that have shaped and continue to shape human growth and social development? I see the production and validation of indigenous knowledges, and the centring of them in the academy, as an important task for educational and social change. It is encouraging that so many educators, students, parents, and community workers are now questioning those modes of conventional knowledge production which privilege some knowledge forms and set up a hierarchy of knowledges. Students in particular are now questioning the devaluations, negations, and omissions that have long been embedded in schooling and school knowledge – for example, the near total absence of teachings on non-European knowledge forms. There is a recognition that educators and learners must start to offer multiple and collective readings of the world. This means exploring multiple and alternative knowledge forms.

My interest in indigenous and marginalized knowledge forms is an academic and political project informed by the realization that we urgently need to rethink the processes of producing knowledge about 'development.' As I stated in the preface to this book, I have come to this discussion of indigenous knowledges after an educational journey replete with experiences of colonial and colonized encounters – encounters that left unproblematized what has conventionally been accepted in schools as 'in/valid knowledge.' In my early education I was confronted with a profound silence about the achievements of African peoples and their contributions to academic knowledge and world civilization. Like many others, I bring to the topic of indigenous knowledges a deep concern about the historic and present-day deprivileging and marginalizing of subordinate voices in the conventional processes of knowledge production, particularly (though not exclusively) in Euro-American contexts.

In this paper I borrow from Roberts (1998: 59) in reading 'indigenous knowledge' as knowledge 'accumulated by a group of people, not necessarily indigenous, who by centuries of unbroken residence develop an in-depth understanding of their particular place in their particular world.' I will make theoretical, discursive, and methodological connections between the notions of 'indigenous knowledge' and 'development.' Such conceptual linkage is based on an understanding that for local peoples, indigenous ways of acting, feeling, knowing, and making sense of the social and natural worlds have significant implications for development. Nowhere are the links between development and indigenous knowledge more prominent than when we examine the micro-level interactions of social, political, spiritual, cultural, and economic activities and institutions in rural communities. Local peoples experience and interpret the contemporary world in ways that are continuous and consistent with their indigenous world views. For the purposes of discussing development issues and indigenous knowledges in 'developing' countries, these links between micro-level and macro-level practices and structures are based on much more than a simple leap of faith. In fact, it has long been argued in African contexts (see Taylor and Mackenzie, 1992) that the search for general solutions to human problems (i.e., development) must proceed from an understanding of local specificities (i.e., indigenous knowledges).

This paper views the indigenous cultural knowledges of African peoples as counterhegemonic knowledges to the conventional discourse on 'African development.' I intend to examine African cultural resource knowledge as a means of epistemological recuperation for local peoples.

I am particularly interested in connecting our understanding of local/indigenous knowledge to development issues in Africa. It is no exaggeration to say that the cultural resource base and knowledge of local peoples have been the least analyzed for their contributions to African development (see also Matowanyika, 1990; Warren, Slikkerveer and Brokensha, 1995). This paper calls for a shift in how we think about development to examine what the indigenous African cultural knowledge base can offer in terms of an African-centred development. By thinking hard about African-centred development[1] we are bound to raise an array of complex and contentious theoretical, methodological, and policy issues. In this discussion I locate 'indigenousness' in the context of applying local cultural-resource information with the goal of developing a genuinely African-centred development. My discursive practice will be to extend analytical debates about 'development' by bringing African indigenousness into both the objectives and the practices of social development.

When I use the term 'Africa,' I do not mean to play down the inherent diversity of African societies and the complexity of the human condition. Without ignoring this diversity, I hope to speak to the overarching concerns that permeate African communities in general. There is no essentialized Africa, nor is there a decontextualized Africa. The histories and processes of African development are diverse, and differ across communities, regions, and countries. Each case has its own unique history and peculiarities. Yet over much of the continent there is also a shared history of colonial and imperial imposition of external ideas and knowledges. It is on this latter point that I seek to problematize, interrogate, and rethink 'African development.' I argue for an approach to African development that is anchored in a retrieval, revitalization, and restoration of the indigenous African sense of shared, sustainable, and just social values. I contend that African peoples must reappropriate their cultural resource knowledge if they are to benefit from the power of collective responsibility for social development.

'Indigenousness' may be defined as knowledge consciousness arising locally and in association with the long-term occupancy of a place. Indigenousness refers to the traditional[2] norms, social values, and mental constructs that guide, organize, and regulate African ways of living in and making sense of the world. Indigenous knowledges differ from conventional knowledges in their absence of colonial and imperial imposition. The notion of 'indigenousness' highlights the power dynamics embedded in the production, interrogation, validation, and dissemination of global knowledge about 'international development.' It also recognizes the multiple and collective origins and the collaborative dimensions of knowledge, and underscores that the interpretation or analysis of social reality is subject to different and sometimes oppositional perspectives. It is important here to reiterate that I am not making a simple/dichotomous distinction between *development* and the African *indigenousness*; rather, I am stressing that conventional development must strive to incorporate indigenous knowledges of African peoples. 'Indigenousness' emerges from an indigenous knowledge system that is based on cognitive understandings and interpretations of the social and physical/spiritual worlds. Indigenous knowledges include concepts, beliefs, perceptions, and experiences of local environments, both social and natural. To speak of 'indigenousness' in the African context is to articulate questions about local cultures and social identities, and to highlight the importance of decolonizing the 'international development' project in Africa. Different forms of knowledge (e.g., knowledge as superstition, knowledge as a belief in the invisible order of things, knowledge as 'science') all build on one another to provide interpretations and understandings of society. This idea that knowledge is accumulative suggests strongly that indigenous knowledges are dynamic. In fact, the so-called 'modern' is embedded in indigenous knowledges. Indigenous knowledges also have moral and cognitive conceptions about nature and society that may be compatible with Western scientific knowledge. As

Prah points out, the worlds of the metaphysical and the physical, the worlds of mystery/'invisible agents' and 'science'/'modernity,' are not 'oppositional realities' (1997: 20). Different knowledges represent different points on a continuum; they involve ways that peoples perceive the world and act on it. Through daily practice, societies 'import' and 'adapt' freely whatever from 'outside' will enrich their accumulated knowledge. In this sense, 'modernity' is embedded in indigenous knowledges.

There are different ways to think about and conceptualize the processes of knowledge production. What constitutes 'valid' theoretical and empirical knowledge in development practice has today become a point of contention for many. Local African peoples are forcefully articulating their concerns about the historical defilement and manipulation of their traditional cultural values. They are asking why Euro-American values and norms are privileged in the development process, and why the value of indigenous African knowledge is not acknowledged (see also Fals-Borda and Rahman, 1991, writing in a different context). In the process of questioning hitherto taken-for-granted assumptions about 'development,' many indigenous and local peoples are attempting to reclaim and reinvigorate their marginalized knowledges. They are challenging commonsense views about 'international development.' They are questioning the institutional ideologies that have tended to obscure and distort their social realities. The political and cultural knowledge these people are displaying – especially in certain rural communities – is acting as a launching platform for such criticisms.

Elsewhere (Dei, 1993a, 1998) I have presented my thoughts about some of the theoretical and methodological issues concerning African development. For the idea of 'development' to have any credibility at all, it must speak to the social, cultural, economic, political, spiritual, and cosmological aspects of local peoples' lives, as well as to their specific needs and aspirations. Debates about 'development' must be situated in appropriate social contexts that provide practical and social meaning to the actors as subjects, rather than as objects of development discourse. This is a critical perspective on development: that local communities should own and control the solutions to their own problems (see also Kankwenda, 1994). This critical perspective also recognizes that real and effective control by the local community over the development process is possible only if the development agenda seeks to centre indigenous knowledge systems in the search for solutions to human problems. This means articulating a conception and praxis of development that does not reproduce the existing total local dependency on external advice, knowledge, and resources. Local input must be from the grassroots, should fully respect women's knowledge, should be ecologically sound, and should tap the diverse views, opinions, resources, and interests manifested in the cultural values and norms of local communities.

African Indigenousness

As already alluded to in any discussion of African indigenousness, it is important to acknowledge the ethnic and cultural diversity of African peoples, as well as their different histories. Also, to remember that some common elements in African indigenous knowledge systems can be found in variant forms among indigenous peoples in other parts of the world (see also Dia, 1991). Furthermore, indigenous knowledge systems and traditions contain sites and sources of cultural disempowerment for certain groups in society (e.g., women and ethnic/cultural minorities; Machila, 1992: 18). Cultural resource knowledge is not frozen in time and space. While I focus on some common underlying sociocultural themes and values (see also Machila, 1992: 16), I also recognize that the actual practices associated with these social values may vary across space and time.

Understanding the social, natural, cultural, spiritual, individual, and collective components of development requires an interrogation of Africa's 'traditional knowledge and know-how, those which have precisely maintained our societies throughout the ages' (Gueye, 1995: 10). The indigenous past is informative. The African past provides positive (i.e., solution-oriented) lessons about sustainable traditions of group mutuality, spirituality, self-help, communal bonding, and social responsibility that can be appropriated to aid the search for an authentic approach to development.

African history speaks to sustainable traditions and social values that can be recovered and reconstituted for social development. Indigenousness does not mean ignorance or backwardness. On the contrary – it provides local peoples with avenues for creativity and resourcefulness. As argued elsewhere (Dei, 1994a), the indigenous African sense of being human speaks about compassion, hospitality, generosity, and the wholeness of relationships, in a world that today is fragmented, polarized, and destructive of people and their social dreams and aspirations. African humanness as a value system speaks to the importance of relating to, rather than mastering, nature and the environment. Many African cultural traditions emphasize and reward individual sensibilities and social consciousness. African civilization was not simply a matter of technological advancement – it was rooted, as well, in social responsibility.

Indigenous African social values privilege *communal solidarity*. Traditional social groupings, such as lineages, clans, age sets, and grades, acted as corporate bodies, protecting the integrity of critical resources (e.g., land) that could not be divided without being destroyed. At times, such social groupings acted as workforces for tasks requiring larger labour pools than individual families could provide. The groups provided social comfort, identity, and a sense of belonging to a community, particularly in times of stress and hardship. One function of such bodies was educating the young – specifically, inculcating communal values and a sense of collective commitment. Similarly, self-help groups of various types exhibited *traditions of mutuality*. Some of these indigenous self-help groups were self-loaning bodies (credit associations). Examples: *upatu* among the Chagga of Tanzania (Bendera, 1991: 126); *susu* among the Akan of Ghana (Goody, 1962); and *esusu* among the Yoruba of Nigeria (Bascom, 1952) and the Krio of Sierra Leone. In many West African societies there were also labour partnerships. Example: the *nnoboa* among the Akan of Ghana were collective self-help groups of age-mates and friends who assisted one another in farming, trading, and marketing activities. In contemporary Africa, traces of such voluntary social groupings (serving as credit associations) can still be found; they continue to enhance community members' limited economic resources for undertaking individual projects and activities.

In indigenous African epistemological constructs, an individual's rights of citizenship have matching obligations and responsibilities to the community in which that person resides. This is the essence of *collective responsibility*. As Mbiti (1982) pointed out, Africans, historically, have been socialized to define themselves by their social obligations to the wider community. These obligations included providing communal forms of labour (e.g., road construction) at any time when called upon by the traditional polity, as well as making compulsory financial and nonfinancial contributions to assist bereaved families in burying their dead. Death, burial, and bereavement are community affairs, and a close examination of the conduct of traditional funeral ceremonies within traditional communities illustrates both collective responsibility and information sharing (see Rattray, 1927, for the Asante of Ghana; Herskovits, 1967: 352–402, for the Fon of Benin; Skinner, 1964: 49–59, for the Mossi of Burkina Faso; and Bascom, 1969: 65–9, for the Yoruba of Nigeria).

In the indigenous African world view, the accumulation of individual property/ wealth does not automatically accord status and prestige. For the wealthy to be accorded community reverence, social prestige, and status, they must share their wealth with the rest of the community (see Dei, 1992; Dia, 1991: 11). Wealthy individuals who want name and status recognition must demonstrate their social consciousness and responsibility by contributing to the society's welfare. In the indigenous African view, the individual is supported by the *family* and the family by the *community*. The family is all of one's kinfolk, while the community comprises both kin and non-kin. As O'Manique and Dotse (1991) point out, Africans reject the Hobbesian image of the competitive, isolated individual who lives in fear of others and is protected from them by the state or community. It follows that the concept of *individual* makes sense only within the concept of *community* (see also Karp, 1986; Gyekye, 1987; Mudimbe, 1988). Individual identity emerges from communion with others (Osagie, 1980). Within African indigenousness, the dichotomy is not between the *individual* and the *community*, but between the *competitive individual* isolated from his or her community and the *co-operative individual* enriched by the community.

African indigenousness cultivates respect for the authority of elderly persons (*genotocracy*), for their wisdom, their knowledge of community affairs, and their closeness to the ancestors (*notion of spirituality*). Many African people believe that with old age comes wisdom and an understanding of the world. It is the duty of the aged to instruct the young and the duty of the young to respect the knowledge of the elders (see Boateng, 1980: 111–18; Mbiti, 1982, 1982: 197). This African world view is based on an intimate understanding and appreciation of the relationship between humans, society, and nature. Indigenous African cultures spiritualize the universe and endow with supernatural powers the forces that threaten people (see Mbiti, 1982; Peek, 1991). Historically, this served to give moral and spiritual grounding to African peoples as social learners. Knowledge production is the outcome of a dynamic, interactive, and reflexive process involving individuals, social groups, and nature.

A Ghanian Case Study

In one contemporary Ghanaian village, local people are utilizing their traditional cultural resource knowledge to empower themselves and to address economic hardships. I provide this case study to illustrate how it is possible for communities to resort to their own social values and norms in order to deal with problems of development. The town of Ayirebi is situated in the forest zone of southeastern Ghana, about 45 km from Akyem Oda and nearly 180 km north of the Ghanaian capital, Accra. The town was the subject of a longitudinal research project that began in 1982–83 with an examination of how the area's peasant farmers adapted to seasonal food supply cycles and other socio-environmental stressors, such as drought, bush fires, and population pressures (see Dei, 1986).

In the early 1980s the people of Ayirebi adapted to domestic economic hardships by applying their endogenous understandings of the intricate links between social and natural forces. They relied heavily on the local environment to supply their household needs; many households had to get by without imported foodstuffs and other economic items. A close examination of the community's apparent success in dealing with the socio-environmental and economic crisis of 1982 and 1983 showed that there were four main reasons why they were able to maintain self-sufficiency in food and other basic requirements.

First, the local farmers were engaged in a strong and viable subsistence farming economy. Their cultivation practices, such as mixed and sequential cropping, crop rotation, and the use of local fertilizers (local manure and wood ash), were designed to ensure that at a minimum, household food supplies would be maintained during periods of drought and scarcity. As well, food-processing methods were devised for local staples – such as cassava – with a view to sustaining household food supplies. Many households also experimented with cultivating semiwild foods such as wild yams (see Dei, 1986, 1988).[3]

Second, many local households adopted hitherto little-used subsistence practices, such as the hunting and gathering of wild forest resources, as a means of supplementing agricultural production. Bush animal protein and wild food plants were collected for household use and for sale at the local markets. Wild forest products were, and still are, important to African rural economies. Africans' ability to resort to them is anchored in a practical understanding of the workings of the social (built) and natural environments. Women in particular were observed using the surrounding environment to supplement household food supplies. Forest products such as snails, crabs, mushrooms, and kola nuts were collected, together with edible and nonedible wild products such as roots, fibres, leaves, bark, fruits, seeds, nuts, insects, molluscs, honey, sap, and syrup (see Dei, 1986). These activities were not new. What was remarkable from the point of view of alleviating economic hardship and ecological stress was the intensity with which forest products were exploited to satisfy household needs. In the absence of imported goods, local households experimented with local products. Examples: the use of palm oil and wood ash to make soap; and the substituting of honey for sugar.

Third, there was a pragmatic dependence on the local market and/or cash economy. This included a resurgence of traditional handicrafts. After meeting their basic household needs, women farmers sold their remaining produce; then they utilized their earnings to pay for their children's education (for tuition, stationery, uniforms, and so on) and also to buy medicines. Young men engaged in basket weaving, and adults in woodworking and other handicrafts, to fetch additional income for both personal and household use. When the government pressured local farmers to sell their farm produce at ridiculously low (controlled) prices at urban markets, many resisted. Those farmers who sold their produce through official channels made certain that they received scarce imported items such as soap, tinned foods, toiletries, medicines, and cloth, rather than hard cash.

Fourth, social relations among townspeople were rebuilt, strengthened, and maintained. Community members redoubled their efforts to help needy individuals and households, as was evident when the town's migrants to Nigeria returned home after being deported from that country in the early 1980s. Community leaders placed 'stool' farmland at the disposal of some households.

(Stool land is community land under the immediate and sole political authority and jurisdiction of local chiefs.) People felt a strong sense of identification and connectedness to the community, and numerous economic exchanges took place among family and community members, as well as between adjacent communities (see Dei, 1986). Townspeople also relied on remittances from family and close relatives in the cities and urban centres, in exchange for local farm produce. Furthermore, individual farmers banded together to form farming co-operatives. During the drought of the early 1980s and through the 1990s, the local women relied on long-established traditions of community solidarity to establish credit associations, working on traditional principles of group mutuality to help relieve the economic pain of households. Research observations in the 1980s revealed that conclusions reached about the state of African economies, when based solely on studies of the cities and their immediate surroundings, perhaps do not always give a true and accurate picture of the health of the local economy. As Posnansky pointed out, the major economic changes taking place in much of Africa, at least in the early 1980s, tended to have far fewer 'long-term deleterious effects on rural areas than they [did] on the urban and peri-urban areas with their expensive, import-dependent social-service infrastructure' (1984: 2163).

In the late 1980s and early 1990s there were follow-up studies to ascertain the extent to which coping strategies were sustained long after the drought and severe national economic contraction of the early 1980s. Research documented the local responses to state policies for reviving the local economy through the promotion of cash cropping and an export-led development strategy. Although many of the economic activities and coping strategies observed in the early 1980s have stayed with the local people, in the late 1980s and early 1990s some households were seen to be relying on individual rather than community and group solutions to social and economic problems (Dei, 1992). That being said, the townspeople's sense of belonging to a community and their identification with the social and natural environments are still very much in place. Households must still live with the contradictions and paradoxes involved in trying to balance local, national, and international interests. This is seen in the current pressures that national and international market forces are placing on the community. One recourse the townspeople have for maintaining their social well-being involves developing a balance between some of the social and traditional values of community membership and the associated individual and social responsibilities of citizenship. Dei (1993b) has discussed how the community has upheld traditions of sustainable forestry. A study of local traditions of forest resource use reveals that the community understands the links between indigenous cultural knowledge and long-term ecological sustainability.

In order to understand the success of local people's coping strategies vis-à-vis broader macroeconomic and political crises, it is important to revisit some of the basic tenets of African systems of thought. As already noted, African-centred epistemologies highlight commonsense ideas about everyday lived realities. African cultural knowledge is rooted in local cultural traditions, values, and belief systems. It is a world view that shapes the community's relationships with its environments. It is a knowledge base that is crucial for group and community survival. For example, African epistemologies perceive knowledge as something that is accumulated by observing and experiencing the social and natural worlds. All humans are seen as learners of their worlds, and in order to develop the intuitive and analytical aspects of the human mind, social learning must be personalized. To understand social reality is to have a holistic view of society – that is, one which connects social, gendered, economic, political, religious, and spiritual dimensions of society. African knowledge systems also teach that history and social change do not lie completely outside the purview and power of human agency. The act of change itself is sacred; even so, humans can predict and cause social change with the blessing of the powers of the natural world (e.g., ancestral spirits). At the same time, the uncertainty of knowledge is also recognized in African systems of thought. The belief here is that the social world and the natural world are both full of mysteries and uncertainties. The importance of this body of knowledge lies in the recognition that social knowledge and human survival go hand in hand. In other words, humans cannot separate theory from practice. What one experiences informs how knowledge is developed in order to deal with daily survival. All of this has implications for how 'development' is conceptualized and promoted. 'Development' in the African context must address locally defined needs and aspirations by embracing the concepts of self-reliance and resource autonomy. It must be pursued in an ecologically sustainable manner and within a framework of equality, social justice, and respect for the fundamental freedoms and rights of all peoples. The challenge for African development is to work with a knowledge of 'globalization' in such a way that 'localization' is still possible.

Implications for African Development

An examination of African cultural resources reveals a body of knowledge about community values, collective responsibility, and social security arrangements, as well as about practices of communal governance and health provision. All of this knowledge is useful for developing social and ecological sustainability. In the remainder of this discussion, in the hope of furthering the cause of new and transformed development, I will briefly touch on *five* significant and interrelated lessons of African indigenousness. African indigenousness constitutes a body of generated, shared, and applied knowledge for thoughtful and responsible action among local peoples.

First, development must take into account local understandings of how culture, society, and nature all work. Devising an African-centred development will require knowledge of African realities and conditions. The material and the spiritual worlds of African peoples cannot be separated. As Gueye notes, there is a specific cultural understanding in diverse African communities that is 'centred around a particular conception of the world which assigns the human being a specific role, around a certain representation of time and space which structures mentalities and behaviours' (1995: 11). Awareness of this is central to effective development practice. Development must be informed by local understandings of the complex linkages between the natural, spiritual, social, cultural, political, and economic forces in society. Local peoples are agents in the construction of their own knowledge. Social development is a project about the social and ecological unity of peoples and their habitats. Social unity entails mutual respect and justice for all. Ecological unity focuses on the responsible use of land and natural resources according to principles of sustainability. African cosmology views humans as part of nature. Therefore, any development approach that affects the natural environment is bound to have consequences for social relations. An emancipatory approach to development should be able to build on the ability of local peoples to generate and apply their own knowledges and cultural and social histories. But for this to happen, there must be an understanding of local conceptions of lived realities and how daily human experiences are sustained by community and individual networks and ties, by political and ecological associations, and by other social support systems. (For a more in-depth discussion of gender equality and African development, please see Patience Idemudia's chapter in this volume.)

Second, the emotional and spiritual well-being of the individual and the social group is the bedrock of any development process. Social transformation is only possible if it proceeds from a development of the inner self and spiritual values. A genuinely human-centred approach to development should examine African philosophies in terms of 'person,' 'personhood,' 'self,' 'individual,' 'community,' 'environment,' 'values,' and 'spirituality.' Development is a complex process that builds on Africans' humanity and social responsibility, as well as their community and spiritual values. For example, an understanding of the philosophical assumptions underlying local conceptions of land and material resources could provide important insights when it comes to developing strategies for promoting natural and human resource management. There is a need for the development process in Africa to address diverse political, moral, spiritual, and ethical concerns and to redefine both individual and corporate responsibilities to the family, the community, the nation, and the world. Development must engender a spiritual awakening, but not in the sense of subscribing to a particular high moral order. An effective development framework is built on strong spiritual values oriented to the satisfaction of the needs, interests, and aspirations of all peoples.

Third, development is a 'socialization of knowledge.' The notion of 'development' must be invoked in the name of the common good. For example, an authentic approach to development in Africa must reassess existing definitions of property and individual ownership, and of rights to social goods and services. The colonial and postcolonial imposition of Western-style property rights continues to bedevil African development, as governments and civil societies attempt to strike a balance between the values of indigenousness and those of modernity. In this era of Africa's full integration into the global capital market, the philosophy of individual ownership and privatization now governs the state's approaches to communal/national property, as well as its definitions of obligations. The commodification and privatization of social knowledge and wealth has alienated and disenfranchised many Africans. Development must seek to appropriate long-standing traditions of mutuality and sustainability as means of meeting local needs and aspirations.

Fourth, authentic development means matching individual rights with social responsibilities. This is democratic development, and it has implications for social justice and political democracy in contemporary Africa. Those accorded the right and privilege to lead and govern have a responsibility to deliver to the people; otherwise, leaders lose their legitimacy and credibility. As political power is allocated to communities, sustainable forms of local representation must be based on indigenous principles of accountability, transparency, and good governance. Unfortunately, this is proving to be enormously difficult in modern Africa, as national governments shed their responsibilities to their citizenry while succumbing to the whims and caprices of the international financial community. States are redefining their obligations and responsibilities to their citizens, with severe consequences for the least advantaged in society (i.e., women, ethnic minorities, and children). The commitment to privatization and private property rights has led to a neglect of social service infrastructures. Private and transnational corporate greed is now being allowed to dictate what should constitute social development, and as a result the emphasis now is on rights rather than responsibilities. While there have always been socio-economic inequalities among individuals, groups, and communities in Africa, the differences have never been as marked as they are today. African indigenousness views ownership of property as an abstract phenomenon. Among

Africans, property is not a 'thing' but a relationship between peoples. Embedded in the African idea of property is the shared notion of what is right for the community and the common good.

Fifth, the idea of 'linkages/connections' that is powerfully entrenched in indigenousness, speaks to the importance of mutual interdependence. African indigenous knowledge systems stress the importance of mutuality and interdependence for group survival. The links between individuals, groups, and society extend beyond the local community. There is a need to connect issues locally, nationally, and internationally. Locally, the issues of poverty cut across class, gender, racial, and ethnic lines. Internationally, the social development concerns of Africans on the continent and of those in the Diaspora converge strongly. Similarly, the South and the North are inextricably linked, particularly in their asymmetrical power relations. There is a broad spectrum of converging interests around social and economic development issues. Therefore, progressive social movements in the North must continually collaborate with forces in the South that are engaged in similar struggles over social and corporate injustice and the yoke of colonialism and [foreign] domination. These movements must find workable grounds for addressing common problems: global racism, structural economic poverty, capitalist and noncapitalist forms of patriarchy, gender and sexual exploitation, and environmental injustice.

Conclusion

The key question is whether 'development' can happen at the level of ideas alone. Thoughts, ideas, and ideals are conditioned by material relations of production, and vice versa. Human agency flows from a material and ideological understanding of the social and natural worlds. The success of African governments' efforts to address the economic problems and issues facing their societies will depend to a great extent on whether nation-states and the international development community are prepared to learn from, and to tap into, the creativity and resourcefulness of diverse local groups. As part of any process of national economic reconstruction, development practitioners will have to examine the accumulated knowledge and varied strategies utilized by local women and men – for example, their strategies for surviving periods of economic expansion and contraction. All of this will provide important lessons in the search for local development alternatives. Development ought to focus on knowledge that is appropriate to local conditions. The processes and principles that local peoples have for years utilized to interpret, explain, and understand their social and natural worlds are valuable for effective development. We need to critically examine conventional development knowledge for what it *includes* and also for what it *leaves out* (see also Kithinji, 1996). Within African contexts, there is a paradox and a contradiction in the development process: we find a continuing transnational/corporate appropriation of local knowledge; at the same time, Africa is experiencing a negation and erasure of its cultural forms of knowledge representation.

As it now stands, conventional approaches to 'development' have not helped local peoples articulate their daily experiences to the outside world (Kankwenda, 1994). As I have argued elsewhere (Dei, 1994b), there is a disturbing failure to recognize that local peoples *do* theorize in their communities as part of community life – that they not only articulate but also *interpret* their experiences. Local peoples have culturally constructed ways of reflecting on their daily lives. They can give their own accounts of what is happening to them and what their needs are, as well as what they are doing, can do, and intend to do about these needs.

Development practitioners and experts should be able to tease out the specific nature of the linkage between indigenous knowledges and local community participation in the development process. Leaders must include local people – particularly women and the poor, whose knowledge and power have been marginalized – at all stages of the conception, planning, implementation, and evaluation of development activities. Local knowledge systems contain invaluable explications of the workings of ecosystems, and of the sustainability of ecologically sound economic production strategies.

A basic challenge is for development theoreticians and practitioners to complement the search for general solutions to human problems, with local specificities. To talk about local specificities is to speak about African indigenousness. The integration of localized, empirical research with theoretical, generalized studies demands that international development researchers begin to accord some importance not only to country-specific research but also to research studies that explore local-level understandings and perceptions of problems, and local strategies to problem-solving.

While community or locality studies by themselves are insufficient to offer a comprehensive understanding of society, they nevertheless provide data that we need in order to ground our theoretical discussions of international development in the everyday lived experiences of people. Such studies provide opportunities for well-meaning development practitioners to hear what people at the grassroots have to say, what their everyday experiences are, and how they make sense of their worlds. For African indigenousness to contribute to an African-centred development process, local peoples must own their past, culture, and traditions. African peoples should be able to critically use knowledges about their histories, cultures, and traditions as a basis for contributing to universal knowledge systems about social development. Like other indigenous communities, African peoples can contribute to universal knowledge systems through a holistic and human approach to society and nature, and through the promotion of communitarian practices. As Prah rightly points out, the process of decolonization requires that indigenous/African peoples confront the 'insulting idea that others know and understand them better than they understand themselves' (1997: 21; and see also hooks, 1991: 22).

NOTES

1 By African-centred development, I am referring to 'development' adapted to the African condition. This must involve adapting to understanding of 'development' – that is, allowing Africans to appropriate the process and objectives of development to ensure that locally defined needs and aspirations are given precedence.
2 In the context of this discussion I use the terms 'traditional' and 'indigenous' interchangeably. As pointed out elsewhere (Dei, 1993b), the term 'traditional' denotes a continuity of cultural values from past experiences that shape the present – for example, how indigenous peoples have accommodated their new form of post-colonial experience. African scholars such as Muteshi (1996) make a distinction between the 'traditional' and the 'indigenous' when arguing that the 'indigenous' past offers a means of staking out a position as an African that is outside of the identity that has been, and continues to be, constructed in Western/Euro-American ideology. In the broader sense of this paper, 'indigenous' is defined as arising locally, primarily from long-term residents in a given community (see also Fals-Borda, 1980; Warren Slikkerveer & Brokensha, 1995).
3 Local communities in Africa have knowledge of local varieties of food crops, wild plants, and food planting cycles that can be harnessed to assist in the formulation of alternative development. The sustainability of these local economic practices has stood the test of time (see Bean, 1992, in another context). For example, local farmers in Sierra Leone have intimate knowledge of planting requirements and yields of local rice varieties. Such knowledge is invaluable in any plan to increase rice production and needs to be taken into account if a change in rice variety is to be advocated (see also Richards, 1985, in another context).

REFERENCES

Bascom, William R. 1952. The Esusu: A Credit Institution of the Yoruba. *Journal of the Royal Anthropological Institute of Great Britain* 82(1): 62–70.
– 1969. *The Yoruba of Southwestern Nigeria.* New York: Holt, Rinehart and Winston.
Bean, W. 1992. Reflections on a Consultation on the Development of Tribals in Asia. *Convergence* 25: 5–17.
Bendera, Stella. 1991. 'Rural Transformation through Education in Tanzania.'

Unpublished EdD dissertation, Department of Sociology, OISE/University of Toronto.

Boeteng, F. 1980. 'African Traditional Education: A Tool for Intergenerational Communication.' Pp. 109–22 in M. Asante & K.W. Asante (eds.), *African Culture: The Rhythms of Unity*. Trenton: Africa World Press.

Dei, G.J.S. 1986. 'Adaptation and Environmental Stress in a Ghanaian Forest Community.' Unpublished PhD dissertation, Department of Anthropology, University of Toronto.

– 1988. Crisis and Adaptation in a Ghanaian Forest Community. *Anthropological Quarterly* 61(2): 63–72.

– 1992. The Renewal of a Ghanaian Rural Economy. *Canadian Journal of African Studies* 26(1): 24–53.

– 1993a. Sustainable Development in the African Context: Revisiting Some Theoretical and Methodological Issues. *Africa Development* 18(2): 97–110.

– 1993b: Indigenous Knowledge Systems: Local Traditions of Sustainable Forestry. *Singapore Journal of Tropical Geography* 14(1): 28–41.

– 1994a. Afrocentricity: A Cornerstone of Pedagogy. *Anthropology and Education Quarterly* 25(1): 3–28.

– 1994b. The Women of a Ghanaian Village: A Study of Social Change. *African Studies Review* 37(2): 121–45.

– 1998. Interogating African Development and the Diasporan Reality. *Journal of Black Studies* 29(2): 141–53.

Dia, M. 1991. Development and Cultural Values in Sub-Saharan Africa. *Finance and Development* (December) 10–13.

Fals-Borda, O. 1980. 'Science and the Common People.' Paper presented at the International Conference on Participatory Research, Ljublana. Yugoslavia.

Fals-Borda, O., and M.A. Rahman (eds.). 1991 *Action and Knowledge: Breaking the Monopoly with Participatory Action Research*. New York: Apex Press.

Goody, Jack. 1962. *Death, Property, and the Ancestors*. Stanford: Stanford University Press.

Gueye, S.P. 1995. Science, Culture and Development in Africa. *CODESRIA* 2: 7–12.

Gyekye, Kwame. 1987. *An Essay on African Philosophical Thought*. London: Cambridge University Press.

Herskovits, Melville J. 1967. *Dahomey: An Ancient West African Kingdom*. Vol. 1. Evanston: Northwestern University Press.

hooks, b. 1991. *Yearning: Race, Gender and Cultural Politics*. London: Turnaround.

Kankwenda, M. 1994. 'Marabouts' and Merchants of Development in Africa.' *CODESRIA* 3: 9–15.

Karp, Ivan. 1986. 'African Systems of Thought.' Pp. 199–211 in Phyllis M. Martin and Patrick O'Meara (eds.), *Africa*. Bloomington: Indiana University Press.

Kithinji, W. 1996. Developing an Endogenous Science in Africa: Beginning with

Women's Needs and Aspirations. PhD research proposal. Department of Curriculum, OISE/University of Toronto.

Machila, M. 1992. Gender and Pluralism in African Development. *Ngoma Ya Mano* (August) 16–20.

Matowanyika, J. 1990. 'Cultural Heritage as a Resource towards Sustaining Rural Africa into the Twenty-First Century.' Paper read at the Annual Conference of the Canadian Association of African Studies, Dalhousie University, Halifax, 9–12 May 1990.

Mbiti, John S. 1982. 'African Views of the Universe.' Pp. 193–9 in R. Olaniyan (ed.), *African History and Culture*. Lagos: Longman.

Mudimbe, V.Y. 1988. *The Invention of Africa: Gnosis, Philosophy, and the Order of Knowledge*. Bloomington: Indiana University Press.

Muteshi, J. 1996. 'Women, Law, and Engendering Resistance: A Pedagogical Project.' Unpublished PhD dissertation, Department of Education, University of Toronto.

O'Manique, John, and Mawuena Dotse. 1991. Development, Democracy, and Decentralization in Ghana: Policy and Legislation of the Provincial National Defence Council. Unpublished paper.

Osagie, Eghosa. 1980. 'Socialism in the African Cultural Context.' Pp. 141–56 in *African Culture: The Rhythms of Unity*. Ed. Molefi Asante and Kariamu W. Asante. Trenton: Africa World Press.

Peek, Philip M. (ed.). 1991. *African Divination Systems: Ways of Knowing*. Bloomington: Indiana University Press.

Posnansky, M. 1984. Hardships of a Village. *West Africa* 3306 (December): 2161–3.

Prah, K. 1997. 'Accusing the Victims – *In My Father's House*.' A Review of Kwame Anthony Appiah, *In My Father's House*.' *CODESRIA* 1: 14–22.

Rattray, Robert S. 1927. *Religion and Art in Ashanti*. London: Oxford University Press.

Richards, P. 1985. *Indigenous Agricultural Revolution*. London: Hutchinson.

Roberts, H. 1998. 'Indigenous Knowledges and Western Science: Perspectives from the Pacific.' In D. Hodson (Ed.), *Science and Technology Education and Ethnicity: An Aotearoa/New Zealand Perspective*. Proceedings of a conference held at the Royal Society of New Zealand, Thorndon, Wellington, May 7–8, 1996. The Royal Society of New Zealand Miscellaneous series #50.

Skinner, Elliot P. 1964. *The Mossi of Upper Volta*. Stanford: Stanford University Press.

Taylor, D.R.F., and F. Mackenzie (eds.). 1992. *Development from Within: Survival in Rural Africa*. New York: Routledge.

Warren, D.M., L.J. Slikkerveer, and D. Brokensha (eds.). 1995. *Indigenous Knowledge Systems: The Cultural Dimension of Development*. Exeter: Intermediate Technology Publications.

PART II

Indigenous Knowledges:
Resistance and Advocacy

While indigenous forms of knowledge drawn from experience traditionally have been passed on for purposes of understanding nature and ways of being in the world, this knowledge can also be understood as articulating a cosmology that contradicts forms of domination such as patriarchy, racism, militarism, scientific and economic colonialism, and imperialism. This section illustrates the formulation of resistance as found in people's experiences as they develop an oppositional consciousness and notions of transformative change.

As McIssac notes here, employing the concept of resistance, particularly as it relates to a counterhegemonic consciousness, requires certain cautions. Within dominant culture there are some resistances that do not challenge structures of power and therefore do not effectively threaten to destabilize the balance of power. It follows that for resistance to be considered a legitimate concept in a discussion of social agency, those forms of resistance which break with dominant culture that need to be identified. It is not a question of whether resistance is expressed, but rather whether it is significant – that is, whether it rearticulates or subverts dominant discourses. In order not to replicate domination, it is important always to examine the processes of both domination and emancipation. For resistance to be politically significant, it must be more than defensive: it must provide for a solidarity of interest and alliances that have the potential to bring about change.

As well in this section, resistance to domination and hegemonic power structures is expressed through visions of social relations and values located within traditional values, knowledges, and practices. Such forms of knowledge can help provide challenges and alternatives to dominant destructive discourses, offer radical alternatives as well as subjective interpretations of historical events, and restore historical agency to cultures and communities.

5

Oral Narratives as a Site of Resistance: Indigenous Knowledge, Colonialism, and Western Discourse

ELIZABETH McISAAC

My point of entry into the discourse of indigenous knowledge is located in an attempt to find resistance to colonialism within the narratives of elders of Kimmirut (formerly known as Lake Harbour), an Inuit community on southern Baffin Island. My approach was to investigate the development of a class/ colonial consciousness within the framework of historical materialism. As a nonaboriginal person located within the parameters of the academy, this method provided me with a starting point for developing an understanding of indigenous knowledge. The difficulty, however, was that in relating colonial resistance to issues of consciousness, I was presupposing a particular philosophy – one that excluded issues that were soon to force themselves through the narratives collected. I may have been pushing the limits of the theoretical framework by expanding the concept of class consciousness to engage elements of a colonial consciousness; questions of cosmological relatedness and centrality of legacy have difficulty lodging themselves within the confines of historical materialism.

This chapter will explore how the barriers created by the theoretical framework impeded a full understanding of the reality confronted. First, the principles and assumptions of a historical materialist framework, and the method of analyzing consciousness within, will be delineated. I will then apply this method to the community, first summarizing the conclusions that I reached through an objective analysis of the group consciousness and then exploring in more depth the subjective expression of consciousness located in the narratives. It is at this point that a rupture occurs, as the notions expressed in the narratives prove to fit badly with the central concerns proposed by the framework. This rupture provides a point of departure for the argument for an indigenous epistemological grounding for theorizing in this context. I argue that the values, interests, and knowledge of indigenous peoples must be accepted as the starting point for developing meaningful social analysis, and that the knowledge systems they possess must be the means of achieving that end.

It is important, first, to contextualize the oral narratives examined in this study. In 1993 I undertook a contract with the Government of the Northwest Territories to compile a Cultural Resource File that would inform the development of an Environmental and Cultural Interpretive Centre in the community. This centre would become part of a larger plan for developing ecotourism in the community. My approach to this research was to rely heavily on the oral narratives of community elders. The interviews I conducted with the elders were oriented toward understanding the land and the people. A problem immediately became apparent: the narratives were collected by an outsider and framed for a particular use. This tension in fact illustrates what I noted earlier: that the expressions and articulations of world view, interests, and values have forced themselves through this discourse. The particular issues related to data collection – mediation of orality, relationship with audience, and framing of questions – will be dealt with in greater detail in the analysis of subjective consciousness.

Theory and Method

Consciousness: Class and Colonial

Any discussion of class consciousness must be prefaced by a clear articulation of the concept of class. Following Ollman (1993: 151–2), class is understood dialectically as having two facets: objectively it involves functional places within the capitalist system, and subjectively, it involves social groups. Regarding social groups, shared interests may include identities that have been constructed through historical experiences or social location. However, the interplay between productive forces and shared interests must be understood as powerful. This leads Ollman (155) to define class consciousness as 'the understanding that is appropriate to the objective character of a class and its objective interests,' on the one hand, and on the other hand, as the group's understanding of who they are and what their actions or practices should be. The relationship between the objective and subjective interests of a group is the central dialectic of class consciousness.

The organizing principles of aboriginal communities have always run counter to hegemonic interest and discourse, and continue to do so. The existence of an indigenous cosmology and its manifestation in knowledge and practice make this form of counterhegemony alive and lived. However, this oppositional force must be recognized as embracing much more than a relationship to capital; it must be understood that political and cultural relations are also major components.

Totalization and Resistance

Using the concept of resistance, particularly as it relates to a counterhegemonic consciousness, requires certain cautions. Within dominant culture there are certain forms of resistance that do not challenge the social structures and therefore do not effectively threaten to destabilize the balance of power. For resistance to be considered a legitimate concept in a discussion of social agency, it must be such that it truly challenges or subverts dominant culture. As Scholle (1990: 96–7) suggests, it is not a question of whether resistance is expressed, but rather whether it is significant – whether it rearticulates or subverts dominant discourses. It is also important to remember that while the totalizing force of capitalism may be understood as pervasive and inclusive (affecting culture, social relations, politics, and so on), this should not lead to a reification of the structures of capital and its power. Rather, as Kulchyski (1992) advises, it is important always to examine the processes of both domination *and* emancipation in order not to reify the totalizing force of capital.

In developing the concept of resistance, Giroux (1983: 108) outlines three basic assumptions. *First*, resistance assumes a dialectical notion of human agency. The dynamic nature of domination demands an analysis of the complex ways that people respond to their experiences and to structures of domination; this in turn involves considering intentionality and consciousness. *Second*, the concept of resistance recognizes that power is never one-dimensional; rather, it is practised as both a mode of domination and as an act of resistance. Thus, there may exist 'moments of cultural and creative expression that are informed by a different logic, whether it be existential, religious, or otherwise' and in which are found 'fleeting images of freedom.' *Third*, resistance contains an expressed hope for social transformation. For the concept of resistance to be useful, then, it must offer an emanicipatory alternative to the present condition of domination. Scholle (1990: 103) insists that for resistance to be politically significant it must be more than defensive: it must be able to foster a solidarity of interests and alliances that have the potential to effect change.

Analysis of Consciousness

Before we can discuss the present consciousness of the Kimmirut community, we must understand the transformations in political economy that the community has experienced. Relations with European and American capital began with the whalers at the end of the nineteenth century and were intensified with the arrival of the Anglican Church, the Hudson's Bay Company (HBC), and the Royal Canadian Mounted Police (RCMP), in 1909, 1911, and 1927 respectively. While the HBC clearly played a fundamental role in the economic colonization of the community, the church and the RCMP also had a strong impact on issues of culture and political sovereignty. Until the late 1960s, most people continued to live on the land; their connection to the HBC post was limited to trading. At this time, however, the government began encouraging the people to settle in the community. Having done so, the people became more engaged in the cash economy. It should be noted, however, that most community members today still rely heavily on the traditional economy for food, as both an economic and a cultural practice.

The objective economic position of the people, which in part conditions their ideas and actions, may be summarized as follows[1]: increasing dependency on the cash economy over time; progressive proletarianization of the population; transformation of the prevalent-use value of production (i.e., prior to contact and subsequent colonization) to exchange value; and marginalization of the traditional economic roles of women under the patriarchal structures of capitalism. These pressures and constraints are highly interrelated, and within a historical materialist framework they impute certain responses. Remember here that the subjective interests of the group must also be understood as affecting the objective ones, so that the interplay between the two creates a dynamic process emerging as a particular consciousness.

Relatedness and Learning – Questions of Ancestry

Before analyzing the narratives in terms of colonial consciousness, it is important to place oral history in the proper cultural context. One elder expressed the significance of oral tradition and memory:

> Men used to talk, like when they talk among themselves, or ... have conversations. Women weren't allowed to [join] the conversations because they would talk mainly of what the men do ... It was strange for a woman to start ... talking [to a man] unless she had questions, a lot of questions that she wanted to know. And like back then, we didn't have papers and stuff, and put information on paper. It all had to do with memory, like ... we haven't lost it because we remember it ... And also, like in terms of land or islands, according to the man and his knowledge about them, then he would give information that he had to another person or another male who's interested. (July 1993)[2]

This comment highlights the role of oral tradition in maintaining social structures – in this case, the gendered divisions of labour and expertise, which were sustained through the selective passing of knowledge. As well, it points out the importance of memory and oral tradition in protecting knowledge necessary for the survival of society. Oral history as a cultural practice and mode of cultural survival is also important when it comes to expressions of cultural resistance.

The use of oral history has been subject to a variety of criticisms. Questions of mediation and power relations surround the process. When oral histories are related in a one-to-one exchange, the problem of power dynamics clearly arises: 'It is a form of history that requires mediation: it is built into it. There is always that power position between the informant and what gets related to the consumer. It places the informant in a very vulnerable position. How that vulnerability is negotiated is of prime importance in how one uses oral history' (Gunew and Sheridan, 1990: 67).

The power relations that influenced the oral narratives collected were those which defined my position as researcher and the elders' position as holders of oral history and traditional knowledge. The tensions characterizing the relationship related mainly to contesting vantage points, one representing dominant Canadian society and the other illustrating the counterhegemonic discourse. I tried to structure the interviews loosely, my intent being to create a space for an indigenous interpretation and expression, and to forestall criticisms of hegemonic textual dominance. Alternatively, the informants negotiated the relationship in terms of both their willingness to speak and the context of their speech.

Lacey relates the issue of performance dynamics in the relating of oral histories to the problem of power relations: 'Any conversational narrative is controlled to such an extent that a person who is asking the questions becomes the audience to whom the person responding speaks ... People tell the same story twice, but differently ... We are speaking of performances and the relationship between people masking and unmasking to each other' (1990: 49).

This allows the critic of oral history to find problems of validity relating to circumstance and audience. Yet at the same time, the issue of validity suggests the *strength* of using oral narratives for investigating consciousness and identifying resistance – particularly when power relations are accounted for in the process. The concern about validity, however, must not be perceived as restricted to the interests of the audience. When legends or old stories were asked for, informants refused to relate them for fear of not telling the story the *right* way. In relating the experience of the sinking of the *Nascopie*, one man repeated throughout the narrative the unique nature of what he had to say and the possible contradictions of other versions: 'Every person has different stories about it, because everyone, like ... if I say something about it, it can be a little different from the real story. I was here during that time so I know how to tell a story about [it], because when I hear some people saying [things] about it, it has been said differently' (August 1993). This disclaimer of absolute validity permitted the speaker to relate the story according to his own experience, subjectively. What is important in this context is the ability to provide alternative histories to those which have been socially constructed by the dominant society; and which position the people as historical subjects.

Legacy and Learning

The question that was put to informants at the beginning of each interview was framed to allow the discussion to be directed by the informant: 'What do you feel are the most important aspects of the history and traditions of the people which you feel are important for your grandchildren and their grandchildren to know?'

Invariably, the women initiated a discussion of their traditional roles prior to settlement in the community. Three (out of seven) of the women interviewed had spent most if not all of their life at the settlement and had done at least some work for the HBC or RCMP. Nevertheless, their discussions began with how to prepare and sew sealskin, how to maintain a *qulliq* (oil lamp), traditional methods of childbearing and the various rituals surrounding it, and, at varying levels of abstraction, the inextricable relationship of the people to the land. A theme that ran through all responses, male and female, was the profound change the community had experienced in living memory. With respect to women, this was perhaps even more exaggerated because of the patriarchal nature of capitalism and the effect this has had on their role. One women emphasized the importance of the traditional roles and knowledge that belonged to women: 'And also the roles of women and what they do, not just cleaning in the house, but in terms of cleaning seals and those things' (August 1993).

The exaggerated effect of change on the role of women may be explained by the fact that while the men continue to hunt and participate in traditional economic pursuits, albeit with modifications, the main tasks of women – keeping the *qulliq*, preparing skins, sewing skins for clothing and tents, and insulating the *qarmagh* (winter tent), to name a few – have for the most part become nearly obsolete. It was important to the women interviewed that knowledge of their traditional roles be passed on to future generations so that they would understand what it once had meant to be Inuit.

Another theme that ran through both the women's and men's narratives was the importance of the learning process in terms of traditional knowledge. Again, change was often referred to in terms of loss:

> There seems to be a gap now, more than before, because back then children didn't have many places to go, there weren't any schools or centres, community centres, recreation centres, and kids back then didn't stay out too late at that time because they spent more time at home, and therefore the grandparents would have more chance to pass their knowledge on to them ... Around the time after we had been born, we did live in outpost camps too, and it was easier to have close relationships with family back then, but this changed quickly when people were in a bigger community where kids spend time with other kids and hang out more together instead of with their grandparents or with the family. (July 1993)

It is important to note that the change in intergenerational relations is traced back clearly to the time of settlement in the community. The social relations of camp life are understood as having encouraged close family relations and, it follows, opportunities to learn from elders. The above comment makes reference to the importance of relationships in the process of learning and for providing a 'container' for the legacy of knowledge.

The men interviewed (twelve in total) spoke consistently about hunting, fishing, and survival, and about their knowledge of the land, weather, and dangers. A central concern for them was that future generations know how to use and survive on the land. Cultural practice through hunting and food sharing was also emphasized. This reveals a concern for the continued practice of culture and the reproduction of meaningful relations inherent in this; for example, kin relations activated for food sharing reproduce the real relations of production in traditional society.

Like the women, the men spoke about the importance of experiential learning for passing on traditional knowledge:

> Back then I didn't realize I was learning, but I went with my father, when he was going hunting. I didn't realize that I was being taught, but I learned it by seeing it and doing it without really feeling like I was learning, like in schools. Like now as an adult I go hunting, I can go hunting by myself. Like my father used to tell me what I'd have to do, or how I'd do it. Like even up to today when I go out, I still remember what he used to tell me, and I follow his advice. (July 1993)

This man highlighted the continued need for traditional knowledge. He referred specifically to the importance of relationships in constructing and transferring knowledge. In this way, he was pointing explicitly to the embodied and timeless nature of knowledge.

Applying traditional knowledge to everyday matters has become a matter of survival in Kimmirut. Tensions develop as modern technology intrudes into traditional practices. For example, traditionally, land areas were travelled slowly, and this allowed travellers to acquire detailed knowledge of dangers. According to one man's story:

> And I've watched TV programs teaching about [hunting], but I thought it could be better. The program that I saw showed a place in open water where there's broken ice, and the [man in the program] was hopping from one bank to the other and he harpooned an animal and he didn't let go. Like I was taught that if I was in an area like that, I had – it did not matter how close the animal was, like a seal – I was taught that I have to let go right away. And the one that I saw on TV, he didn't let go, and that's very dangerous. And I think that would mislead some youngsters, that they could start thinking, 'Oh, that's how I do it.' (July 1993)

Again, it is essential for traditional knowledge to be transferred accurately to the next generation. Also interesting in this passage are the contradictions between experiential learning and watching television. Yet the elder interviewed did not necessarily object to the medium; rather, he was concerned about the validity of the information and the implications that bad information might have.

The examples given here of traditional life represent much more than simple cultural artifacts. They imply a series of relations: to the land, to the community, and to production. For example: traditional winter clothing involves hunting on the land and knowledge of the land. These in turn imply a sense of protection of the land based on use according to need, and the social relations of hunting. Furthermore, preparing skins and sewing winter clothes is the domain of women in terms of their traditional knowledge and roles. The final product, the winter clothing, holds important cultural value in this context. The concern for passing traditional knowledge to future generations perhaps implies a vision of social relations based on principles that challenge the dominant Canadian culture.

Is maintaining traditional knowledge and cultural practices a form of resistance? For this to be so, such knowledge and practices must have the potential to emancipate people, and the people must intend it to do that. Elders recognized that they are situated at a critical moment in terms of this knowledge. The next generation has not lived on the land as they have but has grown up in a hamlet where the dominant Canadian culture has structured much of their everyday life. The elders' emphasis on cultural practice and traditional knowledge is not simply about economic relations; it is also about resisting cultural domination and colonial history.

The Land

Throughout the interviews, the land was framed over and over again as a locus of identity. This suggests that we must look more closely at how the people express their relationship to it. At the end of each interview, I asked the respondents to describe their relationship to the land. It was only months after my stay in the community and after several rereadings of the texts that I realized how redundant the question was. On most occasions the respondents offered a very short answer or simply gave me a puzzled look. Throughout the hours of discussion that preceded the question, they had weaved into their stories very elaborate descriptions of their relationship to the land. My own discourse – my Western constructions of understanding – had prevented me from realizing that the question had already been answered.

Still, the question of the people's relationship to the land did evoke some revealing responses that merit attention for how they express resistance to the totalizing effect of capitalism and cultural imperialism. The first response to be considered draws on an analogy to kin relationships:

Between me and the land means ... I love the land like I love my family, like my own wife or my own children. That's how close it is to me because it has food, it has animals that live on it. I love it like I love my family ... My ancestors are gone, they're dead, and they were buried on the land, and the loved ones are buried. It's almost loving the whole world like I love my family. (August 1993)

This comment transcends the relations of production that the people have with the land and situates the relationship as parallel to kinship and deeply imbued with love. This response calls attention to the fact that ideologically, the land continues to be perceived as more than a means of production. This vantage point provides an understanding of the land that is incongruous with capitalist relations, which involve ownership and exploitation of land. It also invokes a language, one of love and of a particular relationship with nature, that finds no space within the discourse of political economy. The informant expresses a commitment to maintaining this relationship, which speaks of relationships that cannot be addressed within the framework of historical materialism.

The following response puts forward both a cosmological conception of the land and an explicit reference to productive use. It also expresses the tensions that have developed through change over the person's lifetime:

> To me, the land is very important, it has its purpose and use. Nowadays the younger people use snowmobiles and they can travel faster and therefore go further away than what they're familiar with, like in terms of the surroundings, and they're gone too long, like they didn't know the area. Older people tend to worry that something might happen to them ... We had no choice but to use the land and so it's very important to me and if you know where you've left something, then you can use the landmarks and whatever and just, make yourself familiar with the land, like a belonging. But the only thing that's not too useful, that I can say, are the ravens because they're more like raiders, and you don't use them for food and even when they're young, or their eggs, they've never had any relationship with the survival of the Inuit. Like with seagulls, there is their eggs, even though they're scavengers. We'd use these. But ravens, if you leave a camp or something, they'll go right up to it and raid it and mess things up ... You can use everything on the land, and even travelling or having a sense of belonging by using, that you're not in danger or you're not in trouble when you can use these ... I left off with the raven because I want to leave an impression where, as a hunter you go out and work hard and try and get food for your family, then the ravens are there. I like to keep everything neat and prepared for the family to supply the family, but ravens do the opposite thing – they mess things up and they steal and raid and take whatever the hunter's trying to do. (July 1993)

There are three points that should be addressed from this excerpt. *First*, reference is made to the change in land use that has occurred with modern technology. This change affected the production and reproduction of traditional knowledge of the land, which draws heavily from familiarity and experience. The narrative, in itself, may not constitute resistance as the concept is being applied, but it does express a particular acknowledgment of changing reality and the impact it is having. *Second*, the excerpt points out how the relationship between land and the people is conceived of as 'belonging by using.' No relationship of ownership is expressed in this formulation, but rather an accessibility to resources to satisfy needs. *Third*, the allusion to the raven and its relationship to the Inuit is instructive. The response is framed in such a way that the only relationships worth pursuing are those which are complementary to the objective, which is the survival of the people, who are part of a series of symbiotic relationships found in nature. The framing of the ravens as raiders makes it easy to understand the analogy to the experience of the Inuit over time with the various representatives of capitalist and colonial interests, and consequently, then, their overt rejection of this form of exploitative relationship.

Taking into account the central importance of the land to the people, the explicit references to the incongruence of ownership and exploitation to the Inuit conception of the land, the injustice of dispossession, and the fact that these sentiments were expressed in the context of the project and the relations of research, a particular form of resistance may be theorized. Clear rejection of the effects of colonialism, which has disabled the traditional relationship to the land, is evidence of this. The Inuit relationship to the land is described in the accounts as one that defies ownership, provides for the survival of the people, and is cosmologically conceived as a part of a whole of which the people are an equal part. This relationship, which is understood as being of both economic and cultural significance to the Inuit, resists the totalizing logic of capitalism, which works to commoditize everything it encounters – most fundamentally, land. While this value is expressed at the level of territorial negotiation regarding land claims and use, it is important in terms of consciousness to note that it also pervades the discourse at the community level.

Concepts of lineage, learning, generational linkages, containers of legacy, unity of land and people, and relationships of love are central to the creation of knowledge by the elders. Communalistic practices and corresponding relations of production can be identified clearly from the vantage point of historical materialism, and consequent claims about consciousness and resistance can be made. However, notions such as the people being *part* of the land, and love being an organizing principle for relations with the natural world, are situated beyond this framework. These principles cannot be adequately addressed within the discourse of historical materialism unless they are relegated first to the realm of ideology, as the philosophical assumptions do not permit these concepts to be taken up as a legitimate system of knowledge.

Conclusion

The issues that are brought to light through the framework of historical materialism are important. Examining class/colonial consciousness does reveal that indigenous knowledge participates in a political agenda, defines agency, and expresses historical agency. Through the narratives, a particular resistance to domination and hegemonic power structures is expressed through visions of social relations and values located within traditional practices and knowledge. The existence and survival of indigenous knowledges are also evidence of the resistance of the people in the face of colonialism. Indigenous knowledges not only represent alternatives and challenges to dominant discourses, but also restore historical agency. While knowledges drawn from experience traditionally have been passed on for purposes of understanding nature, the land, the animals, and the elements, these knowledges can also be understood as articulating a cosmology that contradicts the logic of colonialism and offers a radical alternative.

Indigenous knowledges are knowledges of experience and relationship that speak to lived, material, and cosmological concerns. In the production of these forms of knowledge, traditional values, interests, and objectives articulate a series of relationships (land/nature, spiritual, and human). The history of indigenous peoples has shown that to sever these relationships is tantamount to genocide. This is a consequence that cannot be ignored. Therefore, for those who participate in producing knowledge that concerns indigenous peoples, there is a moral imperative to become resituated as learners, and to engage in a process and relationship of learning that is based on indigenous knowledges.

NOTES

1 This summary is drawn from a more extensive analysis provided in 'Indigenous Knowledge and Colonial Power: The Oral Narrative as a Site of Resistance' (unpublished MA thesis, Department of Sociology, OISE/University of Toronto, Canada, 1995). Chapter 3 of this thesis examines historically four examples of commodity production in the community: whaling, the fur trade, boat building, and soapstone carving. Changing labour relations as well as the relations of the workers to the product of their labour are explored.
2 All quotes in this paper have been taken directly from the interview transcripts. Quotes have been edited to remove the interpreter's voice and provide consistency. Individuals cited in this chapter are not identified, in order to protect their privacy.

REFERENCES

Giroux, Henry. 1983. *Theory and Resistance in Education*. Westport, CT: Bergin and Garvey.
Gunew, Sneja, and Sue Sheridan. 1990. 'Comment on Troger.' In Shelley Schreiner and Diane Bell (eds.), *This Is My Story: Perspectives on the Use of Oral Sources*. Geelong: Centre for Australian Studies, Deakin University.
Kulchyski, Peter. 1992. Primitive Subversions: Totalization and Resistance in Native Canadian Politics. *Cultural Critique* (Spring).
Lacey, Rod. 1990. 'From Kepai to Margaret – Conversational Narratives in Papua New Guinea and Australia.' In Shelley Schreiner and Diane Bell (eds.) *This Is My Story: Perspectives on the Use of Oral Sources*. Geelong: Centre for Australian Studies, Deakin University.

Livingstone, D.W., and J. Marshall Mangan. 1993. Class, Gender, and Expanded Class Consciousness in Steeltown. *Research in Social Movements, Conflicts and Change* 15: 55–82.

Lukács, Georg. 1979. *History and Class Consciousness.*: Cambridge: MIT Press.

Marx, Karl, and Frederick Engels. 1981. *The German Ideology.* New York: International Publishers.

McIsaac, Elizabeth. 1995. Indigenous Knowledge and Colonial Power: The Oral Narrative as a Site of Resistance. Unpublished MA thesis, Department of Sociology, OISE/University of Toronto.

Ollman, Bertell. 1993. *Dialectical Investigations.* New York: Routledge.

Scholle, David. 1990. Resistance. *Journal of Urban and Cultural Studies* 1(1): 87–105.

6

The Retention of Knowledge of Folkways as a Basis for Resistance

PATIENCE ELABOR-IDEMUDIA

In this paper I will highlight the contribution that indigenous knowledges, embodied in folkways or traditional practices and transmitted through 'sayings of the wise,' have made to the formation of African people's cultural identities. The object of this is to show that knowledge of African folkways, when inculcated in children through socialization, becomes a basis for resistance in later life. For ages, exposure to such knowledge of folkways has given most Africans strength, courage, and a sense of identity. I will show that the sense of cultural identity and belonging that African peoples thereby acquire has always been central to their survival throughout hardships such as those imposed by slavery, colonialism, and the imperialism exemplified by present-day development programs. In this paper I will also discuss how African knowledge and systems of organization have been excluded from mainstream development strategies; and propose that an alternative, *African*-centred epistemology be made the basis for planning and designing development programs and policies.

People brought up in Western societies often equate knowledge with written 'literature,' and forget that oral traditions as embodied in folkways preceded and helped shape written knowledge. In most traditional societies the spoken world is the basis of cultural identity and a means of transmitting indigenous knowledge[1] from one generation to the next. Oral forms of knowledge such as ritualistic chants, riddles, songs, folktales, and parables not only articulate a distinct cultural identity but also give voice to a range of cultural, social and political, aesthetic, and linguistic systems – systems long muted by centuries of colonialism and cultural imperialism.

In Western accounts of African history, the persistent use of Eurocentric discourse continues to be particularly problematic, in that too often its starting point has not been the personal everyday experiences of the people. This point is especially important in view of the fact that experience – with practical images as its symbolic vehicle – is a fundamental epistemological tenet in African thought systems. In contrast to Western 'either/or' dichotomous thought, traditional African world views are holistic and seek harmony. People become more human and empowered only in the context of a community, and only when they become seekers of connectedness – of interactions and meanings of the sort that lead to harmony (Asante, 1987:185). These values form the basis of African philosophy.

African Philosophical Thought and Knowledge of Folkways

In the past (and to some extent the present), the literary heritage and philosophical thought of an African community were enshrined in its folk traditions, especially in its myths, legends, proverbs, tales, and songs. The myths examined and attempted to answer questions about life and death. Desired cultural traits were reflected in characters, which were understood as symbolic representations of these traits. The legends were related to ethnic origins and migrations, and usually proved to be highly accurate and reliable. The proverbs, sometimes presented as questions, encapsulated the wisdom of a group, a wisdom that was often human rather than specifically African and that complemented traditional Western beliefs. The value of co-operation was the theme of many proverbs, because as every African knows, 'One hand cannot tie a bundle' (Todd, 1979: xi). Folktales, often incorporating solo and group singing, were an integral part of African life. So deeply rooted was the folktale tradition in African life that it survived the slave trade and re-established itself wherever Africans settled, whatever languages they adopted.

Modern African literature is suffused with these cultural traits. Modern African drama is characterized by rituals, the supernatural, and spirit possession, and by a language enriched by proverbs. African poetry absorbs rituals, incantatory rhythms, traditional oratory, and symbolic animal and plant imagery originating in folklore (Ojaide, 1994). African literature is utilitarian, based more on social ideals than on individual psychology; it is community-oriented and in the past was a tool for ethical and moral instruction. It draws on the beliefs, world views, and folkloric heritage of African's people. Its allusions to folklore, while often obscure to outsiders, lend it a certain profundity (Ojaide, 1994). Ibrahim Tala rightly observes that in Africa,

'New writers incorporate oral literature in their writing to give a flavour of authenticity to their works and to show that as modern Africans, [they] are conscious of a rich source of literary inspiration. They include oral tradition to link their past with their present experience (as a group), to localize the content of their works, to educate fellow Africans and give them confidence in their cultural heritage and to enlighten outsiders and help them get rid of the false impression about African cultures acquired from years of cultural misrepresentation.' (1984: 95–6)

Although it has been argued that 'African culture' cannot exist because Africa encompasses many ethnic groups, Chimezie (1983) over a decade ago argued that those who expound this view are drawing attention away from the continental African heritage of North American blacks, and from the innovations and cultural integrity of African peoples. As Dei (1994b) and many others point out, underlying the 'fragmentation' of culture along ethnic, religious, ideological, class, and gender lines are a number of common themes. According to Dei (1994a), African cultures, be they Yoruba, Asante, Maasai, or Gikuyu, have more in common with one another than with European or American culture. It should also be noted that culture is a both a product and a reflection of history. It is a product and a reflection of human beings communicating with one another in the struggle to create and control wealth. Africans actively inform African cultural images and pictures of the world of nature and nurture, especially in the minds of children. Our entire conception of ourselves as people, individually and collectively, is based on those pictures and images, which may or may not correspond to the actual reality of the struggles with nature and nurture that produced them in the first place (wa Thiong'o, 1987: 15).

Growing Up as an African Child

I was born in Nigeria, in Irrua, Esan, in the western region of Okpebho local government area. Although an only child of my biological parents, I had several cousins and social brothers and sisters who were part of my extended family. Having grown up in an Esan-African culture, I am able to appreciate how the community in which I was raised helped shape the adult I have become. This is because, as with many African children born into extended families, I was raised as belonging to the community as a whole. As children, we spoke our native dialect as we worked with elders in the fields and in our homes. In the evenings we would sit around the fire and listen carefully as adults told stories. Most of the stories had animals as the main characters and their experiences and adventures reflected the challenges of the natural and social environment. The tortoise was always slow but cunning, full of tricks and good at outwitting all others. The hare, although small and weak, was full of innovative wit and cunning. It often struggled against predators like the lion, the leopard, and the hyena. We children saw its heroic victories as our victories, and thereby learned that the weak can outwit the strong. We followed with keen interest the animals' struggles against hostile natural forces such as rain, drought, sun, and wind; in these confrontations the animals were often compelled to co-operate with one another. But we were also keenly interested in the struggles among the animals themselves, particularly those struggles between the beasts of prey and their victims. These twin struggles – against nature, and against other animals – reflected real-life struggles in the human world (wa Thiong'o, 1987: 11). Co-operation as the ultimate good in a community was a constant theme. Co-operation could unite human beings with animals against ogres and beasts of prey. Through these stories and songs, we internalized many lessons; through them, our parents were encouraging us to be strong and fearless in the face of adversity.

As an African child, my sense of solidarity with others was rooted in wider, kin-based groups. These kin groups comprised people who claimed descent from a particular male or female ancestor, who might be mythical or putative in the sense that his or her historical existence could not be physically proven. However, such ancestorship symbolized the social unity and identity of the membership; this in turn meant that the kin group was central to many of the society's most important functions. The kin group fostered collective responsibility, solidarity, and mutuality; it instilled among us a need to act as a corporate body and to protect the integrity of critical resources (such as land) that could not be divided without being destroyed (see also Dei, 1989, 1994a). The kin group also provided a workforce for those tasks which required labour pools. It provided members with identity, social comfort, and a sense of belonging to a community, particularly in times of hardship.

My feelings of solidarity and mutuality were developed through participation in community rituals, celebrations, and associations. Solidarity was developed through association with non-kin social groupings such as age sets, age grades, and ritually defined generations of age-mates whose major roles in the society were to educate the young, particularly about communal values, and to instil a sense of commitment to the collective. Mutuality, as an indigenous characteristic, was always demonstrated. Within African communities there were many various self-help groups and institutions, many of which would still be useful today. For example, self-loaning bodies and 'credit circles' were common. These loaned money to their members as necessary and prudent; any surplus would be set aside as a reserve to help relieve any sudden hardships, or to invest in other economic ventures.

Collective responsibility was taught by promoting within the community the belief that rights of community membership come with matching obligations and responsibilities. As Mbiti (1982) has pointed out, Africans historically have been socialized to define themselves according to their social obligations to the wider community. Such responsibilities included providing communal labour (e.g. for road construction) at any time when called upon by the traditional polity, as well as making compulsory financial (Dei, 1989) and nonfinancial contributions to assist bereaved families in burying their dead (see also Herskovits, 1967; Skinner, 1964; and Bascom, 1969).

Considering all of the above, it is not surprising that an individual's relationship with the community is also important. The indigenous African philosophy posits that mutual co-operation is vital for both individual and group survival. The fear that the group could withdraw mutual aid and co-operation was a powerful inducement for individuals to conform to societal norms and regulations.

Through my upbringing in the community, I also learned the significance of gender. The gender roles of women in African society are far different from those of the Western tradition. Gender speaks loudly as a 'persistent and visible cultural resource in the folk model of difference' (Mills, 1992: 2). An abundant body of research (Stamp, 1991; Elabor-Idemudia, 1991) exists that highlights the existence in traditional African societies of various forms of domination and exploitation based on gender, ethnicity, class, and sexual inequality; but in those same societies there is also a tradition of women's empowerment. Amadiume (1987) notes that women have a role to play in exposing the contradictions in their societies regarding their own social history; the purpose of these efforts is to challenge, where necessary, discrimination against women, to achieve more power for women, and to foster more egalitarian societies for everyone. Women have been very powerful influences in traditional politics and religion. Historically, women's associations were cultural sources of power for women. Through such organizations, women were able to influence how resources were allocated within their communities. Women influenced the economy by making decisions about the foods to be produced for consumption, marketing, and exchange. This provided them with some autonomy within the community, as well as leverage in terms of their relationships with men (Steady, 1990: 15–16). By relying on the social group, women were able to reduce their dependence on individual men, and this served to reduce general male control of society. Unfortunately, these indigenous institutions were co-opted by colonialists, and their roles were redefined. In some cases the colonial rulers manipulated and exploited existing patriarchal attitudes in African culture.

Colonial Influence and the Destruction of African Culture

Under the colonial administration in Nigeria, new forms of production were introduced and new systems of power relations were imposed. New patterns of inequality were established involving people of different backgrounds, languages, and beliefs. At age six, children of my age cohort were required by the newly imposed colonial policies to go to Western-style schools to acquire 'formal' knowledge through education. At the school we were forced to give up the knowledge of folkways that we had acquired in our homes and from the community, as these folkways were considered primitive. We were also forced to give up our mother tongue and acquire a foreign language – the language of the colonial master. We were not being educated in a way that would encourage us to pursue our own political and economic interests or that would make us a viable part of our own country. We were, in fact, being educated *against* our own interests, in the sense that we were now being educated by outsiders who saw advantages in giving us an education that would make us more susceptible to their control. We were being educated to be individualistic, complacent, subordinate, and unquestioningly obedient: cultural traits that were not only foreign to us but also counter to our indigenous heritage. Our pride in who we were by virtue of our traditions and culture was completely negated. This white-controlled education, which was so highly valued, turned us into defective Africans suffering from false, 'white' consciousness (wa Thiong'o, 1987: 34).

According to Jell-Bahlsen (1994), 'assault on African values, thoughts, achievements, social and economic arrangements, on nutrition and preventative health care, religious beliefs and artistic expression have continued well beyond colonial past.' For example, local farmers traditionally planted several food crops (cassava, yams, and beans) together. In the name of modernization and development, Western 'experts' advised farmers to engage in monocropping – that is, growing one crop at a time. This practice led to the destruction of crops by insects. Had traditional agricultural methods been used, these insects would have been kept in a balanced state by the presence of other crops. As a solution to the problem of destructive insects, the 'experts' recommended the use of insecticides, which created environmental and health problems. The insecticides were more beneficial to Western insecticide producers, whose products, which were banned in Europe, found new markets in Africa. Africans were often told that the new forms of production and subsequent use of chemicals were 'developments' necessary for modern 'progress.'

Land, which had sustained the corporate existence of Africans, was appropriated by colonial administrators for the production of raw materials and cash crops for export to Europe. The loss of land in colonial times was highly resented, as it translated into poverty, rootlessness, and lack of dignity. Land issues gave impetus to the Mau Mau insurrection against British colonialism that ushered in Kenyan political independence. In West and Southern Africa, feelings of alienation grew as people were compelled by economic circumstance to move from rural to urban areas. Colonial organization of production undermined Africans' sense of community.

Similarly, imported Western and Eastern religions (Christianity and Islam) have created conflicts and civil wars in African countries. In Nigeria, for example, several conflicts have arisen in the past decade over religious freedom. Religious freedom, including freedom of traditional religion, is officially recognized; but in practice, being a Muslim or Christian offers economic advantages denied to other religious groups. With the imposition of Christianity, local religions in Africa were devalued and believers were prevented from making offerings to sculptures of local gods and goddesses. Local shrines and sculptures were destroyed by Christian missionaries, while believers were accused of witchcraft. All of this was done without consultation with the believers as to their reasons for adhering to pre-European practices. A child in Nigeria, I was told by elders that idols are adopted for worshipping because the worshippers feel too insignificant and 'unworthy' to address Almighty God directly; thus, they must build sculptures as 'small' gods to serve as mediators between them and the Almighty.

Development Approaches in Africa

Three major development paradigms were adopted in Africa in the 1950s, 1960s, and 1970s respectively. These were the modernization, developmental, and dependency paradigms. Together, these constitute the foundational thinking that has shaped development policies and strategies in African countries. While the approaches to development embedded in these theories were different, their results were much the same.

Modernization Theory

It was presumed that African societies evolved in their social organization and value systems along a continuum. It followed that in order to modernize, they had to rise above their traditional values, institutions, and forms of production, which were preventing them from adopting modern values and technology. According to the notion of social evolution, societies are compelled by changes in their population/resource balance and by competition with neighbours to move toward an increasing division of labour (Parsons, 1970). At one end of the continuum are societies in which people (or institutions) perform a multitude of tasks (simple societies); at the other end are societies in which there are various social units specializing in only a few tasks (complex societies). According to Parsons, complex societies are characterized by higher levels of technology and more formal institutions; while the opposite is the case in simple societies. Thus, increased specialization is equated with higher efficiency and greater increases in productivity. Simple societies, in which there is less differentiation among social units, are regarded as less productive and poorer.

This model of modernization was advanced by the Western powers after their victory in the Second World War. It reflected the values of capitalist democracy: high social mobility in a consumer-based Keynesian economy. Scholars and proponents of modernization theory, such as Rostow (1971), developed five stages of economic growth that a nation passes through along the path to modernization. This model was based on that of nation-states, whose focus has always been on the individual and/or aggregates of individuals. In the Third World, which was still colonized in the 1950s, the agents of modernization were those foreign or local élites (usually men) who had assimilated the values of the industrialized modern world, adopted its technology, and imported its financial, industrial, and educational institutions. These modern-world values favoured men; women were (and still are) neglected and deprived of status because of the resulting social and sexual division of labour inherent in these models of growth and development (Beneria & Sen, 1981). Agents of modernization tended to imitate Western institutions and social structures. In doing so they were embracing Western value systems and cultural traits (Hoselitz, 1966).

Modernization theory is based on the assumption that there is a unilinear route to development and that the social and economic 'fixes' applied in the West ought to be applied in developing countries as well. This assumption is in tune with Marx's thinking that developing nations can see their own future in the developed nations. What is not accounted for in modernization theory are the political, historical, social, cultural, economic, and ecological factors at play in developing nations – factors that are very different from those encountered in the West. Development models fashioned after Western values are doomed to failure because they create and then do nothing to bridge an immense gap between theory and practice – that is, between development policy and people's daily experience. In developing countries, economic and social policies based on modernization theory have been strikingly unsuccessful. They have resulted in low productivity, polarization between the rich and the poor, and poverty and marginalization of poor people (especially women). They have also damaged the environment and people's health. This model focused more on the *nation* as an economic entity than on social and household well-being and on the general quality of life of the nation (Asante, 1991).

The disruptive effects of decolonization during the 1960s, coupled with the widespread emergence of 'authoritarian, totalitarian and military regimes' in most Third World countries, led many scholars to reconsider the assumptions of modernization theory (Gallagher, 1983: 23). The result was the emergence of the developmental theory.

Developmental Theory

This view of development replaced the modernization paradigm by shifting the explanation for underdevelopment to emphasize structural factors. Early proponents of developmental theory followed the tradition of Max Weber. They emphasized individual freedom of action and the importance of individual entrepreneurs as innovators of development. David McClelland's argument (1961) that individual achievement drives development is a classic example of a development framework rooted in these assumptions, although he paid little attention to Weber's concern (1968) for analyzing the constraints of social structure on individual freedom. The assumptions behind developmental theory are in direct conflict with the Afrocentric values of community and co-operation.

Proponents of developmentalism pointed out that few development decisions are implemented by direct intervention, and proposed that decision-making should include individuals as well as governments. Feminist researchers understood quickly enough that modernization affected men and women differently, and proceeded to point out obstacles preventing women from participating in development. Feminists engaged in developmental studies look at women as rational decision makers, and not simply as conservative holdouts, and have criticized the assumptions underlying 1950s and 1960s style development.

Feminist theorists argue that as a result of the developmental paradigm, women's social roles have narrowed, they have lost political power, and their capacity to generate income has shrunk. As a result, society has also suffered, in that it has lost the household as an adaptive, low-cost production centre that can shield its members from the vicissitudes of the market economy (Nash & Safa, 1976).

In the face of various criticisms, proponents of developmentalism changed their emphasis to focus more on the role of the state in promoting development. Consequently, scholars such as Nettl and Robertson (1968), Furtado (1970), Dumont (1969), and Prebisch (1981) looked at development from the perspective of the international stratification system, using the nation as the frame of reference.

When development policies based on structural factors and on the role of the state are critically analyzed, it becomes clear that they have a negative impact on some members of society, and on women in particular. For example, when the state limits women's rights, in particular their right to control land, and when it restricts their access to technology, credit, and extension services, society's ability to maintain and expand production is severely affected (Deere & De Leal, 1981; Westergaard, 1982; Whitehead, 1982). Dependency theory has since been adopted to address the generally negative impact of 'development' on people in developing countries.

Dependency Theory

The original proponents of the dependency paradigm (Frank, 1969; Griffin, 1974; Bernstein et al., 1990) emerged in Latin America. Their goal was to explain underdevelopment on that continent. Underdevelopment within the dependency paradigm is defined as 'a process whereby an underdeveloped country, characterized by subsistence agriculture and domestic production, progressively becomes integrated as a dependency into the world market through trade or investment. Its production becomes geared to the demands of the world market and particularly of the developed countries, with a consequent lack of integration between the parts of the domestic economy' (Wilber and Jameson, 1984: 18).

Underdevelopment in Latin America has been linked to external factors, such as the penetration of North American capital, which has been described as a structural and historical process (Furtado, 1970). During such a penetration, a metropole/periphery structure is established whereby the metropole (the West) exploits the periphery (the developing countries). The Western metropolist powers expropriate large portions of the surplus wealth of the developing countries and also prevent those countries from realizing their potential surplus. In doing so, they undermine their economic autonomy.

In Africa, capitalism was introduced through colonization, and dependency was initiated through the development of 'metropolitan' urban areas, which were serviced by the rural 'satellite' sector. When colonized countries were introduced into the world market system, they were made to serve as sources of raw materials for the developed countries of Europe and North America. According to Wilber and Jameson, (1984: 17), this process created a situation of dependency in which underdeveloped countries became appendages of developed countries. This dependency meant that many of the most important decisions about development – decisions about prices, investment, macroeconomic policies, and so on – were made by individuals, firms, and institutions outside the country (15). According to Bendera (1991: 28), such practices usually benefit certain enterprising social groups at the expense of the masses and contribute to unevenness of growth in the various economic sectors and geographical regions within the peripheral state.

As Ihonvbere (1989) posits, the contact between Africans and the forces of Western capitalism not only distorted, disarticulated, and underdeveloped the continent, but also ensured its structural incorporation into, and peripheralization in, the international division of labour. The processes of underdevelopment and incorporation were fostered through monetization, imperialism of trade (unequal exchange), and metropolitan-directed investment; and through the creation of local institutions and structures to facilitate the attainment of imperialist objectives. As Ake argues: 'The process of monetization went hand in hand with the spread of capitalist relations of production, particularly because it led to the proletarianization of the African peasants as well as some African entrepreneurs ... The monetary system not only helped to create capitalist economy, but also a capitalist economy structurally dependent on foreign economies' (1981: 35).

Dependency theorists claim that from a structural and macrosociological standpoint, it is structural processes and not lack of skills or inappropriate attitudes and behaviours that determine underdevelopment. They insist that the presence of 'modernized élites' with entrepreneurial skills is not necessarily a precondition of balanced development. Quite the contrary – their presence often *reinforces* existing patterns of dependency. Along the same lines Chinchilla (1977) has concluded that one cannot understand power relations between men and women except in the context of modes of production. While the migration of men to urban industries left women with more opportunity to participate in community life, the options open to these women remained severely restricted by the economic position of the community, which was ultimately determined by the international system (Mueller, 1977).

Approaches to development adopted by African countries were based on the advice of Western experts and embodied Eurocentric biases that upheld capitalist values and supported only certain forms of knowledge and production. This is why indigenous African knowledges, modes of production, and social organizations were undermined by the very processes of 'development' and 'modernization.'

Resistance through the Application of an Afrocentric Framework of Development

Existing approaches to development have several inherent weaknesses. *First,* the dominant framework was designed without input from the grassroots. Popular participation ensures at least some degree of commitment on the part of people. When people feel that their interests and needs have not been included in a program, they do not feel committed to that program, which they see as failing to improve their situation. *Second,* the dominant framework is blind to gender and class and assumes that men and women are homogeneous categories. By this, I mean that it assumes that whatever benefits men receive (all men irrespective of class) will trickle down to the women. It does not take into consideration the gender inequalities that have plagued systemic practices as a result of patriarchy. According to the Economic Commission for Africa (1983), development will be achieved if, and *only* if, the continent succeeds in promoting collective self-reliance and self-sustainment.[2]

Modern approaches to development are designed to foist capitalism on emerging nations. They are premised on two assumptions: that economic growth is best achieved through the existing international division of labour; and that the global natural resource base is replenishable. In present vogue the idea is of 'doing something for the poorest'; but this only compartmentalizes the problem and diverts attention from the issues at the centre of the crisis. Through their failure to think in sociopolitical terms, development experts are blindly rejecting holistic solutions to development problems. The practice of 'doing' development for the 'poor' – and now the 'poorest' – has contributed to the many failures to generate successful policies in developing countries. The expansion of capitalism as a new model of development has heightened the polarization[3] between the rich (developed) countries of the North and the poor (developing) countries of the South. The commercialization of Third World economies for the sake of generating surpluses and profits involves not only reproducing a particular form of wealth creation, but also creating poverty and disposition. One can say that concepts and categories about economic development and natural resource utilization that had emerged in the specific context of industrialization and capitalist growth in a centre of colonial power, have been raised to the level of universal assumptions and applicability in the entirely different context of basic needs satisfaction for the people of the newly independent Third World countries.

Afrocentrism, as currently proposed, involves investigating and understanding phenomena from a perspective grounded in African-centred culture and values. The notions of self-reliance and community bonding are highly relevant in the call for all Africans, both continental and diasporan, to use their local creativity and resourcefulness to address contemporary problems of daily survival; and for them to move beyond the problems of postcolonialism by drawing on their cultural heritage and traditions to assert their rights as Africans. Afrocentrism is about Africans taking up their rights. African people have the right to the experiences of the continent, to the enjoyment of their culture, to the celebration of their histories, and to the continued survival and togetherness of African people irrespective of where they reside. Africanist analyses of the black experience generally agree on these fundamental elements of the Afrocentric point of view (Okanlawon, 1972).

There are numerous aspects of Africa's indigenous traditions and collective histories that can be recovered, reclaimed, and reconstituted by African peoples today as they struggle to rejuvenate their lives and livelihoods. Indigenousness does not mean ignorance or 'backwardness.' On the contrary, it provides avenues for creativity, as well as cultural sources of power that African men, women, and children should reclaim and reconstitute for the benefit of their respective societies and communities (see Dei, 1994a). Africans everywhere must begin to appreciate the richness of their past histories, culture(s), and traditions as a source of hope, strength, and resistance.

The revival of the past may be unacceptable to some people. But we must understand that the total rejection of the African heritage – mainly due to slavery and neocolonialism – has created much confusion, as well as a lost sense of identity, community, and sharing, among many African peoples. It will be desirable to apply aspects of indigenous African cultures as epistemological constructs when we gather to formulate the guiding principles for development policy. Some of these characteristics have existed in diverse forms among indigenous peoples in other parts of the world (Dei, 1992). They include notions about solidarity, mutuality, collective responsibility, individual wealth and community status, gender relations, and the individual's relationship with the community. Many of these characteristics were illustrated in my account of what it was like to be a child in Africa, in terms of their centrality to African culture. They can also be useful when it comes to developing an Afrocentric framework to inform development strategies in African communities.

Conclusion

Any development process must be directed by those it is supposed to benefit. This calls for a reconceptualization of the process so that it brings into the centre the roles of Third World people, their local inputs, and appropriate technology. The existing dominant strategies for development are not supportive of peasants who seek access to the means of production and control of the results of their labour; nor of workers who seek the right to organize and to work under safe conditions; nor of women who seek the right to decide what and how they will produce. In general, the conventional development strategies have not adequately taken into consideration the daily challenges confronted by women, such as the need to walk long distances to collect fuel and water, the lack of adequate health care and child care facilities, and the lack of inheritance rights to land. Nor have they acknowledged the agricultural knowledge that women possess as a result of their deep relationship with nature. Under conventional development schemes, women's needs are for the most part never met. The male bias inherent in development practices has resulted in women's increased marginalization and undervaluation (Sen and Grown, 1985; Elson, 1991). According to Sen and Grown: 'It is impossible to obtain sustainable improvement in women's economic and social position under conditions of growing relative inequality if not absolute poverty for both women and men. Therefore, ... equality for women is impossible within existing economic, political and cultural processes that reserve resources, power and control for small sections of people – usually men' (1985: 14).

If development is to promote self-reliance and self-sufficiency through a process that is participatory, equitable, and sustainable, it must support and build on the initiatives taken at the grassroots level. In many developing countries, especially those in Africa, Asia, Latin America, and the Caribbean, grassroots (particularly women-led) organizations are challenging conventional models of development and advancing approaches rooted in local knowledge and realities. These alternative, locally based initiatives must be considered seriously in the present-day discourse of development, which is seeking alternatives to the conventional models, which are limiting and exclusionary in nature.

An alternative model of development will use knowledge of folkways to meet the needs of people based on the values of community, co-operation, equality, and mutuality. This will ensure that Western-based development models are resisted, while knowledge of folkways is brought to the foreground, thereby reducing the contradictions confronted by communities and their people.

NOTES

1 Within the context of this paper, *indigenous knowledge* is the knowledge of folkways embedded in people's everyday experience and grounded within tradition and culture. It also includes traditional community socialization processes.

2 See ECA, *The Revised Framework of Principles for the Implementation of New International Order* (NIEO in Africa, 1976–1981/82, Addis Ababa: ECA, 1983), p. 23.

3 *Polarization* refers to the increasing gap between the centres (developed countries) and the peripheries (underdeveloped countries).

REFERENCES

Ahmed, Zubeida, and M. Loufti 1985. *Women Workers in Rural Development: A Programme of the ILO*. Geneva: International Labour Office.

Ake, Claude. 1981. *A Political Economy of Africa*. London: Longmans.

Amadiume, Ifi. 1987. *Male Daughters and Female Husbands: Gender and Sex in an African Society*. London: Zed Books.

Amin, Samir. 1989. *Eurocentrism: Critique of an Ideology*. New York: Monthly Review Press.

Asante, Molefi. 1980. 'Afrocentricity and Culture.' Pp. 3–12 in Molefi Asante and Kariamu W. Asante (eds.), *African Culture: The Rhythms of Unity*. Trenton: Africa World Press.

– 1987. *The Afrocentric Idea*. Philadelphia: Temple University Press.

Asante, Molefi, and Kariamu W. Asante (eds.), 1980, *African Culture: The Rhythms of Unity*. Trenton: Africa World Press.

Asante, S.K. 1991. *African Development: Adebayo Adedeji's Alternative Strategies*. London: Hans Zell.

Banks, Curtis W. 1992. The Theoretical and Methodological Crisis of the Africentric Conception. *Journal of Negro Education* 61(3): 262–72.

Bascom, William R. 1942. The Principle of Seniority in the Social Structure of the Yoruba. *American Anthopologist* 44 (1): 37–46.

– 1952. The Esusu: A Credit Institution of the Yoruba. *Journal of the Royal Anthropological Institute of Great Britain* 82(1): 2–70.

– 1969. *The Yoruba of Southwestern Nigeria*. New York: Holt, Rinehart and Winston.

– 1992. *African Folktales in the New World*. Bloomington: Indiana University Press.

Bendera, S. 1991. Rural Transformation through Education in Tanzania: Implications for the Workload of Primary School Teachers in Hai District. PhD dissertation, University of Toronto.

Beneria, L., and G. Sen. 1981. Accumulation, Reproduction and Women's Roles in Economic Development. *Signs: Journal of Women in Culture and Society* 7(2): 279–98.

Bernstein, H, et al. (Eds). 1990. *The Food Question: Profit versus People?* New York: Monthly Review Press.

Black, Cyril. 1966. *The Dynamics of Modernization: A Study in Comparative History*. New York: Harper and Row.

Brydon, L., and S. Chant. 1989.*Women in the Third World: Gender Issues in Rural and Urban Areas*. New Brunswick, NJ: Rutgers University Press.

Buck, Pem D. 1991. The View from under the Sink: Can You Teach Anthropology Up When You Aren't Down? *Transforming Anthropology* 1: 22–4, 41.

Chimezie, Amuzie. 1983. Theories of Black Culture. *Western Journal of Black Studies* 7(4): 216–28.

Chinchilla, N. 1977. Industrialization, Monopoly, Capitalism and Women's Work in Guatemala. *Signs* 3(1): 38–56.

Cornoy, M. 1984. *The State and Political Theory*. Princeton: Princeton University Press.

Deere, C., and M. De Leal. 1981. Peasant Production, Proletarianization and the Sexual Division of Labour in the Andes. *Journal of Women and Culture in Society* 7(2): 338–60.

Dei, George J.S. 1989. The Economics of Death and Funeral Celebration in a

Ghanaian Akan Community. *Culture* 9(1): 49–62.

– 1992. The Renewal of a Ghanaian Rural Economy. *Canadian Journal of African Studies* 26(1): 24–53.

– 1994a. The Women of a Ghanaian Village: Studies of Social Change. *African Studies Review* 37(2): 121–45.

– 1994b. 'Reflections of an Anti-Racist Pedagogue.' Pp. 290–310 Lorna Erwin and David MacLennan (eds.), *The Sociology of Education in Canada*. Toronto: Copp Clark Pitman.

– 1994c. Afrocentricity: A Cornerstone of Pedagogy. *Anthropology and Education Quarterly* 25(1): 3.28.

– 1994d. The Challenges of Anti-racist Education Research in the African Context. *Africa Development* 19(3): 5–25.

Dia, Mamadou. 1991. Development and Cultural Values in Sub-Saharan Africa. *Finance and Development* (December): 10–13.

Diop, Chikh A. 1974. *The African Origin of Civilization*. New York: Lawrence Hill.

Dumont, R. 1969. *False Start in Africa*. Translated by P. Naut Ott. Introduction by Thomas Balagh, with an additional chapter by John Hatch. London: A. Deutsch.

Early, Gerald. 1995. Understanding Afrocentrism: Why Blacks Deam of a World Without Whites. *Civilization* (July/August): 31–9.

Economic Commission for Africa (ECA). 1983. *The Revised Framework of Principles for the Implementation of New International Order (NIEO) in Africa, 1976–1981/82*. Addis Ababa: ECA.

Elabor-Idemudia, P. 1991. 'The Impact of Structural Adjustment Programs on Women and Their Households in Bendel and Ogun States, Nigeria.' Pp.128–150 in C. Gladwin (ed.), *Structural Adjustment and African Women Farmers*. Gainesville: University of Florida Press.

Elliot, Carolyn. 1977. Theories of Development: An Assessment. *Signs* 3(1): 1–8.

Elson, Diane (ed.). 1991. *Male Bias in the Development Process*. Manchester: Manchester University Press.

Frank, Andre Gunder. 1969. 'Sociology of Development and Underdevelopment of Sociology.' In Andre Gunder Frank (ed.). *Latin America: Underdevelopment or Revolution*. New York: Monthly Review Press.

Furtado, Celso. 1970. *Economic Development in Latin America: A Survey from Colonial Times to the Cuban Revolution*. Cambridge: Cambridge University Press.

Gallagher, Kathleen. 1983. Canadian Dimension of Development Education. MA thesis, University of Toronto.

George, Susan. 1992. *The Debt Boomerang: How Third World Debt Harms Us All*. Boulder, CO: Westview Press.

Griffin, Keith. 1974. The International Transmission of Inequality. *World Development* 7: 13–16.

Gunew, Sonya (ed.). 1991. *A Reader in Feminist Knowledge*. London: Routledge.

Henry, Annette. 1991. Taking Back Control: Toward a Black Women's Afrocentric Standpoint on the Education of Black Children. PhD dissertation, Department of Curriculum, Ontario Institute for Studies in Education, Toronto.

Herskovits, Melville J. 1967. *Dahomey: An Ancient West African Kingdom*. Volume 1. Evanston: Northwestern University Press.

Hoselitz, B. 1966. 'Main Concepts in the Analysis of Social Implications of Technological Change.' In B. Hoselitz and W. Morre (eds.), *Industrialization and Society*. Mouton: UNESCO.

Ihonvbere, J. (ed.). 1989. *The Political Economy of Crisis and Underdevelopment in Africa: Selected Works of Claude Ake*. Lagos: JAD Publishers.

Jell-Bahlsen, Sabine. 1994. 'This Native Something': Understanding and Acknowledging the African Experience. *Dialectical Anthropology* 19: 373–86.

Laclau, E. 1979. Feudalism and Capitalism in Latin America. *New Left Review* 67: 19–38.

Mbiti, John. 1982. African Views of the Universe. Pp.193–9 in R. Olaniyan (ed.), *African History and Culture*. Lagos: Longman.

McClelland, David. 1961. *The Achieving Society*. New York: Free Press.

Mills, Margaret. 1992. A Twenty-Year Trajectory toward Theory, Maybe Better Called Slouching Toward Theory (Xeno's Paradox?). Paper presented to the American Folklore Society, Jacksonville, Florida, October.

Mudimbe, V.Y. 1988. *The Invention of Africa: Gnosis, Philosophy and the Order of Knowledge*. Bloomington: Indiana University Press.

Mueller, M. 1977. Women and Men, Power and Powerlessness in Lesotho. *Signs* 3(1): 154–66.

Nash, J., and H. Safa (eds.). 1976. *Sex and Class in Latin America*. New York: Praeger.

Nettl, J., and R. Robertson. 1968. *International Systems and the Modernization of Societies: The Formation of National Goals and Attitudes*. London: Faber and Faber.

Ojaide, Tanure. 1994. *The Poetry of Woles Soyinka*. Lagos: Malthouse.

Okanlawon, 1992. *Africian Oral Literature: Backgrounds, Character, and Continuity*. Bloomington: Indiana University Press.

Okpewho, Isidore. 1991. *The Epic in Africa: Toward a Poetics of the Oral Performance*. New York: Columbia University Press.

Oyebade, Bayo. 1990. African Studies and the Afrocentric Paradigm: A Critique. *Journal of Black Studies* 21(2): 233–8.

Parsons, Talcott. 1970. *The Systems of Modern Societies*. New York: Free Press.

Prebisch, R. 1981. The Latin American Periphery in the Global System of Capitalism. *CEPAL Review* 13: 143–50.

Rattray, Robert, S. 1927. *Religion and Art in Ashanti*. London: Oxford University Press.

Rostow, W. 1971. *Stages in Economic Growth: A Non-Communist Manifesto.* New York: Cambridge University Press.

Said, Edward. 1979. *Orientalism.* New York: Vintage Books.

Sen, G., and C. Grown. 1985. *Development Crisis and Alternative Vision (DAWN): Third World Women's Perspectives.* New York: Monthly Review.

Shiva, Vandana. 1989. *Staying Alive: Women, Ecology and Development.* London: Zed Books.

– 1993. *Monoculture of the Mind: Biodiversity, Biotechnology and the Third World.* Malaysia: Third World Network.

Skinner, Elliot P. 1964. *The Mossi of Upper Volta.* Stanford: Stanford University Press.

Smith, Dorothy E. 1990. *The Conceptual Practices of Power: A Feminist Sociology of Knowledge.* Toronto: University of Toronto Press.

Stamp, Patricia. 1991. Burying Otieno: The Politics of Gender and Ethnicity in Kenya. *Signs: Journal of Women in Culture and Society* 16(4): 809–45.

Stasiulis, D. 1991. Theorizing Connections: Race, Ethnicity, Gender and Class. Pp. 269–305 in Peter Li (ed.), *Race and Ethnic Relations in Canada.* Toronto: Oxford University Press.

Steady, Filomena C. 1990. *The Black Woman Cross-Culturally.* Rochester: Schenkman Books.

Tala, Ibrahim Kashim. 1984. *An Introduction to Cameroon Oral Literature.* Yaounde: SOPECAM.

Todd, Loreto. 1979. *Tortoise the Trickster and Other Folktales from the Cameroon.* Boston: Routledge & Kegan Paul.

Vlach, John M. 1979. African Folklore in the New World: A Review. *American Anthropologist* 81: 382–3.

wa Thiong'o, Ngugi. 1987. *Decolonising the Mind: The Politics of Language in African Literature.* London: James Currey.

Weber, Max. [1904] 1976. *The Protestant Ethic and Spirit of Capitalism.* Translated by Talcott Parsons with an introduction by Anthony Giddens. New York: Charles Scribner's Sons.

Westergaard, K. 1982. *Pauperization and Rural Women in Bangladesh.* CDR Report. Copenhagen: Center for Development Research.

Whitehead, A. 1982. A Conceptual Framework for Analyzing the Effects of Technological Change on Women. *Development Research Digest* 7: 58–65.

Wilber, Charles K., And Kenneth Jameson. 1984. 'Paradigms of Economic Development and Beyond.' In Charles K. Wilber (ed.), *The Political Economy of Development and Underdevelopment.* 3rd ed.. New York: Random House.

7

Indigenous Nations and the
Human Genome Diversity Project

SANDRA S. AWANG

The prevailing intellectual property rights system is seen as a new form of colonization and a tactic by the industrialized countries of the North to confuse and to divert the struggle of indigenous peoples from their rights to land and resources on, above and under it ... This is akin to robbing indigenous peoples of their resources and knowledge ... Indigenous knowledge and resources are being eroded, exploited and/or appropriated by outsiders in the likes of transnational corporations (TNCs), institutions, researchers and scientists ... For indigenous peoples, life is a common property which cannot be owned, commercialized and monopolized by individuals ... The indigenous peoples of Asia strongly condemn the patenting and commercialization of their cell lines or body parts, as being promoted by the scientist and institutions behind the Human Genome Diversity Project (HGDP).

(*Indigenous Peoples' Biodiversity Network*, 12–13)

Around the world, development and modernization are contributing to environmental degradation and a loss of diversity. World structures are creating mechanisms that allow the North to plunder the South. The relationship between nature and humans is increasingly based on dominance and exploitation. On account of the unconscionable practices of a minority, life on this planet is becoming more tenuous for the majority. These are some of the truths that led me to this work. I come from the Caribbean, whose peoples' history is one of resistance and survival in the face of tremendous odds. We have named ourselves after the Caribs, one of the indigenous peoples of the Caribbean region, who resisted being decimated by Europeans despite conquest, enslavement, introduction of disease, and near genocide. To replace the First Nations peoples, colonial powers enslaved Africans and transported them over the Middle Passage to the Caribbean, where they toiled for almost 400 years to create wealth for Europe. Indentured Indians and Chinese were also shipped to the area to work. No statues have been unveiled in former bastions of colonialism to honour our freedom fighters. None of the former colonial powers or their institutions are willing to consider making reparations or even public apologies for nigh on 500 years of exploitation.

In this chapter I look at the Human Genome Diversity Project as an imperialist mission and deconstruct its role in shaping science to accommodate capital accumulation. Indigenous knowledges are recognized at international conferences, yet indigenous nations face an intensification of those forces which are seeking to commercialize their biological diversity. Indigenous knowledges offer hope for the survival of the Earth. However, the very survival of indigenous nations is being threatened by those same forces which have brought our planet to the brink of destruction. Indigenous knowledges are now being conceptualized in the North as sources of profit and power. Once this knowledge is commercialized, the holders will find themselves irrelevant to the forces of capital.

In terms of intention, the HGDP exemplifies the colonial, patriarchal, capitalist, racist, scientific/militaristic surge to acquire the living cells and biodiversity of the South. Vested interests prefer to ignore the ethical and political issues surroundng the HGDP; this is precisely why we must delineate and disseminate the connections between biotechnology and biodiversity and between biopiracy and human, cultural, and ecological destruction; and why the ascendancy of genetics and the concomitant marginalization of other knowledges must be made issues for public debate. I focus mainly on the incursions now being made into indigenous nations under the veneer of science. My goal is to unmask the very particular agenda of those who are appropriating the living cells of indigenous peoples. I also examine how indigenous and social organizations, drawing on indigenous values and knowledge, are resisting the bio-prospectors in this contemporary gold rush.

The role of science and technology in precipitating human and ecological destruction has not been made sufficiently clear. Yet at a time when experts in the North are promoting scientific and technological solutions to alleviate growing human and environmental crises, the need has become urgent to scrutinize the forms of knowledge that are embedded in objective and universal solutions. Vandana Shiva theorizes that dominant science and technology is a patriarchal, colonial project with ambitions to control and appropriate (1995). Shiva's critique stresses the neocolonizing impact of technology transference from North to South, and takes into account the ecological disasters that result from resource appropriation and biopiracy. Shiva adds that loss of livelihood, escalating poverty, and community conflicts over diminishing resources are all linked to the destruction of ecosystems by scientific experts. As Moser lucidly points out, science and technology do not exist in isolation from 'social and political structures, cultural projects and ecological relations' (1995). She points out that indeed, science and technology have their political economies. Accordingly, the cultural project of science and technology is 'economic, social and political relations.' Shiva goes further, conceptualizing that science and technology assume a *political ecology*. The political ecology of science and technology defines who we are and interprets, creates, and legitimizes differences. Through the creation of political economies, this political ecology assigns disparate values to peoples and cultures, thus maintaining hierarchies and power differentials.

In its efforts to reshape human evolution, scientific discourse is reconstituting the field of molecular biology so that it is based increasingly on racism and on greater power for the North. Scientific theory, which purports itself to be conventional knowledge, arises within particular discourses and practices and serves the needs for which it was designed. According to Evelyn Fox Keller, theories 'reflect both the subjectivity of human objectives and the objects of human action' (1995: 53). Close examination of the history of science reveals that scientific theory intends a particular world, one that is governed by the subjectivities of a minority. These subjectivities are embedded in a discourse that is presented as factual, truthful, and irrevocable. Keller has demonstrated that there are significant movements within scientific history, movements that allow us to uncover the motives behind the directions charted by the science establishment.

In 1994 the Rural Advancement Foundation International (RAFI) reported on the growth of what it termed the 'genomic industry' – that is, companies engaged in the identification and commercialization of human genes. RAFI indicated that genomic companies, in what it termed a gold rush, are seeking to privatize biological information, thereby reducing human life to a commodity. The global trade in human tissues is an unaddressed issue with profound moral implications. Moreover, this trade, 'especially [the trade in] rural populations and indigenous peoples – has expanded dramatically in recent years and has far outstripped efforts to create policy mechanisms to ensure the rights of tissue donors' (*RAFI Communique*, January–February 1997: 1). The trade in human tissues is a rapid-growth industry in which profits are derived from patenting resources, providing access to genomic information, and selling body parts. Indeed, this aspect of the 'life industry'[1] has been assessed as a critical component of capital accumulation that had never been explored till the present day except, perhaps, within the medical/scientific legacy of the Third Reich. The sale of genetic information for clinical and industrial use, like the sale of tissues, also generates profits. Finally, computer technologies are being used to analyze, store, and retrieve information on DNA sequences.

The Human Genome Organization (HUGO), launched in 1990, is a multibillion-dollar research project whose goal is to map the human genome. In 1991 the U.S. Congress advanced $3 billion toward HUGO's 15-year initiative to map and sequence all genes internationally. HUGO, an intergovernmental body, is the parent organization of the Human Genome Diversity Project (HGDP). The HGDP is 'an informal consortium of universities and scientists in North America and Europe' (*RAFI Communique*, May 1993). Project members include universities in North America and Europe and the National Institutes of Health (NIH), as well as HUGO (Wandell, 1996: 73). When asked to clarify the distinction between the HGDP and HUGO, Anthony Socci, a research associate at the Smithsonian Institute in Washington, told *Akwesasne Notes* (73) that the intergovernmental HUGO is an 'extensive road building project for genetic exploration.' He indicated that 'each region of the world is encouraged to create its own HGDP committee and be responsible for regional fund raising and sample collection.' He added that there were thirteen members on the North American Committee. When the HGDP was brought under the governance of HUGO, a three-person committee was appointed 'to look after its relationship' with the parent organization. Socci stated that one member of the North American Committee was Native American and that another was African American. When the HGDP was being established, the U.S. National Science Foundation provided US$1 million for the convening of four or five planning meetings around the world. No indigenous peoples were apprised of or invited to these meetings. Furthermore, 'Indigenous peoples did not call for a Human Genome Diversity Project' (Lyons, 1996: 91). Below, the *stated* goals of the HGDP are reproduced verbatim:

1 Understand the diversity of human genomes within the human species.
2 Clarify the history of specific indigenous poulations around the globe, from a genetic perspective. Populations will learn what science believes to be their origin and history.
3 Preserve ('Immortalize') DNA cell lines of indigenous populations before these populations and/or their cell lines become extinct either through intercultural marriage, or through the literal demise of the population in question. Consequently, the Human Genome Diversity Project seeks to collect samples of blood, saliva, cells, hair roots, and other biological materials from 500 indigenous populations.

In 1995, Lydia Dotto reported in a discussion of the Human Genome Project that

Canadian researchers, including several at U of T, are participating in this immense international undertaking through the Canadian Genome Analysis and Technology Program (CGAT), a five-year effort that started in 1992 and is funded by $22 million in grants from the Medical Research Council, the National Sciences and Engineering Research Council, the Social Sciences and Humanities Research Council and the National Cancer Institute of Canada. (1995: 10)

Dotto's article provided an overview of some of the work being undertaken by researchers at Mt Sinai Hospital in Toronto at the new Centre for Human Genome Research and Molecular Medicine (funded with $5 million from the Canada/Ontario Infrastructure Works Program, with additional monies from the $10.3 million awarded to the Samuel Lunenfeld Research Institute from Bristol-Myers Squibb). Dotto also referred to the Hospital for Sick Children, where 'gene mapping research' is underway. It would seem that Dotto was speaking of the HGDP when she referred to the Human Genome Project. If so, scientific involvement in the HGDP has been facilitated in Canada both by governments and by the TNCs. It must be noted that I am unaware of any public statements having been made vis-à-vis the role of the Canadian government in the HGDP, either by the government itself or by the scientific establishment. It follows that if the public is aware of research such as Dotto described, they can only assume that these efforts are independently driven.

Keller identifies three shifts that have contributed to the modern-day understanding of molecular biology. In these shifts, physicists provided what Keller terms 'social authority' for a new concept of biology. In brief, the shifts were as follows: first, the essence of life was relocated in the gene; second, life was redefined as 'instructions,' a 'code,' a 'puzzle,' a 'cryptogram'; and third, the goals of science were recast, away from representation and toward intervention in the process of making and remaking life (1995: 54, 55). According to Keller, early advocates of these shifts, H.J. Muller and D. Bernal, both expressed that in the future, the central question in biology would be how to control the evolutionary process.

H.J. Muller, acclaimed as the founder of molecular biology, was awarded the Nobel Prize for his work on X-ray-induced mutagenesis[2], which he developed in 1927. According to Keller, this classical geneticist had a clear vision of a biology dependent on physics and premised on the three shifts identified above. In 'The Gene as the Basis of Life' Muller posited that the gene is a 'biological atom' that accounts for higher life forms, variation, and growth. He contended that in order to penetrate this unit of life, mutations should be studied. It was his recommendation that the

secret of ... gene parts may perhaps be reached first by an upward thrust of pure physical chemistry, or perhaps by biologists reaching down with physico-chemical tools through the chromosome, the virus, of the bacteriophage ... The beginning of the pathway to the micro-cosmic realm of gene-mutation study thus lies before us. It is a difficult path, but with the aid of the necromancy of science, it must be penetrated. (1926: 200–2, quoted in Keller, 1995: 57)

Having been rewarded with the Nobel Prize, Muller was vested with the scientific authority to pursue his previously articulated obsession. In 1916 this geneticist had expressed that the 'keystones ... to power' lay in the ability to control mutation and transmutation. If this control were achieved, 'any achieve-ment with inanimate things' would be possible (Keller, 1995: 56). On winning the Nobel Prize, Muller wrote that

Those working along classical genetic lines may be drawn to the opportunity, afforded by the use of X rays, of creating in their chosen organisms a series of artificial races for use in the study of genetic ... phenomena ... for the practical breeder, it is hoped that the method will ultimately prove useful. The time is not ripe to discuss here such possibilities with reference to the human species. (1927: 87, quoted in Keller, 1995: 57)

With the opportunities afforded by genomic software, it appears that selected communities of the 'human specie' have been earmarked as the raw material for creating 'artificial races.' The artificiality of which Muller speaks, I suggest, lies in the ability of science to induce changes to the genetic codes of entire peoples, having collected and analyzed those peoples' DNA. It is no secret that nation-states, in staking claims to land and resources, have subjected indig-enous nations to genocidal policies. From a scientific point of view, once *artificial* changes begin to be wrought in peoples' bodies[3], Muller's projected gene-mutation study will have become a modern-day reality.

Computer technology is, of course, vital to the success of the HGDP. Leaps in computer technology and the recognition of intellectual property by the World Trade Organisation (WTO) have unleashed a torrent of market forces falling under the general rubric 'globalization.' When we assess the concept of intellectual property, which is marketed as a key new system of knowledges, in the context of industrialized countries' efforts to institutionalize their *Western orientation toward information as a world system of thinking*[4], we find that it has been formulated as a means to appropriate genetic knowledge and turn that knowledge into a commodity for economic gain. Owing to the specifics of globalization and privatization, profits are now to be made from the sale of the genetic information of indigenous nations. It is against this backdrop that the informational gap on indigenous peoples – a gap that the HGDP, a 'consortium of universities and scientists in North America and Europe,' seeks to bridge – is to be evaluated. RAFI reports, tellingly, that the draft of the Second Human Genome Diversity Report made no reference to intellectual property rights. Insultingly, this draft referred to peoples as 'isolates of historic interest' (IHIs); emphasis was to be placed on 'preserving' their DNA, since many or most of the nations carded to be sampled were, it was stated, destined for 'extinction.' Indigenous nations make the following straightforward analysis of the interest now being expressed in their very cells:

> The international concern about indigenous knowledge has arisen because of several factors. The increased efficiency in screening the genetic make-up of living beings has made bio-prospecting a profitable concern, and the facility for utilising DNA in the bio-technology industry has given rise to a worldwide interest in gathering raw materials for study ... The recent concern about the use of indigenous knowledge, life forms, cultural heritage and resources for nefarious purposes has taken place in a context of a neo-liberal dogma which is sweeping the world, extending property and free marketing everywhere. Patenting of life forms, bio-prospecting and free trade arrangements are aspects of this neo-colonial wave ... The reasons for the anger felt by indigenous peoples is that the external power of the state and market are entering aspects of life which are sensitive and mark the uniqueness and dignity of indigenous peoples. (Gray, 1995: 2,3)

In *The Medical Mafia*, Guylaine Lanctôt discusses the objectives of 'world authorities in destroying people's health, both in industrialised countries and in the Third World' (1995: 126). She argues that world financiers control health. In her chapter 'The Trilogy of Lies,' which looks at the profoundly destructive impact of vaccination programs on human immune systems, she presented information with which the Quebec College of Physicians took issue. That group forced this doctor to appear before their disciplinary committee on charges of disseminating 'wrong and misleading information.' Lanctôt is no longer practising medicine. She is being harassed because she believes that the medical system exists largely to create sickness. She also expresses the view that vaccinations encourage 'the moral and financial dependence of Third World countries' on the industrialized world. Referring to 'targeted genocide,' Lanctôt warns that vaccinations have the ability to 'kill people of a certain race, a certain group, a certain country. And to leave others untouched' (1995: 127). In apartheid South Africa, which also benefited from the largesse of 'Project Paperclip,'[5] it was disclosed that genocide was the aim of the fascist government.

The HGDP has been scheduled to collect DNA from 165 peoples in Africa.

The African continent has been drawn into a vortex of diseases, many of which are new and devastating, at an alarmingly quickly rate. Interestingly, one of the HGDP's stated goals – to 'immortalize' indigenous peoples because of their imminent extinction – has some rational basis: the spread of AIDS in countries of the South may well indicate that mortality rates in that region are about to skyrocket. *Working People's News* (Duffy, 1997: 3) provides an exposé on research in the South against which Lanctôt's concerns may be measured:

> An experiment on pregnant women in Africa, Thailand, and the Dominican Republic was harshly criticized by Dr. Marcia Angell, executive editor of the prestigious *New England Journal of Medicine*. Her editorial in the September issue compares the cruelty of this research with the notorious Tuskegee experiment in Alabama, in which poor Black men were studied with untreated syphillis ... More than 1,000 infants who could have been saved will contract the AIDS virus needlessly ... Such an experiment was not conducted in the United States, where it would have raised an outcry. Instead it was imposed on poor women in Africa, Asia and Latin America. (November 1997: 3)

It is easy to dismiss revelations such as these as 'conspiracy theories.' Yet as Leonard G. Horowitz states in 'AIDS: A Planned Plague? Fear, Denial and Indifference!' (1997: 21), evidence exists that governments have engaged in hideous nuclear, germ warfare, and mind control experiments. There were the experiments on African Americans at Tuskegee; the mind control experiments conducted in Canada on Canadian citizens by the U.S. Central Intelligence Agency (CIA); similar experiments conducted in the United States under the names BLUEBIRD, ARTICHOKE, MKULTRA, and MKNAOMI (Ross, 1996), now available for public scrutiny as declassified CIA documents; the injecting of developmentally delayed children at Willowbrook School in New York with Hepatitis B viruses during cancer experiments; and the infecting of Native Americans with smallpox. Horowitz documents in his article how he traced the development of AIDS and Ebola-like viruses to 'Nazi-linked researchers at the U.S. National Cancer Institute (NCI) and their colleagues from Litton Bionetics.' Litton is the principal supplier of monkeys and monkey viruses to the U.S. National Institutes of Health; in 1969 it was also the sixth-leading biological weapons contractor in the world – this at a time when the Nixon Administration, through its security advisor, Henry Kissinger, was proceeding to 'develop immune-system-destroying micro-organisms for germ warfare.' This Nixon/Kissinger project fell under the auspices of MKNAOMI, referred to above, which was administered by the CIA.

Horowitz's article is significant because it clarifies some of the murky history associated with the development of vaccines. It also shows how proponents of Nazism were selected to play leading roles in American chemical and biological development during the Cold War. Furthermore, the revelations made by Horowitz show us the necessity of situating current projects such as the HGDP within the broader context of biomedical history, given the 'numerous Nazi-American biomedical biowarfare connections' (23). This history, which extends back as far as the CIA's postwar efforts to safely transport Hitler's virologists and biological weapons developers into specific countries, demands that the personnel and governments involved in the HGDP be compelled to open their work for inspection. Considering the human rights abuses that have already occurred through the patenting of tissues taken from indigenous peoples, these inspections should be undertaken under the auspices of the United Nations with the same vigour as those directed toward Saddam Hussein in the 1990s. Naturally, international public dissemination of the 'international' HGDP undertaking must be an integral part of disclosure. Writing about AIDS, Horowitz highlights the need for vigilance as he draws an important link between Litton and Merck: 'Since contaminated Litton monkeys and chimpanzees were used to produce ... contaminated vaccines, it is reasonable to theorize that some of Litton's AIDS-like viruses might have contaminated ... Merck-made vaccines giving rise to the AIDS epidemic we have today' (22).

The struggle for the land in which indigenous nations are engaged suggests that indigenous peoples have been singled out by the HGDP to be studied because they are being *disappeared*, as has happened already in El Salvador, Chile, Guatemala, Mexico, Brazil, and Peru. While the HGDP offers the rationale that it is seeking to 'immortalize' the cell lines of 'isolates of human interest' should they become 'extinct,' the agenda of the consortium engaged in the project is hardly benign. One fact provides a good basis from which to derive this observation: The core computer for storing the records of the HGDP, GenBank, is located in the national laboratories at Los Alamos, New Mexico. In other words, the depository for indigenous peoples' DNA sequences is within a major U.S. weapons laboratory, 'the premier U.S. nuclear research center' (Churchill, 1994).

Evidence is being unearthed in the Americas, as in Africa and Asia, that military oppression is being directed toward the very same communities of indigenous peoples whose DNA is being sampled. The lands of indigenous nations in the Americas are being encroached on and engulfed by transnational corporations. At the same time, violence is being directed toward those who reside on these lands. Meanwhile, the military are standing close by to contain the revolts by dispossessed peoples, and are providing storage space for data and blood samples from the same people the HGDP has targeted. The following note illuminates the militaristic nature of the HGDP, which is undertaking its work under the veneer of science:

> The Rural Advancement Foundation International (RAFI) ... has recently discovered that research units of the US Navy have collected blood samples in Peru and in Indonesia occupied West Papua (or Irian Jaya), while the Naval Medical Research Institute in Washington has obtained blood samples from the Philippines ... The National Institutes of Health, a US government agency believed to control some of the world's largest collections of indigenous peoples' blood and tissue samples, carries out much of its research on these materials at Fort Detrick, Maryland. These facilities are managed by Science Applications International Corporation, a private contractor working for US and international militaries and intelligence agencies. Along with two units of the NIH, Fort Detrick is also home to Department of Defense projects related to biological and chemical warfare ... Under the terms of the 1972 Biological Weapons Conventions, the US government officially halted development of biological weapons at Fort Detrick. However, some of the military agencies which now share the facilities have been set up to research vaccines and other counter-measures to biological warfare agents, research which necessarily involves creating and studying active agents of biological warfare. Furthermore, the Armed Forces Medical Intelligence Center, also working out of Fort Detrick, has been specifically directed to investigate the vulnerability of 'foreign' populations and states to disease and infection. (Benjamin, 1996: 1)

The web of secrecy in which the HGDP is shrouded, and the locating of genetic information from indigenous peoples in a military computer, leads me to conclude that the HGDP may be a weapon of genocide constructed by racism and supported by capitalist patriarchy and scientific militarism, whose purpose is to subdue the South while advancing the 'evolution' of the North. The two-thirds of the world that has a claim to rich natural resources and biodiversity has to be exploited in order that the privileged in the North and the élites in the South may have untramelled access to the Earth's diminishing resources. This is the underlying construct of the HGDP. This is why it must be halted by any means necessary. Indigenous nations have made their position clear on this count: if this project is not terminated, and if the DNA of communities is not returned immediately, all people of colour must expect that their turn to be subjects in scientific experiments will soon follow. After that, it will be poor whites; then the aged, homosexuals, the differently abled, and so on. Hitler tried something similar on unionized workers, Communists, the Jews, the Roma people, Blacks[6] and homosexuals. He was inspired in part by the treatment meted out to the indigenous peoples of the Americas by the settler newcomers.

It seems that the HGDP is taking U.S. policy that has always been internally directed toward the indigenous nations of the Americas and extending it, based on Hitler's overt eugenics experiment that intended the extermination of those considered inferior. As Churchill (1994) has warned, the United States is in a position to impose on the entire South the relationship that it has maintained with indigenous nations 'at home.' The neutral free science that the HGDP purports to embrace is, in fact, a science with the potential for taking life and leaving death in its wake.

Many in the indigenous communities are worried that the research may identify genetic information capable of being used against genetically distinct populations. The HGDP raises the possibility that genetic materials or data will be misused for racist purposes, and even raises the possibility of genocide by biological warfare. While scientists disagree on the feasibility of such uses, it is difficult to predict what will be technologically possible in ten years, or in twenty. Biological warfare has been used on indigenous peoples in the past – a reminder of the threat posed by such scientific projects (Harry, 1995: 31).

Resistance: Building Momentum

The HGDP reflects a rise in an implicitly scientific form of knowing that negates diversity and alternative ways of knowing. Seen in that light, the existence of this project is closely linked to the destruction of indigenous knowledges. However, modern forms of oppression, bioprospecting, biopiracy, and biotechnological colonialism are being contested by the majority world in the South. As the momentum of resistance grows, and new methods of resistance are found, people in the North are being confronted with the stark realization that to save two-thirds of the world is to save themselves. The growth model of development is destroying the Earth and creating a planet unable to support life. One planet, one fate, one future, is compelling reason for action. Increasingly in both the South and the North, people are choosing life and its traditional values over the current paradigm.

In June 1993 the World Council of Indigenous Peoples (WCIP) and RAFI spoke at the United Nations Human Rights Conference in Vienna, where they called for a halt to the HGDP until indigenous peoples had themselves assessed and addressed the ethics of such a project. Even as indigenous peoples were condemning the HGDP, the U.S. government was applying for world patents on the cell line of a 26-year-old Guaymi woman from Panama, who had not been informed of this action. The Guaymi Congress in Panama, the World Council of Churches, and a growing number of organizations across the world, opposed the U.S. government's patent claim (WO 9208784), to human genetic material appropriated from this indigenous woman. In October 1993, RAFI and the president of the Guaymi General Congress protested the action of the U.S. government in Geneva at the intergovernmental meeting of the Biodiversity Conference, and also at the GATT Secretariat. Isidro Acosta, the Guaymi president, was informed that human genetic material is not excluded from GATT (which has since been superseded by the WTO). In October the European Greens introduced an emergency resolution in the European Parliament opposing the world and U.S. patent claims. They called for a halting of the HGDP. Faced with mounting pressure, the United States withdrew its patent claim in November 1993. It refuses, however, to return the cell lines to the rightful owner. Furthermore, the United States has secured two other patent claims, WO 93/03759 and W-9215325-A, filed in the name of the U.S. Department of Health and Human Services and the U.S. National Institutes of Health, and the U.S. Department of Commerce, respectively. The first claim arose from blood samples taken from twenty-four Hagahai people from New Guinea; the second is for the human cell lines of a man and a woman from the Solomon Islands. These cell lines are on deposit at the American Type Culture Collection in Washington, D.C.

In September 1994 the Coordinating Body for Indigenous Peoples' Organizations of the Amazon Basin (COICA) met in Bolivia to discuss the patenting of life and the threat this poses to indigenous nations. In February 1995 representatives from twelve Asian countries met in East Malaysia with this same purpose. In April 1995 in Suva, Fiji, a third meeting took place at which fourteen Pacific countries were represented. All participants at these meetings opposed the patenting of life, and sent a strong message to the European Parliament on the eve of its voting on the European Directive on 'The Legal Protection of Biotechnological Inventions.' The participants at these meetings have issued statements committing themselves to research, education, and action to protect themselves and their peoples from biopiracy, for it seems that reparation and restitution have no application to the South.

Since RAFI's press release of 4 October 1995 pointing out the U.S. government's attempt to patent the cell lines of a Hagahai man, there has been no statement issued by the U.S. government regarding this human rights violation. On 15 June 1996, Debra Harry, a Northern Paiute researcher, Jeanette Armstrong, an Okanagan writer and educator, RAFI, and Cultural Survival (Canada) held a press conference in Ottawa to publicize the implications of the HGDP. The mainstream press has not seen fit to expose this matter as a subject of serious urgency.

The Samuel Lunenfeld Research Institute of Mt Sinai Hospital in Toronto has begun collecting blood from Anishnabi communities in Canada. According to the centre's director, Canada has entered a 'golden age of medical research' (Brady, 1997: 35). In a special report on health care carried in the *Post* it was stated that the Medical Research Council (MRC), the main federal agency funding medical research in Canada, funded more than $130 million worth of research by Canadian academic institutions in 1997. [Of this figure, more than 85 per cent of in-kind support or money had come from the Pharmaceutical Manufacturers Association of Canada (PMAC).] It was also reported that the U.S. government's National Institutes of Health, together with the Howard Hughes Medical Institute (HHMI), were funding Canadian academic institutions. In 1996, HHMI supported over 300 research programs in Canada, with each grant averaging $1 million per scientist – more than the total budget of the MRC. Could it be sheer coincidence that the HHMI had also funded the Montreux, Switzerland, meeting of HUGO in September 1988? Judging from financial contributions to medical research in Canada, it might be concluded that pharmaceutical TNCs, the U.S. government, and private American research institutions are shaping the research agenda of the Canadian health care system. It may be, then, that the role played by the NIH and HHMI in the HGDP has been exported, along with its funds, across the border into Canadian institutions.

Harvard, Cornell, Johns Hopkins, Yale, and Texas Technological University all have collections of blood from Colombia's indigenous peoples. The NIH, in addition to 1,773 samples from indigenous nations in Colombia, also holds blood collections from African Colombians. RAFI has revealed that the South has not been exempted from the 'Vampire Project.' The Center for Disease Control in Atlanta, Georgia, holds Colombian material from Colombia's indigenous and African communities. The U.S. National Cancer Institute (NCI) holds tissue samples from China, the Francophone Caribbean, Mauritania, Guinea-Bissau, Ivory Coast, the Central African Republic, Congo, the Guianas, the Solomon Islands, and Papua New Guinea. The CDC has used blood samples in HTLV research from Brazil, Jamaica, Ethiopia, Somalia, Peru, Panama, Indonesia, Japan, and Mexico. Kyoto University in Japan is conducting research using blood samples from Gabon, Ghana, and India, and from the Ainu people of Japan. Kyushu University in Japan holds human tissue samples from Jamaica and Chile (RAFI, March–April 1996).

The struggle against the trade in human tissues, a struggle spearheaded by RAFI and indigenous peoples, has resulted in the dissemination and critique of previously hidden information. The HGDP has stated that its interest in commercializing tissues is negligible; yet estimates are that the market for human tissues is expected to climb to over 'US$80 billion within a generation' (RAFI, January–February 1997: 11). Also, the HGDP has maintained that it is impossible to target specific populations for biological warfare. Yet the British Medical Association and the World Medical Association view this as a serious possibility (11).

Indigenous nations, RAFI, and other alliances in the South and the North are preparing to take the issue of life patenting of native peoples to the UN International Court of Justice in the Hague. This action will have a direct impact on TNCs, which see the privatization of the resources and genetic materials of the South as essential to their accumulation of capital. It will mobilize public opinion and thereby encourage an open and visible political debate – a debate for which there is great urgency. In Canada this debate is especially critical, for the patenting of life has found in Canada a comfortable environment in which to proliferate. (Such patenting, once rejected in Europe, has been legal again there since 1998.) This action will challenge the model of capital accumulation being forced on indigenous nations and the South through globalization. It will raise concepts that are fundamental to the survival of human beings and the planet, such as justice, peace, equity, and the meaning of life itself. For indigenous and other peoples, life is sacred. It is their belief in the sanctity of life that has given rise to their resistance. The HGDP has put us on alert that other 'international' projects of similar ilk vis-à-vis their position on the sanctity of life, may well be in the offing.

The collaboration between indigenous nations and RAFI has made it clear that the HGDP is a gross infringement of human rights and that the tissue trade should be brought under examination and control of the United Nations Human Rights Committee. RAFI has also contended that the International Court of Justice in the Hague should determine whether the patenting of human tissues, considered legal according to international trade instruments, contravenes human rights. No doubt because of these actions and ongoing lobbying by indigenous peoples, the National Research Council (NRC) in the United States reported on 21 October 1997 that the HGDP is 'ethically and scientifically inadequate' (RAFI, September–October 1997: 8). The NRC, however, does not support a prohibition of patents. Rather, it supports a global survey on diversity originating in the United States. Given the extensive collections of indigenous peoples' blood held in American depositories, the halting of the HGDP, although a moral victory, may not forestall 'business as usual.' Since the names of universities and researchers involved in the HGDP are not widely known, who will know in which direction the research will be turned? Since reparations have not been discussed, since disclosure has not been international, and since UN inspection of the HGDP and HUGO has not occurred, it would be folly to let the HGDP escape our scrutiny. Perhaps the *raison d'être* for this seemingly 'humane' move is to lull us into a false sense of security.

NOTES

1 Transnationals that buy, sell, utilize, and control food, agricultural, and health products globally in a market driven by the application of genetic technologies against biological materials.
2 A permanent alteration in a gene or DNA molecule.
3 See, as one example, Churchill (1992: 296) for an elaboration of the extent to which birth anomalies, cancer, and other diseases have increased among the Dene and Métis of Saskatchewan.
4 Prior to the completion of the GATT (Uruguay) round of negotiations, led by Ed Pratt, chair of Pfizer, the United States began to bully countries into according more protection to patents and copyrights of business interests, threatening noncooperation, with accompanying loss of access to export markets. To get intellectual property onto the GATT agenda, Pratt formed the Intellectual Property Rights Committee (IPC), an alliance of thirteen major corporations such as Bristol-Myers Squibb, Hewlitt-Packard, DuPont, General Electric, IBM, Time Warner, Pfizer, Rockwell, Monsanto, Johnson & Johnson, Proctor & Gamble, FMC Corporation, and Merck. The committee that Pratt led co-ordinated its efforts with Clayton Yeutter, the U.S. ambassador for international trade negotiations. Despite resistance from the South, codes protecting American claims to property were included in the final draft of the Uruguay Round of GATT, tabled on 20 December 1991 by the director. The draft Trade-Related Intellectual Property Rights Code (TRIPs) did not meet with the satisfaction of the IPC, which sought to further its interests, demanding amendments to the TRIPs text while seeking negotiations within NAFTA to improve its position. In particular, the IPC cited that it did not agree with the exclusion of biotechnological inventions from the GATT text. Chapter 17 of NAFTA, which duplicates and extends the precedents set out in the draft GATT text, is viewed by the IPC and transnationals as a considerable advance. The IPC has requested further 'improvements' in NAFTA in future negotiations.
5 In September 1946 under a special Presidential Directive, President Truman authorized the Pentagon's Joint Intelligence Objectives Agency (JIOA) plan to recruit German Nazi scientists to work in America. The code name of this program was Project Paperclip. Although known Nazis were supposed to be banned from recruitment, the directive stated that 'position or honors awarded a specialist under the Nazi Regime solely on account of his scientific or technical abilities' would not disqualify a candidate (Simpson, 1988:36).

6 See Delroy Constantine-Simms, 'Blacks and Hitler – A Forgotten Story' (*Pride*, 2–8 October 1997: 2, 6). This article refers to the documentary film 'Hitler's Forgotten Victims,' made by David Okuefuna and Moise Shewa of Afro-Wisdom Films. The film links Hitler's obsessions with racial purity to views expounded by Ernst Haeckel, a German Darwinian zoologist who wrote of racial imperialism. Haeckel also wrote of 'Papuans and Hottentots fast approaching extinction.' The film reveals German genocidal activities in Africa, particularly in Namibia, where, after the massacre of 80 per cent of the Herero people, the survivors were 'imprisoned in concentration camps, or used as human guinea pigs for medical experiments, a foretaste of things to come for Germany's Blacks and Jews.' To date, the film reveals, the 'horrific experiences of Black people in Nazi Germany are virtually unknown or ignored.' Okuefuna and Shewa tell that 'thousands of Black Germans, as well as Black soldiers captured as prisoners of war, became 'Hitler's Forgotten Victims.' When Hitler came to power, the 24,000-strong Black German community was the first to be targeted for sterilization. Black German survivors of the Holocaust document in the film that they were sterilized as children of mixed race in a program pioneered by a Nazi geneticist, Dr Eugen Fischer, who had developed his ideas in South West Africa (German) prior to the First World War.

REFERENCES

Awang, Sandra S. 1997. The Impact of Biotechnology, Intellectual Property Rights and NAFTA on Selected Economies of the Americas. PhD dissertation, University of Toronto.

Benjamin, Craig. 1996. Submission to Native Americas. June (unpublished).

Brady, Margaret. 1997. 'Medical Research Flourishes in Canada. *Financial Post*, 9 October: 35.

Churchill, Ward. 1994. *Indians Are Us? Culture and Genocide in Native North America*. Toronto: Between the Lines.

Diprose, Rosalyn. 1995. 'A "Genethics" That Makes Sense.' In Vandana Shiva and Ingunn Moser (eds.), *Biopolitics: A Feminist and Ecological Reader on Biotechnology*, 162–74. London: Zed Books.

Dotto, Lydia. 1995. 'Genome Quest: An International Collaboration.' *University of Toronto Magazine* 22(4): 8–13.

Duffy, Eileen. 1997. Racism in International AIDS Experiment: Women of Color as Guinea Pigs. *Working People's News*. November: 3.

Gray, Andrew. 1995. Whose Knowledge Is It Anyway? *Indigenous Affairs: International Work Group for Indigenous Affairs* 4: 2–4.

Harry, Debra. 1995. Patenting of Life and Its Implications for Indigenous Peoples. *Information about Intellectual Property Rights*, 7.

136   Sandra S. Awang

'HIV Injections for TT, Bahamas.' 1998. *The Caribbean Camera*, 5–11 March: 20.

Horowitz, Leonard G. 1997. AIDS: A Planned Plague? Fear, Denial and Indifference! *Alive: Canadian Journal of Health and Nutrition* 182. December: 21–3.

Indigenous Peoples' Biodiversity Network. Indigenous Peoples' Perspectives on Intellectual Property Rights and Indigenous Peoples' Knowledge Systems. Discussion Paper No. 1, Cultural Survival Canada and UNDP.

Keller, Evelyn Fox. 1995. 'Fractured Images of Science, Language and Power: A Post-Modern Optic, or Just Bad Eyesight?' Pp. 52–68 in Shiva and Moser (eds.), *Biopolitics*. London: Zed Books.

Lanctôt, Guylaine. 1995. *The Medical Mafia*. Miami: Here's the Key.

Lyons, Oren. 1996. Ethics and Spiritual Values and the Promotion of Environmentally Sustainable Development: 50 Years of the World Bank, Over 50 Tribes Devastated. *Akwesasne Notes: A Journal of Native and Natural Peoples* 2(1): 88–93.

RAFI. 1997. 'Biopiracy Update: The Inequitable Sharing of Benefits. *RAFI Communique* (September–October).

– RAFI. 1997. The Human Tissue Trade. *RAFI Communique* (January-February).

– RAFI. 1996. Collecting the World Over ... Human Tissue Samples used by U.S. Government Institutions. *RAFI Communique* (March–April): 10.

– 1993. 'Patents, Indigenous Peoples and Human Genetic Diversity.' *RAFI Communique* (May).

Ross, Colin. 1996. The CIA and Military Mind Control Research: Building the Manchurian Candidate. Lecture given at 9th Annual Western Clinical Conference on Trauma and Dissociation. 18 April.

Simpson, Christopher. 1988. *Blowback: America's Recruitment of Nazis and Its Effects on the Cold War*. London: Wiedenfeld & Nicolson.

Waerea-i-te-rangi Smith, Cherryl. 1996. When the Resources Run Out, the West Goes Shopping: Indigenous Environments and Knowledge. *The Big Picture* 7: 2–4.

Wandell, Jack. 1996. Tracking the Vampire Brigade. *Akwesasne Notes: A Journal of Native and Natural Peoples* 2(1): 73–6.

8

Toward Indigenous Wholeness: Feminist Praxis in Transformative Learning on Health and the Environment

DOROTHY GOLDIN ROSENBERG

This essay introduces a feminist critique of the dominant biomedical/techno-logical corporate approach to health and how it marginalizes and largely suffocates indigenous knowledges in many parts of the world by serving the medical/industrial complex. It then illustrates how some women are reclaiming traditional paradigms of environmental health consciousness and social responsibility, thus contributing to knowledge and praxis for social/political transformation in justice/health/Earth relationships.

I write as a Jewish-Canadian feminist educator and activist of over three decades in the areas of peace, equality, ecology, health, and social and economic justice. The Nazi Holocaust in Germany, which was supported and perpetuated by many other countries of the world, was my earliest lesson in anti-Semitism, the destruction of cultural heritage, and genocide. It was but the first of my lessons about abusive systemic power, domination, and oppression; and about environmental and military racism; as well as about the possibility of incredible resistance, bravery, and cultural survival in the face of despicable evil. From this tragedy, unfortunately the world has learned little about curbing patriarchal power, racism, militarism, greed, violence, and the destruction of ecosystems, all of these having been perpetrated since the Second World War, in North, South, and Central America, South Africa during decades of apartheid, and the Gulf War, Bosnia, and Rwanda, to name but a few examples. In addition, as a health professional, I am well aware of medical tragedies such as thalidomide, tainted blood, DES, medical X-ray-induced cancers – tragedies arising from mistakes of science and technology.

The term 'feminist critique' refers here to ecological/feminist analysis that draws from traditional knowledge, which views all of life as an interconnected web enriched by diversity; and which understands power relationships and domination from critical cultural perspectives such as sexism, racism, classism, ageism, homophobia, and anthropocentrism. Ecological feminist praxis challenges patriarchal institutions of power such as corporations, militaries, and governments, which are largely responsible for toxic pollution, which is known to weaken immune systems and to cause hormone, genetic, and behavioural disruptions, illness, and often death. It draws links between violence against women and against the Earth, structural adjustment policies, the debt crisis, and militar-ism, seeing all of these as forms of institutional and systemic violence in most contemporary societies. Largely due to breast cancer and other related epidemics, feminist activists are challenging environmental destruction and the tenets of economic growth, as well as promoting a more traditional societal paradigm of respect for the Earth and all species on it. Many are demanding that the medical establishment replace its largely singular focus on testing (machines) and treatment (drugs) with more balanced, just, and holistic approaches to health.[1]

Towards Indigenous Wholeness: The Context

The indigenous principles of ecological integrity and health have been clearly enunciated: the health of the planet is the primary context for the health of all life on it; the life support systems of the Earth are severely threatened; what we do to the planet, we do to ourselves (Colorado, 1989; La Duke, 1995). These principles are largely ignored in the segmented thinking of military/corporate/government decision makers and the medical establishment (Bertell, 1985; Moss, 1989). Thus, the ecological/health crisis is seen as a crisis of cultural pathology precipitated by the thought processes and institutions that shape modern life. In the industrial world, conditions associated with technological growth – chronic and degenerative diseases such as heart disease, cancer, and diabetes – are called 'diseases of civilization' because they are related to lifestyles and environmental pollution in those societies (Capra, 1982). Ecological health crises have their roots both within and outside medical science and are inextricably linked to larger social and cultural crises: 'The environmental crisis is not just a problem of physical ecosystems; it is an example of power, profit and political wrangling, of institutional and bureaucratic arrangements, settings and cultural conventions that create conditions of environmental destruction' (Seager, 1993).

Most significant ecological harm can be traced to modern patriarchal cultural, scientific domination, beginning with the Age of the Enlightenment, during which both women and nature were perceived as passive, worthless, and dispensable, and therefore to be controlled, exploited, and then disposed of, as exemplified by the witch burnings and the commencement of ecological destruction in that era (Merchant, 1990). Yet in most cultures, indigenous knowledges in women's (witches') hands were integral to the maintenance of health. Caring, midwifery, herbalism, and other modalities included the interplay of body, mind, spirit, and the Earth. The disappearance of such forms of knowledge suggests that cultural values and attitudes may reflect the imbalances in social, economic, and political structures affecting societies today (Shiva, 1993).

The cultural transition proposed by feminist activists reflects a 'paradigm shift' – that is, a profound change in thoughts, perceptions, and values away from those associated with the different streams of patriarchal Western culture: the Scientific Revolution, the Enlightenment, and the Industrial Revolution. Most forms of indigenous knowledge are based on holism; in contrast, current biomedical/technological health models are firmly grounded in Cartesian thought, in which there is a separation of mind and body and the body functions as a machine of many parts. This mechanistic view of the human organism, and the resulting engineering/corporate approach to health, have led to an excessive emphasis on medical technology and drugs, which are perceived as the only way to treat illness (Capra, 1982; Sherwin, 1992). This view embraces a belief in the scientific method as the only valid approach to knowledge. It perceives the universe as a mechanical system, and social life as a competitive struggle for existence. It embraces the notion that unlimited material progress can be achieved through economic and technological growth and competition. This mechanistic paradigm of Western industrial society is often described as dualistic, dependent on rationality, and exploitative of women, nature, and indigenous and other marginalized peoples. In contrast, in most indigenous cultures, rational and intuitive thought are regarded as complementary.

The Suffocation of Indigenous Knowledges by the Dominant Biomedical/ Technological Approach to Health

Historical Background

Scientific/archaeological methods now make it possible for us to document how people lived in prehistoric times. Evidence now strongly suggests that for the greater part of civilized history, traditional societies were based on co-operation and reverence for life and nature, not on competition and an obsession with death and technology. There was respect for the life-giving and life-sustaining powers of the Earth – a respect rooted in a social structure whose values reflected caring, compassion, and nonviolence rather than conquest and possession. For millennia – a span of time much longer than the 5,000 years conventionally counted as history – societies based on spirituality, nature, and orality were structured according to what now we would call an 'ecological consciousness.' They were not ideal or utopian; but at the same time, and unlike today, they were not warlike. Women were not subordinate to men and the Earth was not an object for exploitation and domination. Our earliest estrangement from nature actually began around 4500 BC, when Indo-European nomads from the Eurasian steppes began invading Europe, the Near East, Persia, and India. Thus the nature-based, female-honouring religions of the Goddess, which revered the life processes of the Earth, were supplanted by the omnipotent male sky-God (Eisler, 1987).

The ancient cradles of civilization were highly creative societies in which women held important positions as priestesses, craftspeople, healers, and elders. In many different cultures, the sacred Mother Earth was seen as a living being with a life force of her own (Spretnak, 1991). Most societies have legends about an earlier, more harmonious time. An example is the Chinese legends from the Tao Te Ching, which tell of the time when the 'yin' or feminine principle was not yet subservient to the male principle 'yang' – a time when the wisdom of the mother was honoured above all (Eisler, 1987). However, the aggressive and destructive motives of domination, conquest, control, and profit have been presented to us as human nature by historians as well as by social scientists (Sahtouris, 1987).

In traditional matriarchal cultures, healing was associated with the life-giving capacities of women (Eisler, 1987). For most of human history holistic healing was practised largely by women. This knowledge, which was passed from generation to generation, made use of substances of the Earth to fortify health. For many women, knowledge of herbal preparations was as common as knowledge of cooking today (Griggs, 1982). Women and nature were revered, and plants and animals were closely associated with goddesses. In many cultures, from the North American Indian to the ancient Hebrew and the Greek, the snake has been associated with the deities of healing. The two main goddesses of healing, Hygea and Panacea, were also the names of the Great Goddess's milk-giving breasts. The word 'nurse' carries this age-old associa-tion with women's life-giving, nurturing powers (Walker, 1983).

The spiritual traditions of native peoples, Africans, Asians, and other cultural groups, and the pre-Christian traditions that survived in Europe, shared a common world view in which the sacred was seen as part of the living world. Whether referred to as Goddess, God, Great Spirit, or Creator, nature was a basis of spirituality (Starhawk, 1989). Historically, most aboriginal cultures have integrated these principles in their lives, and they continue to do so even today despite colonization and subjugation. For example, the Gitsan people of

British Columbia understood these relationships respecting a 'Power Larger than Ourselves,' and looked upon the land, the sea, the air, and all creatures as life. They copied nature because they saw all life, large and small, as an interconnected cycle, and saw as well that the system itself punished any breaking of that cycle. They saw and understood the checks and balances; and based their fundamental truths, authorities, and responsibilities on something that had worked for millions of years; and fit themselves into this cycle of life. This is something that most in the West have yet to learn.

The commodification of values by the corporate mass media has led to the stimulation of unmet needs and wants. Frustration is created when people feel unsatisfied, and this is often reflected in destructive lifestyles. More and more young women are developing unhealthy habits such as smoking and over- or under-eating (Mies, 1993). As well, most people in Western cultures adhere to biomedical models because they are afraid to examine their wasteful consumerism and to challenge the status quo. Thus, they delegate responsibility for their health to doctors and drugs, and accept ever-increasing rates of diseases such as cancer rather than investigating how the chemical industry poisons our food to increase profits (Capra, 1982). While more and more people are returning to traditional health values, a critique of capitalist political economy remains elusive in mainstream society and media. Consumer liberation and a changed lifestyle would mean choosing different satisfiers that promote equality, human/Earth relationships, self-reliance, and life enhancement (Mies, 1993).

Modern medicine is dominated by the biomedical model, which has acquired the status of dogma. This is inextricably linked to the common cultural belief system of the day. Interestingly, a basic tenet of Chinese, other Eastern, and other holistic medicine is that illness does not strike mysteriously from nowhere, but arises from clearly identifiable imbalances (Scott and Scott, 1991). In Chinese medicine, sages did not treat those who were sick; rather, they were paid to instruct those who were well. If the patient became sick, it was considered partly the doctor's fault and payments ceased (Huang, 1949).

The transition from holistic health to drugs and the transfer of power from women to men that accompanies it reflects the world view from which both are derived. Indigenous approaches to health nearly vanished during the late nineteenth century with the rise of the pharmaceutical industry. As physicians put their faith in science, holistic approaches fell by the wayside (see chapters by Ng and Shroff in this volume). Pharmaceutical companies convinced doctors to prescribe their drugs; in return, doctors began a campaign to discredit holistic practitioners for failing to fulfil the requirements of science.[2] They also shut down holistic schools and centres that were the training ground for many women and minority cultures (Kheel, 1989). Later, the U.S. National Cancer Institute shifted its focus away from prevention toward treatment – mainly the testing of chemotherapy regimens (Batt, 1994). In recent decades, many scholars and activists have demanded that the limitations of the biomedical model be recognized and that more research be done on holistic approaches to health. Throughout the world, new questions are being raised, rooted in the knowledge and experience of women[3] and of ancient and aboriginal cultures with their millennia-old knowledge systems (Shiva, 1993).

Biomedical/Technological Patriarchal Models: Impacts on Women's Health

If we are to understand health and illness, it is not enough to reduce life to molecular phenomena. This is especially true in the field of women's health. Most women in Western society have lost knowledge of their own bodies as experts dictate procedures to be followed. So-called old wives' tales, herbal recipes, and simply listening to our own bodies are arts that modern medicine has negated. The increasing dependence on technologies has accelerated the trend toward specialization; it has also reinforced a tendency to look at particular parts of the body and to neglect the whole person or how the environment affects health (Harcourt, 1992). The development of gynaecology and obstetrics (by mostly male doctors) during the twentieth century has led to a high degree of medical inter-vention. Examples: synthetic contraceptives and procedures such as genetic engineering and manipulation of eggs, sperm, and embryos outside the human body. The 'pill' and other medical treatments are all part of a modern 'technical fix' and have led to side effects that are often worse than the problems they were designed to solve. Despite evidence that hormone replacement causes uterine cancer, and despite the documented risk that the pill and menopausal estrogen place on all stages of women's reproductive cycles, doctors continue to treat women with synthetic hormones (Hynes, 1989). Feminist health advocates criticize this medicalization of the female body and the failure of health professionals to focus on the broader social and political questions in women's lives. In this climate, more and more women are taking control of their health and their bodies, and often are returning to the traditional health practices of earlier times (Harcourt, 1992; Weed, 1996).

Patriarchal Science and Research

A feminist examination of medical research shows clearly that it embraces masculinist presumptions about society's power structures (Sherwin, 1992). Questions are now being asked about how topics are chosen, and which ones are neglected, and whose interests are served, and who controls decisions, and to whom researchers are accountable. Nor can the myth of the neutral, apolitical scientist be accepted, since research is a social and political activity that has repercussions for our collective lives (Eichler, 1994).[4] Most research and funding institutions are controlled by members of the dominant class and reflect their class, gender, and racial backgrounds. Scientists shape their research interests to serve the orientations of the funding sources, and a significant amount of funding comes from national defence departments and is linked to military interests. Also, much research is funded by pharmaceutical companies and biotechnology industries. Even public research money reflects the clout of special interests; although primary prevention[5] promises to save far more lives than treatment, vastly greater resources are directed at finding cures than at prevention, because cures promise greater profits to industry, whereas prevention threatens to reduce them (Hynes, 1989; Sherwin, 1992). The relatively powerless position of women in society illustrates how health can be sacrificed to the profits of the pharmaceutical industry. Research is geared to high-tech solutions, and careers are made on technological breakthroughs promising opportunities and profits. Little support is available for holistic approaches and primary prevention; medical research speaks of fighting wars against diseases, not of avoiding them. (Sherwin, 1992; Moss, 1989). A feminist health model would be user-controlled and responsive to women's and oppressed groups' concerns (Sherwin, 1992). It would encourage indigenous values and the need for healthy living rather than trying to correct the consequences of opportunities denied.

*The Political Economy of the Medical/Industrial Complex
and the Limitations of Science*

In 1962, biologist Rachel Carson wrote *Silent Spring*, in which she alerted the world to the health hazards caused by pesticides, fungicides, and insecticides.[6] She challenged the right of corporations to make profit over people's health: 'This is an era dominated by industry in which the right to make money at whatever cost to others is seldom challenged and we shall have no relief from this poisoning of the environment until our officials have the courage and the integrity to declare that the public welfare is more important than dollars and to enforce this view.' Carson was called an ignorant woman by the chemical industry (Hynes, 1989). She died in 1964 of breast cancer. That year, the World Health Organization estimated that 80 per cent of cancers were due to synthetic carcinogens in food, water, air, homes, and workplaces (Proctor, 1996). In 1979 the U.S. National Institutes of Health Report stated that environmental factors were thought to be the cause of most cancers. Rather than decreasing, toxins have increased, as have other environmental dangers and diseases. Today one in three people will get cancer and one in four will die from it.[7]

The medical/industrial establishment has been the subject of numerous investigations (Epstein, 1979; Proctor, 1996). The Memorial Sloan Kettering Cancer Center, the world's largest private cancer centre, is an illustration of the allegiances of industry.[8] The centre's board of directors was closely tied to the oil, chemical, and automobile industries (all major polluters); its members included bankers, stockbrokers, venture capitalists, top officials of drug companies, and influential members of the media, as well as leaders of the $55 billion-a-year cigarette industry. Cancer research, diagnosis, and treatment have become a big business in which screening and intervention are the preferred 'prevention' routes.[9] The medical establishment is reluctant to put research money into efforts toward 'zero discharge' of toxics and holistic genres of prevention because of its incestuous relationship with the pharmaceutical corporations and their public relations operations (Epstein, 1979; Hynes, 1989). Instead of preventing the production of toxic materials, the industry and governments have focused on 'managing' the problem through sophisticated public relations (Epstein, 1979; Hynes, 1989).

The International Agency for Research on Cancer (IARC, 1993), which is part of the World Health Organization, has identified a number of health-damaging environmental agents. These include chemicals, mixtures of different chemicals, radiation, drugs, and industrial processes or occupational exposures (see also Misch, 1994).[10] However, routine emissions of these known carcinogens are permitted; while industries lobby policymakers to demand proof of harm of individual chemicals before agreeing to legislate a halt to toxic emissions (Paulson, 1993). This is evidence that science serves mainly as a prop for the status quo (Seager, 1994).

Militarism, Racism, and Maldevelopment

Militarism

As the twentieth century draws to a close, the dominant ideology is facing a cultural crisis with implications for health (Robbins, 1991). This crisis is manifested in the following: 'It is predicted that by the year 2000, weapons related environmental radiation will produce 90,000 cases of cancer, two million miscarriages and infant deaths, 10.4 million children with genetic diseases, and another 10 million who are physically deformed or mentally retarded' (Bertell, 1993). This serves to illustrate a central and vitally important fact of our modern era: military activities are the largest polluters and destroyers of resources in the world (Renner, 1991).

Environmental and Military Racism

Environmental injustice and/or environmental and military racism are reflected in how the health of marginalized people is damaged because they live or work near major streets and highways, toxic emissions or dumps, landfills, incinerators, sewage treatment plants, uranium mines, and farms that use pesticides and herbicides (Bullard, 1993). In the early 1970s in the United States, this type of injustice came to public attention during the California grape boycott, when Mexican farmworkers and their families were exposed to toxic chemicals as they worked in vineyards. (These chemicals were similar to Agent Orange, which was used in biological warfare by the United States during the Vietnam War.) But this type of injustice has a long list of antecedents: for example, Zyklon B gas was developed and used by the Nazis to exterminate Jews, gypsies, and homosexuals during the Second World War; atomic bombs were dropped on the Japanese people by the United States in Hiroshima and Nagasaki in 1945; low-level flight testing by NATO countries is increasing over Innu lands in Labrador and Quebec; uranium is mined on aboriginal land all over the world; and toxic wastes are shipped to poor regions in both postcolonial and industrialized societies. Many marginalized sectors of societies, North and South, are fighting this trend by seeking social and economic compensation and safe alternative development (Bullard, 1993).

Reclaiming Traditional Paradigms of Environmental, Health, and Social Responsibility

The cultural shift required for change reflects principles of transformative feminisms that critique *all* structures of oppression, including sexism, racism, classism, homophobia, and anthropocentrism. Ecological feminisms are transformative in that they go beyond the struggle for equality within current structures and challenge patriarchal institutions (Merchant, 1990; Shiva, 1993). Women's indigenous knowledges and participation are integral to this analysis (Starhawk, 1982; Shiva, 1993). For example, prior to the United Nations Fourth Conference on Women, the Women's Global Strategies Meeting working group on women, science, and technology declared:

Women must be given at national and international levels the opportunity to conceptualize and design science and technology strategies and set priorities in scientific research to support their gender-specific needs, interests and aspirations. There must be recognition of women's indigenous knowledge and traditional techniques as scientific and as a'basis for technological development and intervention. Protection of local community knowledge systems from unfair exploitation is needed to ensure mutually beneficial integration of both local and modern knowledge systems and natural resources for the benefit of people and nature.[11]

Many women's organizations, critical of destructive capitalist development structures, are building alliances to promote healthy-community models that incorporate the best of the old and the new (Bullard, 1993; Nozick, 1992; Roberts and Brandom, 1995).

Ecological feminisms also have much to teach us in an interrogative rather than in a prescriptive mode. Because of shared concerns for health and freedom, a new 'we' has emerged from those feminists, ecologists, peace activists, and scholars who are challenging institutions of power. For example, Wilmette Brown demonstrates the value of such questioning by combining the political insights of the Black civil rights movement, lesbian feminism, ecology, peace movements, and holistic health movements. Writing as a Black American activist and theorist and as a cancer survivor, she sees the issue as how to transform cancer from a preoccupying vulnerability into a vindicating power for everyone determined to reclaim the Earth. That involves making visible the links between sex, class, and health. We have already noted the marginalization of the poor, who are often forced to work and live in high-risk areas and who do not have access to adequate health care. Brown's analysis of convalescence from the perspective of a black, working-class, lesbian feminist explores the limitations of (American) holistic health movements, which have been myopic to race, class, and gender issues as defined by white, middle-class heterosexuals. In her view, despite their critiques of the medical industry, these movements have largely ignored the necessity to struggle against the military/industrial complex. They mostly assume financial access to self-healing experiences as well as the time, skills, and money to obtain healthier diets, and they have too often ignored traditions of herbal remedies that have been practised for centuries among peoples of colour. Her own site of struggle is the international women's peace movement, which she feels has learned to reject the sexist and racist assumptions of most peace and holistic health movements (Brown, 1983).

Brown's analysis and activism exemplify a politics of resistance that runs counter to the will to totalize. They illustrate the necessity to limit essentialist tendencies in an effort to develop a 'coherent' theory (quoted in Quimby, 1983). This must apply to all voices of subjugation so as to enable us to better question our own political and personal practices. It must also extend to anthropocentric assumptions that only human beings have truths to tell. The cries of factory farm animals and of fish suffocating in poisoned waters are among the other voices we need to heed (Quimby, 1983).

An ecofeminist perspective offers a new cosmology that recognizes that life in nature is maintained by co-operation, mutual care, and love. To this end, ecofeminists use metaphors like 'reweaving the world,' 'healing the wounds,' and 'reconnecting the web' (Mies and Shiva, 1993).

The Old and the New: Modern Science from Indigenous Knowledges

Today, increasingly, indigenous health knowledges are spreading as people have become dissatisfied with conventional Western medicine. Holistic practice honours a wisdom whereby the healer not only can provide 'cures' but can be a guide in working with the healing powers of the natural world. There is a growing recognition of centuries-old plant-based remedies, which reflects that science has caught up with indigenous knowledge regarding medical drugs. Through the process of learning about the old, new knowledge is being discovered. Examples: The foxglove plant, the source of digitalis, is one of the most successful drugs in the treatment of heart disease. Essiac, a tea made from bark, is used by native people as a cancer treatment; it contains inulin, an enzyme that breaks down the mucous coating on cancer cells and allows the body's defence system to penetrate them. A natural anti-inflammatory agent in shark cartilage alleviates pain and suffering (Williams, 1995). Plant remedies used by indigenous people to fight mycobacteria, the bacteria responsible for tuberculosis and leprosy, have been well documented (McGuire and Franzblau, 1996). Unfortunately, too often plants are not valued in and of themselves; instead, their most powerful properties are isolated, extracted, and synthesized into chemicals and drugs for profit. Nature is seen as a resource that only becomes useful when transformed by the rational minds of men (Kheel, 1989). This raises ethical, cultural, and economic concerns regarding intellectual property rights and the commodification of indigenous knowledge.

Nonetheless, in some cultures the wisdom of living in harmony with nature and of drawing on natural vital forces possessed by ancestors has never been lost. Different cultures call this wisdom by different names: Prana (India), Chi (China), or Ki (Japan). In fact, the word 'physis,' from which the word *physician* derives, refers to both 'nature' and this 'vital force' (Kheel, 1989).

In addition, indigenous healing practices maintained by lay women for thousands of years remain among the most important healing practices in most rural parts of the world. According to WHO, these practices provide 95 per cent of the world's health care needs (Kheel, 1989). Elsewhere, people are beginning to reclaim holistic approaches to health, and are thereby generating new visions of social transformation. In this way, an understanding of indigenous local experiences is providing the building blocks for health, social, and economic change.

For example, in the Pacific Islands, although many women work profession-
ally in modern economies, the great majority still live in coastal villages or
mountain settlements where traditional ways continue. Plant species often
endemic to single islands or ecosystems are used in traditional methods.
Practical knowledge about local plants and animals, and the physical environment, is often stored in the heads of older women in Pacific communities.
According to the Fiji School of Medicine, 80 per cent of the population are being
treated by traditional medicine and only 20 per cent by modern drugs and
methods. Clinical trials are being carried out on local medicines with the full co-
operation of the healers, who have the confidence of the local people. Their
natural healing approach recognizes environmental, social, and emotional factors in disease, and treats the person as a whole being. As outside influences
change societies, women have often been deprived of knowledge and therefore
of power by lack of access to suitable education. They have also been displaced
by foreign systems that do not care about or are ignorant of their position, status,
activities, and lives. Women often perceive themselves as being without power;
but where they can still practise and apply traditional knowledge, they are active
and confident (Lechte, 1992). In India, the women's community-based Centre
for Health Education, Training and Nutrition Awareness (CHETNA) acknowledges that poor health results from deep-rooted physical, social, and economically based exploitation and discrimination. It takes an intersectoral holistic
approach to health through indigenous systems of medicine while promoting
community educational, economic, environmental, and agricultural programs.
In Thailand, in projects such as Traditional Medicine for Self Reliance, villagers
preserve their community forests by planting trees and edible and medicinal
plants. They take a holistic approach to primary health care, herbal medicine
production, and organic farming, and this leads to individual and community
self-sufficiency and well-being. Traditional medicines can replace imported
expensive Western pharmaceutical products (Reesor, 1991).

For example, in Kenya, the Green Belt Movement has developed widespread
programs of tree planting, food production, and environmental protection.
During the past two decades over 50,000 women have been involved in
providing millions of tree seedlings to schools, churches, and small farmers.
This movement's success is linked to the financial incentives it incorporates, as
well as to a holistic approach in which tree planting is seen in the broader
context of well-being (Ofosu-Amaah, 1992). Since the 1970s the women of the
Chipko ('tree hugging') Movement in India have used nonviolent resistance to
halt the cutting down of their forests, which for centuries have provided their
fuel, fodder, and food. They have slowed deforestation by challenging the
linked timber and mining corporations and by resisting dam projects, mining,

and irresponsible road building. They are engaged in ecological management, forestry planning, tree planting, and soil retention projects. Their movement symbolizes the struggle against the control that Western science has long exercised over resource management everywhere in the world; it has become an inspiration for other such resistance and reclamation (Shiva, 1993).

Conclusion: Healing Ourselves and the Earth

Education and advocacy at the grass roots as well as at the national and international levels are required to promote the political will needed to move away from the dominant patriarchal biomedical models toward a model that embraces holistic health and traditional well-being. This goes hand in hand with the need to replace the dominant world view with a global cultural ethic that gives highest priority to equality, social and economic justice, public health, demilitarization, peace making, and ecological sustainability. A return to spiritual values is needed; as well, we must develop models of co-operation and conflict resolution, and enhanced community relationships (Nozick, 1992; Sahtouris, 1989; Mander, 1991). Against long odds, feminism/equality, peace/ justice, and environmentalism/health emerged as powerful social movements in the late twentieth century. The vision and promise of these movements is that personal interactions and institutional arrangements may be transformed into non-exploitative, nonhierarchal, traditional co-operative relationships and thereby foster equality, sustainability, peace, and health (Seager, 1994). In recent decades, women have been holding forums on these issues at local and United Nations (UN) conferences (UNCED, 1992; UN Women's Conferences, 1975, 1980, 1985, 1995). Increasingly, the experiences of women of the South and other marginalized women are being acknowledged.

There is much yet to be done in building these bridges. That being said, health concerns are providing a means for bringing diverse interests together (Arditti and Schreiber, 1994). Breast cancer and other women's health issues are creating a new sisterhood all over the world,[12] in which women are demanding a say in health in its widest personal and planetary sense (Arias, 1995.) We can observe these philosophical, spiritual, and political strains from the many paths that people in both the North and postcolonial societies are taking in their efforts to protect themselves and the Earth against the encroachments of destructive imperialistic practices. There is also growing evidence of a renewal of indigenous knowledges and practices, and of a commitment to the empowerment of women, which will be a central force in the search for equity, justice, and peace among the peoples of the Earth, and for a balance between all biological species and the life support systems that sustain us.

NOTES

1 Most cultures traditionally espoused holistic traditions, from which healing
   evolved and which honoured not only the power of the body to heal but that of
   the mind, spirit, and nature.
2 Western medicine has made medical casualties routine. In the United States,
   prescription drugs have become a major cause of iatrogenic (doctor induced)
   disease and death (Martin, 1977).
3 In recent years the concept 'women' has become problematic insofar as it hides
   the differences between different categories of women: of colour and white,
   working class and middle class, Third World and First World, disabled and able-
   bodied, lesbian and heterosexual, and so on (hooks, 1984).
4 Most of the thousands of approved chemicals have not been evaluated for their
   effects on pregnancy, hormonal cycles, and breast development; nor have their
   synergistic effects been examined in view of the likelihood that cancers arise
   from multiple factors. A scientific bias exists in how regulatory agencies review
   chemicals, relying on exposure in chemical plants where most workers are male,
   and perform lab tests using male rats. Findings are presented as doctrine that the
   levels of toxins in our bodies present no danger, and then used as excuses for
   delays and inaction (R.H. Hall, 1995).
5 *Primary prevention* consists of activities directed toward decreasing the probabil-
   ity of specific illnesses or disfunctions in individuals, families, and communities.
   It includes actively protecting against stressors. N. Pender, *Health Promotion in
   Nursing Practice*. Norfolk: Appleton & Lange, 1987.
6 Carson (1962) warned that these chemicals remain in the soil dozens of years
   after they are applied. She described how they are stored in the fatty tissues of the
   vast majority of humans, later turning up in breast tissue, in mothers' milk, and in
   the tissues of unborn children.
7 For women, over 40 per cent of these are cancers of the female reproductive
   organs. In industrialized countries, one woman in eight will get breast cancer over
   her lifetime, up from one in twenty three decades ago. In men there are rapidly
   declining sperm counts, increases in prostate and testicular cancer, undescended
   testes, smaller penises, and other related immune and endocrine disruption
   conditions, which also have devastating repercussions on future generations.
8 An example is National Breast Cancer Awareness Month, conceived and funded
   by Imperial Chemical Industries (ICI). Zeneca, the American subsidiary of ICI,
   produces Novadex tamoxifen, a breast cancer treatment drug. ICI, with over
   $18 billion in annual sales, is one of the world's largest producers and users of
   chlorine, a substance believed to contribute to the breast cancer epidemic. CIL, a
   subsidiary paint factory, dumps toxic wastes into the St Lawrence River (Batt,
   1994).

9 Cancer's overall cost is more than $100 billion a year in the United States alone (Epstein, 1993).
10 There is now evidence that various chemical interactions affect toxicity, producing synergistic, additive, or antagonistic effects (Arnold et al., 1996).
11 Women's Environment and Development Organization (WEDO). 1995. *News and Views* 7(3): 23.
12 Devra Lee Davis, PhD, at the 'Pollution Knows No Boundaries' Conference, Niagara Falls, Ontario, November 1995.

REFERENCES

Arditti, R., and T. Schreiber. 1994. 'Breast Cancer: Organizing for Resistance.' *Resist Magazine* (October).
Arias, M. 1994–95. 'Breast Cancer and Pesticide Poisoning in Central America.' WHO *News and Views* (December–January).
Arnold, S.F., et al. 1996. Synergistic Activism of Estrogen Receptor with Combinations of Environmental Chemicals. *Science* 272(7).
Batt, S. 1994. *Patient No More: The Politics of Breast Cancer*. Charlottetown: Gynergy Books.
Bertell, R. 1985. *No Immediate Danger? Prognosis for a Radioactive Earth*. Toronto: Women's Press.
– 1992. 'Breast Cancer and Mammography,' *Mothering* (Summer).
– (1993). *Nuclear Testing and Human Rights: The Movement for a Comprehensive Test Ban Treaty*. Geneva: Women's International League for Peace and Freedom.
– 1996. Speech at the conference 'Mapping and Mobilizing: Women's Health and Environmental Justice.' Toronto, March.
Brady, J. 1991. *One in Three: Women with Cancer Confront an Epidemic*. San Francisco: Cleiss Press.
Brown, W. 1983. 'Roots: Black Ghetto Ecology.' In Caldecott and Leland (eds.), *Reclaim the Earth: Women Speak Out for Life on Earth*, London: Women's Press.
Brundtland, G.H. 1987. *Our Common Future: The World Commission on Environment and Development*. New York: W.W. Norton.
Bullard, R.D. 1993. *Confronting Environmental Racism: Voices from the Grassroots*. Boston: South End Press.
Capra, F. 1982. *The Turning Point: Science, Society and the Rising Culture*. New York: Simon and Shuster.
Carson, Rachel. 1962. *Silent Spring*, New York: Houghton Mifflin.
Centre for Health Education, Training and Nutrition Awareness (CHETNA). 1996. *News*. Gujarat: 1996.

Chu. C., and R. Simpson (eds.). 1994. *Ecological Public Health: From Vision to Practice*. Toronto: ParticipACTION.

Colorado, P. 1988. Bridging Native and Western Science. *Convergence* 21(2,3).

Davis, D.L., and H.P. Freeman. 1994. An Ounce of Prevention. *Scientific American* (September).

Eichler, M. 1995. Feminist Methodology. Toronto: Ontario Institute of Studies in Education.

Eisler, R. 1987. *The Chalice and the Blade: Our History, Our Future*. San Francisco, Toronto: Harper and Row.

Epstein, S.E. 1979. *The Politics of Cancer*. New York: Doubleday.

– 1993. In L. Clorfene-Casten, 'Inside the Cancer Establishment.' *Ms Magazine*. May/June.

Griggs, B. 1982. *Green Pharmacy: A History of Herbal Medicine*, New York: Viking.

Hall, R.H. 1995. Speech at the 'Pollution Knows No Boundaries: Breast Cancer and the Environment' conference. Niagara Falls, Ontario.

Harcourt, W. 1992. 'Sex, Lies and Population Control: The European Debate.' In G. Phillips (ed.), *Power, Population and the Environment: Women Speak*. Montevideo: NGONET.

hooks, b. 1984. *Feminist Theory: From Margin to Center*. Boston: South End Press.

Huang Ti, Nei Ching Su Wen, 1949. *The Yellow Emperor's Classic of Internal Medicine*. Trans. Veith. Baltimore: Williams and Wilkins.

Hynes, P. 1989. *The Recurring Silent Spring*. New York: Pergamon Press.

IJC. 1996. *Eighth Biennial Report on Great Lakes Water Quality of the International Joint Commission/Commission mixte internationale.*

International Agency for Research on Cancer (IARC)/ World Health Organization. IARC monographs on the Evaluation of Carcinogenic Risk to Humans, 'Preamble,' and 'Lists of IARC Evaluations.' IARC Lyon: May 1993.

Kheel, M. 1989. 'From Healing Herbs to Deadly Drugs: Western Medicine's War against the Natural World.' In J. Plant (ed.), *Healing the Wounds: The Promise of Ecofeminism*. Toronto: Between the Lines.

La Duke, W. 1995. Impact of Northern Development on Indigenous Communities and Women. Second World Women's Congress for a Healthy Planet. Beijing.

Lechte, R.E. 1992. 'Women, Environment and Population: Women, Environment and Reproductive Issues in the Pacific.' In G. Phillips (ed.). *Power, Population and the Environment: Women Speak*. Montevideo: NGONET.

Lorde, A. 1988. *A Burst of Light: Essays by Audre Lorde*. Ithaca: Firebrand Books.

Mander, J. 1991. *In the Absence of the Sacred: The Failure of Technology and the Survival of the Indian Nations*. San Francisco: Sierra Club Books.

Martin, E.W. 1977. Drug Information for Patients. *Drug Information Journal* 11, Special Supplement. January: 2S–3S.

McGuire, M., and S. Franzblau. 1996. In Colman Jones, 'Paying for Penicillin Addiction,' *Now Magazine*. 30 October, 1996.

Merchant, C. 1990. *The Death of Nature: Women, Ecology and the Scientific Revolution*. Toronto: Harper and Row.

Mies, M. 1993. 'Liberating the Consumer.' *Ecofeminism*. Halifax: Fernwood Publications.

Misch, A. 1994. 'Assessing Environmental Health Risks.' In *State of the World 1994: A Worldwatch Institute report on Progress Toward a Sustainable Society*. New York: W.W. Norton.

Moss, R.W. 1989. *The Cancer Industry: Unravelling the Politics of Cancer*. New York: Paragon House.

Nelson, J. 1989. 'The New Global Sweatshop' *Canadian Forum* (September).

Nozick, M. 1992. *No Place Like Home: Building Sustainable Communities*. Ottawa: Canadian Council on Social Development.

Ofosu-Amaah, W., and W. Philleo. 1992. *Women and the Environment: An Analytical Review of Success Stories*. United Nations Environment Program (UNEP) and World Wide Network, Inc., Washington, D.C.

Paulson, M. 1993. 'The Politics of Cancer: Why the Medical Establishment Blames Victims Instead of Carcinogens.' *Utne Reader* (November–December).

Plant, J. 1989. 'Wings of the Eagle: A Conversation with Marie Wilson, Gitsan-Wet'suwet'en Tribal Council (British Columbia).' In J. Plant, (ed.). *Healing the Wounds: The Promise of Ecofeminism*. Toronto: Between the Lines.

Proctor, R., 1995. *Cancer Wars: How Politics Shapes What We Know and Don't Know about Cancer*. Toronto: HarperCollins.

Quimby, L. 1990. 'Ecofeminism and the Politics of Resistance.' In I. Diamond and G.F. Orenstein (eds.), *Reweaving the World: The Emergence of Ecofeminism*. San Francisco: Sierra Club Books.

Reesor, S. 1991. 'Thai Villagers Work towards Self Reliance.' *Quaker Concern* 17(2) (Summer).

Renner, M. 1991. 'Assessing the Military's War on the Environment,' *1991 State of the World; a Worldwatch Institute Report on Progress Toward a Sustainable Society*. New York: W.W. Norton.

Robbins, A. 1991. *Radioactive Heaven and Earth: The Health and Environmental Effects of Nuclear Weapons Testing in, on, and above the Earth*. New York: Apex.

Roberts, W., and S. Brandom. 1995. *Get a Life*. Toronto: Get a Life Publishing.

Sahtouris, E. 1989. *Gaia: The Human Journey From Chaos to Cosmos*. New York: Pocket Books.

Scott, J., and S. Scott 1991. *Natural Medicine for Women: A Practical Guide to Good Health*. New York: Avon Books.

Seager, J. 1993. *Earth Follies: Coming to Feminist Terms with the Global Environmental Crisis*. New York: Routledge.

Sherwin, S. 1992. *No Longer Patient: Feminist Ethics and Health Care*. Philadelphia: Temple University Press.

Shiva, V. 1993. In Mies, *Ecofeminism*. Halifax: Fernwood Publications.

Shiva, V., and Ingunn Moser (eds.). 1995. *Biopolitics: A Feminist and Ecological Reader on Biotechnology*. London: Zed Books.

Spretnak, C. 1991. *States of Grace: The Recovery of Meaning in the Postmodern Age*. New York: Harper Collins.

Starhawk. 1982. *Dreaming the Dark: Magic, Sex and Politics*. Boston: Beacon Press.

Thornton, J. 1993. *Chlorine, Human Health and the Environment: The Breast Cancer Warning*. Washington: Greenpeace.

Walker, B. 1983. *The Women's Encyclopedia of Myths and Secrets*. San Francisco: Harper and Row.

Waring, M. 1988. *If Women Counted: A New Feminist Economics*, Toronto: HarperCollins.

WEDO. 1996. *Breast Cancer: The Global Agenda*. Action for Prevention Campaign, The Women's Environment and Development Campaign (WEDO), New York.

Weed, S. 1996. *Breast Cancer? Breast Health! The Wise Woman Way*. Woodstock, NY: Ash Tree Publishing.

Williams, P. 1995. 'Cancer: New Frontiers.' *Homemakers*. October.

PART III

Indigenous Knowledges and the Academy

The complex interactions between the rich and varied contributions of indigenous forms of knowledge and the form and content of contemporary academic life can be understood in several ways. As Joseph Couture, first chair of Native Studies at Trent University, shares, 'everyone has a song to sing which is no song; it is a process of singing.' Indigenous knowledges within the academy are more than content. They are more than a new course to be added to the curriculum; more than a new set of readings to be added to the course bibliography; more than a fresh topic for papers being written. The notion of indigenous knowledges within the academy is about uncovering the aboriginal story. Indigenous knowledges are a way to recover from the artificial split between mind and body brought on by the theorizing of the western European Enlightenment, and a challenge to the ways in which Western knowledges have become hegemonic. Such knowledges can be taken up in work on health, the environment, and spirituality, and indeed at all levels of academic reflection.

In a similar vein, the challenge to international development theory represented by African literature demonstrates that returning to traditions is also a movement forward. It is worth noting that a rapid expansion in relevant new materials is making life increasingly easy for busy scholars and for community groups searching for ideas. As an example, the Legacy Project of the Royal Commission on Aboriginal Peoples offers scholars, students, and readers a resource never before available: direct testimony by women, men, young people, and elders about ways of living, recommendations for change, and aspirations for life seven generations into the future.

9

Native Studies and the Academy

JOSEPH COUTURE

This essay follows from an earlier effort to draw attention to the practical, alluring relevance of native ways of 'knowing' and to do so within a general social science perspective (Couture, 1991b). Frequent reference to psychology, then as now, simply reflects my professional interest and conventional training. A continued focus on perceived traditional views and practices derives from my ongoing apprenticeship since 1971 in aboriginal healing ways.

My previous writing was an attempt to explore aspects of the direct experience of spiritual realities and dimensions. My stated intention was to propose some features of a 'psychological geology' – that is, some of the underlying realities and processes that mould the topography of the traditional, aboriginal mind. Emphasized also was that a pluri-dimensional approach seemed necessary before it was possible to consider general, current issues of identity and survival. It seems to me that indigenous knowledge, as ageless process and content, has eminently practical implications for aboriginal existence in this sophisticated technological and politically manipulative if not oppressive world. As T. Berry declares, it does seem important to appreciate that: 'the Indian ... has established a creative response rooted in his [sic] ability to sustain life in its moment of high tragedy and to continue the basic path of his human development in its most distinctive aspects' (1976: 135).

I continue to hold the above point of view, and reiterate it here so as to provide a context to the considerations that follow regarding Native Studies in general.

This essay also reflects an intense personal experience, ongoing since 1975, in what remains a fresh, pregnant, and exciting event – that of my appointment as chair of the Department of Native Studies at Trent University.[1] Some twenty years later, while its emergence as a legitimate academic endeavour is no longer in question, Native Studies continues to suffer from uncertain footing. This seems to stem from the immensity and complexity of its task. This chapter suggests guide points, thoughts, and feelings, which I group under such headings as Native Philosophy (worldview; assumptions) and Role-related Difficulties (for universities, curriculum development, and teachers).

My views are biased, personal, and suggestive at best, and derive in part from what the chosen focus of Native Studies *is* – the simple, stark fact of aboriginal peoples in change. My views also stem from the acknowledged pressures of on-campus academic habit and attitude, which bear strongly on Native Studies as it struggles to establish itself as a bona fide discipline.

To varying degrees, community and academic stake holders perceive and strive to relate to what is characteristically high drama for peoples whose histories are unique and remarkable, and who are presently intensely engaged in inner/outer, individual/collective changes and growth, away from degradation and despair toward to individual self-determination and group empowerment. As First Nations, aboriginals are both subject and object of intense transition, of great stress and radical changes. They are moving away from an intolerable situation and beginning to establish conditions in which they will be responsible for their destiny.

At the core of all this change is unprecedented healing and expression. The reality of complex human needs and aspirations relentlessly goads Native Studies.

Native Studies Philosophy

The Fundamental Task

By the late 1960s aboriginal peoples around the world were beginning to discover inspiration and the means to rise above oppressive, devastating influences. To their astonishment, they were making these discoveries in their own backyards. Their dawning awareness through a return to traditions has since expanded to become a bracing and creative movement.[2] The institution of Native Studies is located within that context.

The more one enters traditional sources, the more one perceives their world view concepts and values as foundational – as able to incite and guide an entire continuum of aboriginal development and learning needs.

The 'constants' for 'living a good life' are carried by a timeless traditional reflection that has been renewed continuously through the ages. In turn, native traditions manifest themselves as principles such as spiritual awareness and values development. These constants underlay widely diverse native languages, customs, and ways, which are understood as paramount to 'living-life' – that is, as engendering patterns of connecting responses to self, others, family, community, and the cosmos. The 'stuff' of relationships is revealed as the 'ground' to aboriginal being and becoming, and provides a sure footing, a step at a time, for the necessary walk into and through contemporary dilemmas.

Since its inception in the early 1970s, Native Studies has toiled carefully in a trial-and-error fashion to implement strategies for uncovering and describing the Aboriginal Story in all its dimensions. This daunting task presented a second intimidating hurdle – that of moderating a university-based critical analysis. The goal became one of rendering systematically a convincing translation of culture-based knowledge, skills, and attitudes, measured against traditional teachings, under the scrutiny of elders. Native Studies sought a new existential paradigm, impelled by a culture-rooted sense of both worlds in all their dimensions, expressed in the mode of bicultural survival.

The responsibility for interpreting and applying the content of tradition is a sanctioned enterprise. In the early 1970s, after twelve days of discussion, elders from Seven First Nations of Alberta stated:

> We would like to say that in order to survive in the 20th century we must really come to grips with the White man's culture and with White ways. We must stop lamenting the past. The White man (sic) has many good things. Borrow. Master and use his technology. Discover and define the harmonies between the two general Cultures, between the basic values of the Indian Way and those of Western civilization – and thereby forge a new and stronger sense of identity. For, to be fully Indian today, we must become bilingual and bicultural. We have never had to do this before. In so doing we will survive as Indians, true to our past. We have always survived. Our history tells us so ...
>
> On a given day, if you ask me where you might go to find a moose, I will say 'If you go that way you won't find a moose. But, if you go that way, you will.'
>
> So now, you younger ones, think about all that. Come back once in a while and show us what you've got. And, we'll tell you if what you think you have found is a moose.

The characteristic attitude and posture of Native Studies is one of upbeat, continuing evolution. A practitioner of this discipline may be likened to a savvy broker, one who is both a pulse taker and a keen translator, and who conveys world view meanings and ways both to the dominant society and to university faculty and students.

Assumptions

Western science arose from the struggle to develop human knowledge. From this, it follows that the seeking of knowledge is guided by assumptions about reality. These assumptions amount to a set of 'beliefs,' the validity of which cannot be demonstrated.

Assumptions are largely utilitarian in that they are necessary to all human investigative endeavour, serving as points of departure and later as reference points. Their 'truth' is mainly a function of their usefulness. Assumptions are like a map – a matrix of conceptual and experiential indices that provide a sense of direction; the searching mind can use them to methodically explore, and thereby incrementally build up human knowledge. In a burgeoning discipline like Native Studies, a number of assumptions play then a crucial role. For example, it is assumed that Native Studies expresses a philosophy that has several corollaries; and that it reflects a total 'way of life,' which to be lived successfully requires unified or holistic learning.

A second assumption is that Native Studies seeks to show the inherent validity and usefulness of the native heritage, which manifests itself in ways of knowing, which Native Studies draws from in order confront and assess present conditions.

That the 'aboriginal way' embraces mutuality without subordination and forms a comprehensive 'way of life' is a fundamental point. This keystone position is illustrated by the following traditional native axioms:

There are only two things you have to remember about being Indian. One is that everything is alive, and the second is that we are all related.

Eets aull 'dar in dee sareemohnees! Der's a raht time, a raht puhlace, wit' de raht peepool!

Walk in Beauty on the Blessing Way. Find your home, and when you do, you will know everything there is to know.

When a Navajo experiences the sacred mountains, inner forms kindling a new strength within himself, he says, 'I am invincible. I am beautified.' To be invincible is masculine. To be beautified is feminine. These two concepts together are a powerful entity. There is no strength from only one. Power comes from the interaction between them. When you have strength, you recognize your opportunity, you know what you must do, and you have the grace to do it.

Each person has a purpose and a place. Don't worry. Take it easy. Do your best. It will all work out. Respect life. Respect your Elders. It's up to you. You have all the answers within you. Walk the talk. Work hard. Old time learning was very hard. You can do anything when you put your mind to it.

What is life but a journey into the Light. At the center of life is the Light. When I pass over, I will cross the River and go up the Mountain into the Light.

Everybody has a song to sing which is no song at all. It is a process of singing, and when you sing, you are where you are. I dance, I sing, I am. There is within me a voice which tells me who I am and where I am.

We know that the white man does not understand our ways. One portion of land is the same to him as the next, for he is a stranger who comes in the night and takes from the land whatever he needs. The Earth is not his brother, but his enemy, and when he has conquered it, he moves on ... He treats his mother, the Earth, and his brother, the Sky, as things to be bought, plundered, sold like sheep or bright beads. His appetite will devour the Earth and leave behind only a desert.

We didn't know for a long time that we were equal. Now, we know, and there's no stopping us any more. We had forgotten our Story. Now, we're starting to understand.

Another assumption is that universities prefer that subjects have immediate relevance. To the institution, Native Studies brings an ages-old understanding that 'useful' learning is comprehensive and leads to the development of mind, attitude, and adaptation in conduct.

A fourth assumption is that Native Studies is a new expression of the characteristic themes of the North American aboriginal tradition. Accordingly, Native Studies seeks to articulate a deep, comprehensive perception of all levels of reality. The native world view, like beauty, has an inherent power to enliven.

A fifth assumption is that today's native person, whatever his or her position on the long continuum of native experience, on encountering the university milieu needs to understand that certain insights and skills are necessary prerequisites to surviving and prospering in a bicultural system. It is felt that such a person can become tuned to the spiritual and psychocultural nature of traditional existence as well as to the demands of the Western tradition. Those who master these insights and skills can move forward to a better future – albeit amidst a swirl of intertwining and often conflicting trends – in constant relationship and dialogue with the past. By re-establishing harmony, by restoring and healing relationships, by regaining self-reliance and social competence, and by taking back self-determination and control over family, community, and the Nations, native people can ensure for themselves a more fulfilling future.

It is believed also that the native way of 'seeing' and 'knowing' is valid both from general Western philosophical and traditional perspectives and from a social science perspective. This assumption is crucial to the development of a contemporary native way of knowing, as well as to a faithful reinterpretation of traditions.

In the native way of knowing, elders and tradition are primal givens. Our perceptions and grasp of such 'first principles' can shape our response to twenty-first-century realities. When asked what was the 'right' way, an old man replied, 'All ways are good when they are done in a right way!'

Comments to this point highlight the importance of 'oral literature' as basic data. Oral tradition is a medium in its own right and can be studied on its own terms, parallel to the mastery of the written word. However, this presents a major challenge to long-established academic analytic style, which is based on the printed word.

'Core culture' is another marker concept. In some regions the term 'pan-Indian' is used in reference to generic values and attitudes. The increasing numbers of students of diverse aboriginal and nonaboriginal backgrounds is a fact that begs recourse to this underlying dimension. Many students need help (via courses and programs) in order to ensure the development of an authentic identity. In some regions, the term 'core culture' may suggest a state of breakdown or irretrievable loss (or at best a loss retrievable only through long effort). In the eyes of some, to be anchored in this 'something-less-than' is to be less than 'Indian.' However, a flip-side suggests that a state of 'something-more-than-less-than' may be attained.

To increasing numbers of seekers, including many students in Native Studies, accessibility and attainability are possible through learning ways and customs and through applying spiritual development teachings and techniques. This recent development is seen as a path to inner balance and health, as a way out of cultural anomie and individual alienation. 'That-which-is-better' – which includes fluency in the language and its mind patterns – may be beyond the immediate reach of many native people. Even so, to settle for 'that-which-is-less-than' need not be simply a forced choice; rather, it may be an authentic beginning in a positive direction. That notwithstanding, the issue of 'core culture' does pose a dilemma.

One illustration arises in classrooms and training programs at all educational levels. Native students, as well as the faculty in any Native Studies program or course, usually represent a variety of aboriginal backgrounds. What 'culture' then is to be conveyed? What are the choices regarding values? What happens when the native teacher is not of their culture?

A second conundrum arises from the experience of many city-born and city-raised natives, who are without rural or community-based cultural ties. With which aboriginal culture should they identify as their starting point? Are those who have lost or who never had a native language, and for whom English or French (in Canada) is their 'native' tongue, any less 'native' than those who are language endowed? Yes and no. It is still true that in the spirit of the ages, fullness of identity seems to require a bicultural and bilingual base.

Thus, for example, there is a risk in the classroom, when expounding from a Cree perspective, of placing undue pressure on non-Crees. However, when students are held to a generic level (i.e., that of commonalities such as a life philosophy based on relationships with self/family/community/nation/nature/cosmos, trust and respect, stories and legends, dance and song, and ritual and ceremony), it is appropriate to advise, 'Now, you're into the basics. Go home to your elders for help to put a Blackfoot face or shaping on all that.' Or 'Go find a spiritual teacher for the specifics. Find an opportunity to learn the language if you can.'

Finally, it seems that the disadvantage of being city-based is no longer limited to native students. More and more native people, including aboriginal prison inmates, are seeking their cultural roots in an effort to discover or to reclaim their native heritage and knowledge.

Role-Related Difficulties

Universities

Universities tend to be nervous about the intellectual vice of absolutism. Their experience, based in the hard sciences, the social sciences, and the humanities, is with the ambiguous – that is, with the tentativeness of theory and with the shortcomings of method and inquiry.

Their wariness is understandable. One of the primary tasks of universities is to question assumptions. Because of that there arises between Native Studies and the university an unavoidable yet necessary tension. Therefore, a 'dialogal dialogue' is required of both parties (as opposed to a 'dialectical dialogue,' which seeks to convert) – an open, ecumenical positioning charged by a willingness to find complementary means of learning, understanding and interpreting the traditions of others.

Our era seems to be one of much scepticism, of intellectual restlessness, and of defensive retreat into conservatism. The élitism of faculty environments and the penchant for 'value neutrality' are pervasive. Universities tend often to emphasize organization, efficiency, competition, quantitative results, and a concern with *how* at the expense of *what* and *why*. These organizing principles manifest themselves through institutional mindsets, which in turn foster social institutions and social structures in which attitudes and values too often go unquestioned.

In such a milieu, it is not easy to enunciate native understandings in Western language. Besides the working hazards that derive from the class attitude of universities, both parties must contend with the uncertainty that attends any human action in 'naturalistic' circumstances – specifically, they must contend with the flux and turmoil of everyday native life in the 1990s. In a university environment, neither élitism nor value neutrality is appropriate to Native Studies. Native Studies must insist on freedom in intellectual search if it is to formulate and communicate to the various communities – including the community of scholars – fresh and more inclusive models congruent with the traditional paradigm.

Curriculum Development

That Native Studies curricula do not present themselves à la Bloom (1956) as an established canon is largely due to their relative recency. Native Studies programs are still evolving and expanding, and it takes time to amass relevant, accurate data for courses and publications. To accelerate curriculum development, Native Studies readily looks to the humanities and the sciences for tools for uncovering, developing, and enhancing insights.

The acquisition of skills necessary for unearthing and then articulating meaning draws on knowledge from many areas, including oral tradition. Curriculum delivery must take into account the requirements of the primary traditional learning modes of 'experiential learning' and 'learning by doing.'

Teachers

Attentiveness to and involvement in the ordinary life of the peoples as equals is of vital importance; community involvement is vigorously pursued. This demands from native academics compassion, competence, and critical intelligence, as well as moral and spiritual sensitivity to the family, the community, and the nation in the context of oral tradition. The teacher must reconcile the demands of mainstream academic life, such as teaching, research, and publishing (as bearing on academic promotion, for example) with the forthright claims of local community and regional groups.

Academics committed to Native Studies continue to face a demanding apprenticeship. They must learn to access oral literature through learning by doing; yet at the same time, they face limits as to what they can legitimately reflect and expound on in courses and programs. Also, they must acquire an intelligent grasp of how the European contact affected native life, and of contemporary issues such as human rights, worldwide aboriginal emergence, and globalization generally. The gross and still-resonating destructiveness of the European contact is a front-and-centre fact. It is not so much that teachers need to be apprised of the social breakdown in native communities (e.g., increasing rates of incarceration, suicide, drug addiction, sexual abuse, and family breakdown). Rather, teachers must perceive at the deepest levels the degree and extent of the present trauma and dysfunction. It is in light of this that traditional values and learning processes, including healing approaches, must be instilled. Thankfully, this process is now underway across the land; traditional ways can revitalize, and *are* revitalizing, the savaged and degraded soil of the native psyche.

It is helpful to distinguish between traditional behaviour and contemporary comportment. However, in more and more communities the two correspond less and less, if at all. For example, in virtually all aboriginal communities, interpersonal relations and child rearing practices have all been markedly altered by schooling and by decades of welfare. Native Studies teachers must learn to swim in a sea of variables. They are faced with analyzing and integrating all aspects of native life and then finding ways to pass on their findings. The people rightfully demand that analysts/teachers be consistently innovative in gathering their research and articulating the needs and aspirations of native people.

In teaching Native Studies, educators must critically assess not only their knowledge but also their experience of self, others, and social contexts. In the case of social service professionals, success can arise only out of a deep respect for others as *equals*, in all their complexity. Comprehensive preparation in diverse disciplines – including the arts and humanities – shaped by traditional knowledge and methods, can help one arrive at causative factors and short-term and long-range solutions.

An advantage we have, in our desire to transcend personal and group limitations, is that we can look to those respected people who in their visions, emotions, thoughts, and actions, in both a traditional and classical Western sense, are the 'educated.' These people are the elders, the philosopher-historians, the carriers of oral tradition, the teachers and healers, whose attitudes and activities overarch Native Studies and provide sanction and support.

Conclusion

The 'electronic interconnection of humankind' (Mooney, 1998–9)[3] is presently fostering new and very different perspectives on life, and is demanding that educated people be capable not only of providing specialized answers but also of asking the big questions of life itself regarding what is good and valuable about living in a world moulded and controlled by Euro-Canadian culture. Fortunately for native students, tradition offers 'large,' phenomenologically oriented answers in ways that are intellectual, spiritual, moral, and sociopolitical all at once.

In its many expressions, native traditions are being discovered and investigated, or rediscovered and reclaimed. A leading role in this process is devolving to Native Studies. Native Studies professors, as part of a forward-moving academic initiative, have begun to uncover those constants (e.g., laws of Nature/Energy), meanings, and processes that animate and sustain from within the core of Native American life, past and present. This is a 'story' – a concrete, ongoing human saga sustained by traditional values. Some key themes of the story can be outlined in some broad strokes. There does seem to be a core of commonalities, an essential heritage, shared by many if not all Native American cultures – a core of skills and behavioural traits comprising ways of knowing and of being/becoming a human being. Somehow these have endured through the ages, among the nations.

The Native Studies researcher J.E. Brown once stated: 'With our overemphasis on mental activity we are apt to think that the Indian, without any written language, lacks something important or necessary in not possessing a scholastic or dialectical type of doctrinal presentation' (1982: 31). Tom Berry, Elder and internationally regarded scholar in cultural history, declares that 'extensive human resources that are available to these original inhabitants of this continent ... intimate communion with the depths of their own psychic structure is one of the main differences between the psychic functioning of the Indian and the psychic functioning of the Euro-American in modern times (1976).

NOTES

1 In 1975 I was appointed chair of the Department of Native Studies, Trent University, Peterborough, Ontario. The substance of this chapter was originally published as a required reading for a Laurentian University correspondence course on aboriginal families.
2 The native return to ritual and ceremony is now a continentwide phenomenon. The People have begun to dream again (see Couture, 1991a, 1991b).
3 See also S. Turkle for an excellent, intriguing socio-philosophical analysis of modern man and the computer as machine.

REFERENCES

Berry, T. 1976. 'The Indian Future.' *Cross Currents*. Summer: 133–42.
Bloom, B., et al. 1956. *Taxonomy of Educational Objectives*. New York: David McKay Company. Pp. xv–196.

Brown, J.E. 1982. *The Spiritual Legacy of the American Indian*. New York: Crossroad.

Couture, J. 1989. 'Native and Non-Native Encounter: A Personal Experience.' Pp. 186–201 in W. Cragg (ed.), *Challenging the Conventional: Essays in Honor of Ed Newbery*. Burligton: Trinity Press.

– 1991a. 'The Role of Native Elders: Emergent Issues.' Pp. 201–17 in J.W. Friesen (Ed.), *The Cultural Maze: Complex Questions on Native Destiny in Western Canada*. Calgary: Detselig Press.

– 1991b. 'Explorations in Native Knowing.' Pp. 53–73 in J.W. Friesen (Ed.), *The Cultural Maze: Complex Questions on Native Destiny in Western Canada*. Calgary: Detselig Press.

Mooney, C. 1998–9. 'Education's prism.' *Cross Currents*. Winter: 88–9.

Turkle, S. 1984. *The Second Self: Computers and the Human Spirit*. New York: Simon & Schuster.

10

Toward an Embodied Pedagogy: Exploring Health and the Body through Chinese Medicine

ROXANA NG

'The Personal Is Political' ... and More

This chapter reports on my objectives, strategies, and experience teaching a graduate course on 'Health, Illness and Knowledge of the Body: Education and Self-Learning Processes'(heretofore 'Health and Illness') since 1991. My interest in undertaking this course emerged out of at least two tensions: First, I was concerned with balancing a demanding academic career with my political activism as an antiracist feminist and with my personal well-being. Second, I wanted to experiment with ways of teaching that do not privilege the mind/intellect over the body/experience.

My decision to include Chinese medical knowledge and practice (TCM for short) as part of the core content of the course grew out of my own recovery from one of the many health crises I had experienced since 1979 as a result of the tensions mentioned above. In 1990 I again encountered serious health problems as various demands became intolerable. In addition to the therapies (Swedish massage, shiatsu, chiropractic, and homeopathy) that I had integrated into my health regime, I turned to and (re)discovered Chinese medicine. I say (re)discovered because when I was growing up in the British colony of Hong Kong, TCM was not completely alien to me. We were given herbal teas and soups in certain seasons, and we described our bodies in terms of climatic conditions, using terms such as *heat, cold* and *damp* to describe internal bodily states. However, these were considered merely linguistic expressions. In Hong Kong at the time, allopathy[1] was the dominant medical system in the colony; also, my paternal grandmother was an allopath who firmly believed in the superiority of science. This explains, perhaps, why I did not realize that TCM is a rational healing system developed and refined in

China over 5,000 years ago. By *rational* I mean it is a systematic medicine whose logic, diagnostic procedures, and treatment modalities are internally coherent and consistent – albeit radically different from Western notions of diseases and treatments.

Teaching this course gave me an opportunity to explore and reclaim an aspect of my cultural heritage. It allowed me to experiment with a form of teaching that attempts to overcome the body/mind split in intellectual endeavour that is an endemic part of university education. Finally, it helped me bring the public (my career and activism) and private (achieving balance and well-being) spheres of my life together.

Although I did not include TCM in 'Health and Illness' consciously as a way of introducing indigenous knowledge into the Western classroom, I did design the course as a way of disrupting students' 'commonsense' notions about health, the body, and what constitutes graduate education. My use of TCM corresponds to the editors' definition of indigenous knowledge, in that TCM is associated with the long-term occupancy of a place. In the present context, TCM also poses a challenge to what the editors are calling 'conventional knowledge.' As the editors rightly point out in their introduction, indigenous knowledges do not pertain only to the *content* of knowledge; they are also about *how* we know, *how* we learn and 'how our lives are both sustained year after year and transformed over time.' It follows that discourses on indigenous knowledges also have implications for teaching and learning, as I illustrate in this chapter. Furthermore, until Maoist China, Chinese medicine was seen as 'folk medicine' and was subordinated to allopathic medicine as a result of the process of colonization. Preparing and teaching the course made me more fully appreciative of how scientific knowledge has become disembodied and of how feminist and postcolonial scholarship participates in the privileging of the mind over the body. It allowed me to explore ways of re-embodying the knower as subject in scholarly pursuit.[2]

In this chapter, I first outline the content and pedagogical methods of the course. I offer considerable detail here to give the reader a sense of how TCM offers a different way of knowing and learning. I then discuss some of the limitations and problems involved in introducing such a different mode of learning into the conventional classroom. TCM shares some values with aboriginal knowledge in North America (see Couture's chapter in this collection). That being said, TCM is not a legitimate academic subject in the university (unlike Native Studies, which has been integrated into the higher education system, albeit with problems), and so presents a different kind of challenge to conventional knowledge. I end by discussing the possibility of including other systems of knowledge in educational contexts dominated by the Western rational scientific framework.

Course Design and Content

Since this is a course on health, illness, and the body, I begin the first class by asking the students to define health, healing, and illness. As I refined the course, I deleted the definition of illness from this initial exercise. This was after one student, a health educator for a labour union, explained that society's predominant notion of health is the absence of illness and that it is important for people to learn to conceptualize health beyond illness and disease.

The course proceeds on two assumptions: The first assumption is that our understanding of our bodies is mediated by the systems of knowledge, including medical knowledge, that are available to us. Thus, how we know our bodies changes as our knowledge base shifts. The second assumption is that different systems of healing allow, encourage, discourage, and prevent us from understanding our bodies in definite ways. Having made these assumptions, we are able to reach beyond Western notions, which in the modern era are shaped by scientific and medical knowledge systems, to see how health, illness, and the body are conceptualized and experienced in non-Western societies.

To accomplish this, I begin by introducing materials on health systems and healing practices from a variety of cultures (including Western cultures), beginning with homeopathy (see Weil, 1988, 1995, and Kaptchuk and Croucher, 1986, which are the texts used for the course). Students are often ignorant of the Western healing practices that fall outside of allopathy, such as osteopathy; and are amazed to find that faith healing (such as in Christian Science) is a Western healing practice. For many, these readings are a startling revelation. We then take a cursory look at healing systems in other cultures (e.g., Weil, 1988: Chs. 12–14; Kaptchuk and Croucher, 1986: Chs. 1–4; Stacey, 1988, Ch. 2; Mallock, 1990). A great deal of time is devoted to examining TCM to give students a deeper appreciation of how a different healing system can conceive of the body in a drastically different way. To this end, I offer readings, as well as physical exercises that are compatible with and part of the branch of TCM called 'Qi Gong' (for a rationale, see below).

In accordance with the standard graduate seminar format, the class spends much of the time discussing assigned readings, which are organized by topics. However, the emphasis is not on the structure and argument of the materials, rather, it is on how the readings alter the participants' original thinking (or not). Reflection is a key element and aim of the course. Participants, including myself, are encouraged to reflect constantly on how the experience of the course (in terms of readings, lectures, discussions, films, audiotapes, physical exercises, etc.) is changing how they think about health and the body – *their* body.

To accomplish this end, two reflective methods are used. First, I require the participants to keep a reading notebook, which serves as a record of the readings, lectures, and exercises. I ask them to use the following key words to guide their entries: (a) what I see/read/experience, (b) how I feel, and (c) what I think. Second, I ask the participants to keep a health journal – that is, a record of their physical and emotional health at least during the course. I ask that journal entries be made at least on a weekly basis, and preferably daily if students have a specific purpose in mind (for example, if someone wishes to use them to trace her menstruation cycle).

I encourage students to use the materials recorded in the notebook and health journal as 'data' for their term papers, especially if they wish to integrate their experiences into their scholarly inquiry or to explore writing as embodied subjects. For example, one student used her term paper to work through her experience of being sexually abused by her father; the paper was subsequently published (Transken, 1995) and is now part of the reading materials for the course. In fact, I now include the topic 'Learning to Write as Embodied Subjects' in the course content, and use pieces of social scientific writing (e.g., Paget, 1990; Wendell, 1993; Tansken, 1995) to legitimize this form of writing and to show how such an account can constitute more than a self-absorbed autobiography.

A common question raised by my students, and by others with whom I feel comfortable sharing my teaching methods, is why I selected TCM as a major area for exploration. As can been gleaned from the introduction, I have a personal attachment to TCM as a result of my cultural and medical history. But this is only a starting point. I decided to focus on TCM for several reasons.

First, I do not want to give students only a superficial glance at alternative healing practices by allocating a week for each healing system. This I characterize as the 'boutique approach' to knowledge acquisition (that is, you *wander* from one shop to another to purchase what you want/like). My intention is for the participants to gain a more in-depth understanding of a system other than allopathy so that they acquire some familiarity and comfort with a different set of concepts and theories. This knowledge base can then be used for reflecting on their health and body. Interestingly, this is not a point appreciated by all, in spite of my clear declaration of intent. Indeed, many do want a boutique approach.

My second reason for choosing TCM is that by now I have acquired a fair knowledge base of this healing system and so feel competent to incorporate it into my pedagogical repertoire. Apart from the ongoing (now somewhat irregular) consultations I have with a TCM physician and the readings I have done since 1990, I have also attended TCM seminars and workshops. Furthermore, I have taken up Tai Ji Juan and Qi Gong on a regular basis. Reading about TCM and learning Tai Ji Juan has motivated me to study Taoism as a philosophy and to relate it to TCM and other Chinese philosophies. Also, I receive regular shiatsu treatments[3] and insist that my therapist explain all the meridians and acupuncture points he works on, the point being to acquire an experiential knowledge of this treatment. Finally, having to teach TCM and Qi Gong has compelled me to study these related fields in more depth. In other words, as noted, the two separate domains of my life are now integrated. My professional and personal journeys are moving along the same trajectory, and thus this course is helping me with my own healthful journey.

My third reason for choosing a system such as TCM is that it is fundamentally different from allopathy and Western science. Whereas allopathy focuses on disease control and approaches body parts as discrete and mechanical (see Beinfield and Korngold, 1991), TCM focuses on disease prevention and health maintenance and perceives the body as an energetic entity whose parts are interrelated (for a contrast, see Kaptchuk, 1983: Chs. 1 and 10). When I first designed the course, I knew I wanted to juxtapose allopathy with a completely different system to draw attention to how our knowledge of the body is *really* mediated by epistemological presuppositions. Eastern healing systems present a dramatic contrast. At the time I became involved in TCM, I also began to explore other healing practices, such as Ayurveda and the Medicine Wheel; but I ruled out teaching them due to my lack of detailed knowledge. Also, I was concerned about cultural appropriation.[4] I feel a little this way with other medical systems.

In light of the above, TCM lends itself nicely to my overall academic goal and personal requirements. Most students have good things to say about its incorporation into this course:

As a North American-raised woman with persistent exposure to Western scientific medicine and thinking, Traditional Chinese Medicine and philosophy challenges my understanding of health and the environments within which I live and interact at the level of my body and beyond. (Herschler, 1996: 4)

For many years, I have felt a sense of hopelessness and disenchantment because Christianity offers no support for re-connecting with Nature; for understand its intrinsic value or why it so important to my spiritual and emotional well-being.[*sic*] Moreover, I have suffered with an ailment which allopathic medicine says exists only in my mind. Having thus reviewed the strengths of Chinese philosophy and medicine, I will begin the next phrase of my journey on the road to restoring balance in my own life. (Clover, 1996: 19)

What is TCM? According to some scholars and practitioners (Flaws 1992), traditional Chinese medicine (TCM) is a modern term that refers to a *style* of medicine that emerged after the Communist Revolution in 1949. Many of the healing practices have a common philosophical origin, one based in Taoism. That being said, prior to this time the modalities used varied according to local customs, plant life (in the case of herbology), and climatic conditions, to name only a few variants. It is perhaps because of its variability that Chinese medicine, like many other forms of indigenous medicine, never gained the visibility and prominence that allopathy did in the West.[5] The origins of TCM cannot be dated precisely. Although this *style* of medicine can be traced back to the late Han Dynasty, some scholars say that its current practices were created around 1953, while others argue that the conscious beginning of TCM occurred around the time of the Cultural Revolution (Flaws, 1992). In any case, TCM refers to a standardized style of medicine that is codified by means of common terms (such as the names of herbs and acupuncture points). The purpose was to establish a common system of communication and education among practitioners across the diverse regions of China, and to make it possible to transfer treatments as China established itself as a modern nation-state. TCM took the different regional styles of Chinese medicine and transformed them into a national standard style. In the process, those elements that were considered 'unscientific' or superstitious, such as astrology and geomancy, were eliminated from the mainstream of TCM. In modern China, TCM is composed of these aspects or branches: physical medicine (such as *tui na* massage), acupuncture, herbology, and diet and exercise (such as Qi Gong).

Some would argue that because TCM has now gained legitimacy as an alternative medicine vis-à-vis allopathy, it is no longer a form of indigenous knowledge. Certainly within China, TCM is a state-imposed form of medicine (alongside allopathy). However, I want to distinguish the practice of TCM from its philosophical roots. In 'Health and Illness' I use the conceptual aspect of TCM to establish a contrasting framework for exploring the implications of an embodied way of learning.[6]

Briefly, TCM is based on the Taoist principle of unity of opposites – Yin and Yang. According to Chinese creation myth, the universe in the beginning was an undifferentiated whole. Out of this emerged Yin–Yang: the world in its infinite forms (Beinfield and Korngold, 1991: 50–1). In both Taoism and TCM,

Yin–Yang is a symbolic representation of universal process (including health in the latter case) (Beinfield and Korngold, 1991; Kaptchuk 1983; Maciocia 1989). Kaptchuk puts it succinctly thus:

> Yin-Yang theory is well illustrated by the traditional Chinese Taoist symbol. The circle representing the whole is divided into Yin (black) and Yang (white).
> The small circles of opposite shading illustrate that within the Yin there is Yang and vice versa. The dynamic curve dividing them indicates that Yin and Yang are continuously merging. Thus Yin and Yang create each other, control each other, and transform into each other. (1983: 13)

The important thing to understand is that the two opposite states are not mutually exclusive or independent of each other. They are mutually dependent, and they change into each other (Maciocia, 1989: 2–6). Therefore extreme Yang becomes Yin and vice versa. Health is seen to be the balance of Yin–Yang aspects of the body, and disease is the imbalance between these aspects. This form of dialectical thinking is radically different from the causal linear thinking and logic of allopathy and positivist science. In TCM, the body is seen as a dynamic interaction of Yin and Yang; it is constantly changing and fluctuating.

Proceeding from this fundamental understanding of the nature of Yin–Yang, and of health as balance, TCM views illness not so much in terms of discrete diseases[7] as in terms of patterns of disharmony. Thus, TCM goes on to outline eight guiding principles for determining these patterns of disharmony (see Beinfield and Korngold, 1991: 77–80; Maciocia, 1989: Ch. 18). Again, these are not mutually exclusive, but can coexist in a person.

It is impossible to outline all the components of TCM theory in this chapter; therefore, I will highlight only those aspects of particular interest to my pedagogical purpose in 'Health and Illness.'

TCM differs greatly from Western medicine in how it conceptualizes the body. The Chinese conception of the body does not correspond in the least to Western anatomy. For example, Chinese medical theory does not have a concept of the nervous system; yet it can treat neurological disorders. It does not perceive an endocrine system; yet it is capable of correcting what allopathy calls endocrine disorders (Kaptchuk, 1983: 2–3). Although TCM makes reference to what the West recognizes as organs – the lungs, liver, stomach, and so on – these are not conceptualized as discrete physical structures and entities located in specific areas within the body. Rather, the term 'organs' is used to identify the functions associated with them. TCM does not distinguish between physical functions and the emotional and spiritual dimensions governed by the 'organ' in question. Furthermore, it describes organs not only in terms of their physiological processes and functions but also in terms of their orbs (i.e., spheres of influence).

The body, then, is conceptualized not so much in terms of distinct parts and components, as in terms of energy flow (Qi). Qi, a fundamental concept in TCM and Chinese thinking, is frequently translated as 'energy' or 'vital energy'; however, there is no Western term that precisely corresponds to it (Kaptchuk, 1983). Qi is what animates life (Beinfield and Korngold 1991: 30). Thus, while there is Qi, there is life; when there is no Qi, life ceases. It is both material and immaterial (Maciocia, 1989: 35–7). Qi is present in the universe in the air we breathe and in the breaths we take. It is the quality we share with all things, and thus connects the macrocosm with the microcosm. Qi flows in the body along lines of energy called 'meridians' or 'organ networks' (Beinfield and Korngold, 1991). Another way of conceptualizing disease is that it arises when Qi is not flowing smoothly, leading to blockage and stagnation, which if persistent will lead to disease (i.e., pathological changes in the body). Thus, an important part of the healing process is to unblock Qi and facilitate its free flow. Different treatment modalities (massage, acupuncture, and herbology) all aim at promoting the smooth flow of Qi and recovering balance.

Together with these notions of health and the body, the Chinese have developed exercise forms called Qi Gong (or *chi kung*, depending on the system of translation used). These exercises have been around for at least two millennia. Again, it is impossible to provide a comprehensive description of what Qi Gong entails in this limited space. Briefly, Qi Gong is a system of exercises aimed at regulating the breath, the mind, and the body simultaneously. There are literally thousands of forms of Qi Gong, from sitting postures similar to what the West recognizes as meditation, to Tai Ji Juan, which in its most advanced form is a martial art aimed at honing the body/mind to respond to external attack without force. Indeed, Qi Gong is a recommended exercise form in TCM and is taught widely as a healing art in China.[8]

Practitioners of Qi Gong believe that by disciplining, activating, and regulating the normally automatic, involuntary way of breathing, they are able to regulate and alter other functions of the body such as heartbeat, blood flow, and other physical and emotional functions. Thus, Qi Gong is not simply a physical exercise, but 'gives physiological and psychological balance and the balance of *yin* and *yang*' (Zi, 1986: 3).

During the course, as a complement to the assigned readings on TCM, I conduct Qi Gong exercises. The purpose is to integrate the body with the mind not only in theory but also in practice.

'Health and Illness' begins with gentle stretching and breathing. The purpose is to direct attention to the parts of the body that are normally ignored in carrying out intellectual activities. Then I introduce some simple Qi Gong exercises that activate most major meridians, and ask students for feedback regarding how they feel. I also encourage them to record their sensations and reactions in the notebook and health journal and to observe physical and emotional changes over time as they practise the exercises.

This part of the class lasts about thirty minutes, gradually increasing to about an hour as the course progresses. The aim is to reach a balance between the practice of Qi Gong and discussions of the readings.

While conducting the exercises, I explain how the Chinese perceive the body in terms of meridian theory (which is explored through readings later in the course), as well as the reasoning behind the exercises. For instance, to complement the readings on the Five Element Theory of TCM, I teach a set of Qi Gong exercises called the Five Seasons Exercise, which corresponds to the major meridians of Lung (autumn), Kidney (winter), Liver (spring), Heart (summer), and Spleen (late summer).[9]

This exercise begins with autumn. The movements of the autumn exercise are aimed at stretching and contracting the Lung meridian (i.e., the line of energy flow that influences the function of the lungs). The Lung is the body's first line of defence against the external environment. Autumn signals the end of the summer and the movement into winter, when we are more susceptible to invasion by cold, which can lead to colds and flus. Strengthening the Lung reduces the likelihood that we will encounter these maladies.

I talk about acupuncture as a treatment modality in TCM, and about the location of selected acupuncture points and their functions, and I show students how to find these points on their bodies in relation to these exercises. Through this kind of experiential learning, students obtain a different view of the body and are encouraged to acknowledge and value their physical/emotional experiences in addition to their intellectual experience. As well, in an attempt to close the body/mind divide, I ask the students to use their experiences in the exercises to reflect on the course's readings and discussions.

Problems, Limitations, and Possibilities

Space does not permit a thorough discussion of the problems and limitations that 'Health and Illness' encounters and the possibilities it offers. In this section I will list some of the issues arising from the course for myself and for the students. Resolving these issues and improving the course is an ongoing process that will continue beyond the discussion here.

Conceptually, the structure of the course seems quite ideal. In practice, it doesn't always work. In fact, student evaluations of the course in the first couple of years were mainly negative. The major reason, judging from student feedback, was that the two parts of the course (reading and discussion, and physical exercises) did not relate clearly enough to each other. Some students complained that the purpose of the exercises was unclear. I now make a much more conscious attempt in the first few weeks to state why we are doing the exercises and how they connect to the unit on TCM they will encounter later on in the course.

At least three pedagogical issues are reflected here. The first is student expectations, which have been built up through their educational experiences. Students expect to be told, even at the graduate level, that there is *one* right way (to feel, to know, etc.), and they are uncomfortable with the possibility that there is more than one version of 'truth.' The notion that there is certainty in scientific knowledge, be it in education or medicine, is so ingrained that it is almost impossible to shake this belief even when people's experiences run contrary to this dominant belief. This shows precisely the hegemonic power of scientific knowledge as it is normally transmitted, and how scientific knowledge becomes normalized and thus hegemonic – becomes 'common sense' (see Ng, 1993 and 1995). When our bodily sensations are rendered irrelevant to the intellectual process, the result is a mind/body split (see e.g., Walkerdine, 1988; Levine, 1991).

With this educational ethos, students learn not to trust their own feelings. They want to be told how they are supposed to feel, and when I tell them they feel what they feel, that feelings cannot be prescribed, they initially get very upset. The fact that each person may experience the sensation triggered by an acupuncture point or the Qi Gong exercise differently, that experience is not uniform, is unsettling. As well, students find it difficult to take the exercises on faith and to trust their feelings in the beginning of the course without an accompanying theoretical framework (which they will learn over the duration of 'Health and Illness').

A third issue the exercises raise involves body image. Drawing the body into an academic subject experientially evokes people's preconceived ideas about body image – *their* image of *their* own body, which may or may not conform to the cultural ideal. The principles and practice of Qi Gong disrupt our internalized notion of the ideal body – a process too complex to describe here. Suffice to say that physical exercises that raise questions about body image can be extremely personal *and* political.

As a result of feedback from students, I now incorporate readings from different Western philosophical traditions and scientific paradigms into the course (e.g., Paget, 1990; Moore, 1992; Chopra, 1989). The aim here is to expose students to different ways of knowing within the West, in addition to familiarizing them with non-Western healing systems.

A more serious charge is that what I am doing is not scholarly. This charge implies that knowledges that do not conform to the accepted form and content of 'science' and scholarship are inappropriate for graduate school.

It is interesting and revealing that some students cannot not see that some of the materials we cover based on phenomenology (Paget, 1990) and quantum mechanics (Weil, 1998; Chopra, 1989), as well as the growing literature on the sociology of the body (Turner, 1992; Schilling, 1993), are theoretical – albeit from different paradigms than positivism. It is not surprising that they find it hard to accept alternative forms of knowledge as legitimate and do not appreciate that TCM has its own, admittedly different, theoretical foundation.

These students' comments should not be treated as deviant or ignorant. In fact, they represent the prevalent view of education – that it involves the transmission of a set of agreed upon (by whom?) information. Paulo Freire (1970) has called this the 'banking' method of education. Rather than viewing education and knowledge production as a contested process, the assumption is that there is only one version of reality that is truthful and scientific, and thus legitimate. Also, what constitutes 'research' is defined narrowly. In his latest book, *Spontaneous Healing*, Andrew Weil (1995), an allopathic physician and Professor of Medicine at the University of Arizona College of Medicine, recommends the use of anecdotes, especially those pertaining to spontaneous healing, as a starting point for medical investigation into the healing process. He asserts that in its preoccupation with clinical trials (mainly for drug-based therapy), contemporary medical research has consistently ignored how people activate their bodies' innate healing processes. These processes must become an area central to scientific inquiry if medicine is to begin concerning itself with healing rather than with disease control.[10]

Thus, one limitation of introducing alternative forms of knowledge into a mainstream educational setting is that they will always be resisted and delegitimized. This will happen, I conclude, however excellent the materials and pedagogical skills of the teacher may be.

Meanwhile, I suggest that 'Health and Illness' indeed disrupts hegemonic knowledge precisely *because* it is unexpected and foreign. Sociologist Donald Levine (1991) describes the pros and cons, and results, of incorporating aikido, a Japanese martial art, into his course 'Conflict Theory and Aikido.' He argues that although at first glance the Western discipline of sociology and an Eastern martial art form seem completely incompatible, in fact students learn, through experience on the mat, an entirely different understanding of the nature of conflict and its resolution. Although 'Health and Illness' contains different materials and has different pedagogical goals from Levine's course, it is precisely the juxtaposing of the East and West in both courses that presents both a challenge to standard modes of knowledge acquisition and an opening for traditional knowledges to be inserted into Western educational settings. Some of the participants in 'Health and Illness' (Spring 1995 – the same class where I received two negative reviews) commented on their personal growth – particularly in learning to integrate physical activity back into academic processes, learning the politics of health care in Canada, experiencing journal writing, connecting personal experience and growth with theory, and critiquing positivist reasoning. Some enjoyed the practicum in the course as a refreshing change, and suggested that the exercise portion of the course be increased.

Another problem encountered when introducing TCM and Qi Gong into a mainstream Western educational setting is that it has the potential to reduce both East and West to caricatures. The danger is that the stereotypes of both allopathic medicine and TCM may be reinforced (and perhaps even produced). This is especially so given the short school term (twelve or thirteen weeks) and class durations between two-and-a-half and three hours (depending on the instructor's preferences). The time available makes it difficult to delve into any topic in much detail. I have tried to counter this tendency by not assessing either allopathy or TCM in relation to each other. The spring term of 1995 was the last time I used materials that explicitly criticized allopathic medicine. This was partly due to the negative reactions from students (some of whom were totally committed to the efficacy of allopathy and Western science), and partly due to the fact that this approach created a dichotomy of the two healing systems that need not exist. Given the dominance of allopathy in our society, any healing method that does not fit into its accepted treatment model tends to be seen as 'naturally' oppositional rather than complementary.

I rely on students' comments in class discussions to further our understanding of the complexity of each healing system. Example: the issue of cultural appropriation was raised as an opportunity to open up a discussion on how TCM may be understood and used in a context dominated by Western knowledge. In this way we also explore the history of colonialism and the political economy of health care in Canada.

Conclusion

I began this chapter by describing my own need to integrate the two previous separate spheres of exploration in my life. When I took up TCM personally for health reasons, and later on when I incorporated it into my professional and academic life, I discovered as a feminist antiracist educator a different way to rupture what I have called elsewhere 'common sense knowledge,' and to do so without having to define alternative epistemologies and ontologies merely as a critique of Western scientific knowledge. In the process of developing, refining, and teaching 'Health and Illness,' I have reintegrated my life.

Thus for myself and for some students in the course, 'Health and Illness' is ultimately about empowerment, in the authentic rather than the rhetorical sense of the word. One student concluded her term paper with the following remarks:

> My participation in this journey of self-discovery and the opportunities I have been given to be self-reflective, self-critical and self-aware are what has given me the insight to my mind and body, health and illness. However, it is those types of processes that we avoid when we look entirely outside of ourselves, to the 'experts' to tackle our problems on our behalf. (Roberts, 1996: 22)

In spite of or because of the resistance and difficulties I encountered in teaching 'Health and Illness,' it is clear that teaching TCM as an indigenous healing system is one way of disrupting commonsense assumptions about science and education. As I have tried to show in this chapter, the conceptual foundation of TCM and Qi Gong offers a means of bridging the body/mind divide as well as the divide between the personal and the theoretical, which have become taken for granted in the scientific knowledge that is endemic to Western education, especially in North America. Obviously, what I do in 'Health and Illness' is not the only way of disrupting the dominant knowledge system. It does, however, offer an alternative, as well as some tools for us to break out of the confines of 'conventional knowledge.'

NOTES

My friend and TCM physician, David Bray, has been endlessly supportive in my personal and professional journey. He has read and commented on many versions of this chapter. I also thank the editors, especially Dorothy Goldin Rosenberg, for their helpful comments on an earlier draft. But needless to say, I alone am responsible for its shortcomings.

1 I am using *allopathy* or *allopathic medicine* to refer to biomedicine, in recognition of the fact that Western medicine is made up of two branches: homeopathy (treatments based on the principles of 'like cures like' and the administration of minimal dosages) and allopathy (commonly perceived as the totality of Western medicine, which since the turn of the century has relied increasingly on drug therapy and surgery). For an introduction to these systems, see Weil (1988) and Kaptchuk and Croucher (1986).

2 Due to space constraints, I cannot elaborate on how 'malestream' (O'Brien, 1981) knowledge dominates Western intellectual thought, which bifurcates the body and the mind (Bordo, 1987; Smith, 1987). For the privileging of mental over manual labour, see Marx and Engels (1970).

3 Shiatsu is a form of massage developed in Japan that involves pressure placed on meridians and acupuncture points. It is distinct from Swedish massage, which is concerned with muscle manipulation.

4 Term paper by Abby Hershler, 1996. See references.

5 One central force, too complex to describe here in detail but nevertheless significant, that led to the disappearance of many traditional healing systems is the expansion of Western, notably British, imperialism in Asia (see Shroff in this volume).

6 Interestingly, as I was writing the first draft of this chapter, a student was writing a critique of the course, which she titled 'Body as Content and Pedagogy' (Gustafson 1997). In it she discussed both her resistance to the course and the insights gained from it. The paper was subsequently published (Gustafson, 1998).

7 Here I make a distinction between illness and disease, following Kaptchuk's definition: 'Illness is the state of a patient, beyond discomfort, but defined in the patient's terms. Disease is an objective condition, independent of the patient's judgement, which many medical models often assume to be the whole of illness' (Kaptchuck and Croucher, 1986: 9).

8 See 'The Mystery of Chi,' the first in a six-part series *Healing and the Mind*, narrated by Bill Moyer.

9 The Chinese calendar is divided into five seasons, with two summer seasons (early and late summer), not four seasons as in the West.

10 One recent branch of allopathic medicine that does investigate how the mind affects soma is PNI (Psycho-neuro Immunology), more popularly known as body/mind medicine.

REFERENCES

Beinfield, H., and E. Korngold, 1991. *Between Heaven and Earth: A Guide to Chinese Medicine*. New York: Ballantine Books.

Bordo, S.R. 1987. *The Flight to Objectivity: Essays on Cartesianism & Culture*. New York: State University of New York Press.

Chopra, D. 1989. *Quantum Healing: Exploring the Frontiers of Mind/Body Medicine*. New York: Bantam Books.

Clover, D.E. 1996. Environmental Related Illness and Disharmony: Re/creating Positive Relationships Through Traditional Chinese Medicine. Term paper for

'Health, Illness, and Knowledge of the Body: Education and the Self-Learning Process,' OISE. December.

Flaws, B. 1992. *Before Completion: Essays on the Practice of TCM*. Boulder: Blue Poppy Press.

Freire, P. 1970. *Pedagogy of the Oppressed*. New York: Herder and Herder.

Gustafson, D. 1997. The body as content and pedagogy. Unpublished ms., OISE.

– 1998. Embodied Learning about Health and Healing: Involving the Body as Content and Pedagogy. *Canadian Woman Studies* 17(4): 52–5.

Herschler, A. 1996. Health, Traditional Chinese Medicine and Our Bodies. Letter to Marianne Cheng. Term paper for 'Health, Illness, and Knowledge of the Body: Education and the Self-Learning Process,' OISE. December.

Kaptchuk, T. 1983. *The Web that Has No Weaver: Understanding Chinese Medicine*. New York: Congdon and Weed.

Kaptchuk, T., and M. Croucher. 1986. *The Healing Arts: A Journey Through the Faces of Medicine*. London: British Broadcasting Corporation.

Levine, D.N. 1991. 'Martial Arts as a Resource for Liberal Education: The Case of Aikido.' In M. Featherstone, M. Hepworth, and B. Turner (Eds.), *The Body: Social Process and Cultural Theory*. London: Sage.

Maciocia, G. 1989. *The Foundations of Chinese Medicine. A Comprehensive Text for Acupuncturists and Herbalists*. London: Churchill Livingstone.

Mallock, L. 1990. Indian Medicine, Indian Health: Study between Red and White Medicine. *Canadian Woman Studies* 10(2 & 3): 105–12.

Marx, K., and F. Engels. 1970. *The German Ideology*. New York: International Publishers.

Moore, T. 1992. *Care Of the Soul: A Guide for Cultivating Depth and Sacredness in Everyday Life*. New York: HarperCollins.

Ng, R. 1993. A Woman Out of Control: Deconstructing Sexism and Racism in the University. *Canadian Journal of Education* 18(3): 189–205.

– 1995. 'Teaching Against the Grain: Contradictions and Possibilities.' In R. Ng, P. Staton, and J. Scane (eds.), *Anti-Racism, Feminism, and Critical Approaches to Education*. Westport, CT: Bergin & Garvey.

O'Brien, M. 1981. *The Politics of Reproduction*. London: Routledge and Kegan Paul.

Paget, A.M. 1990. Life Mirrors Work Mirrors Text Mirrors Life ... *Social Problems* 37(2): 137–48.

Roberts, M. 1996. Stress: How It Led the Way for a Journey of Self-Discovery. Term paper for 'Health, Illness, and Knowledge of the Body: Education and the Self-Learning Process,' OISE. 23 December.

Schilling, C. 1993. *The Body and Social Theory*. London: Sage.

Smith, D.E. 1987. *The Everyday World as Problematic: A Feminist Sociology*. Toronto: University of Toronto Press.

Stacey, M. 1988. *The Sociology of Health and Healing.* London: Unwin Hyman.

Transken, S. 1995. *Reclaiming Body Territory.* Ottawa: CRIAW.

Turner, B.S. 1992. *Regulating Bodies. Essays in Medical Sociology.* London: Routledge.

Walkerdine, V. 1988. *The Mastery of Reason: Cognitive Development and the Production of Rationality.* London: Routledge.

Weil, A. 1988. *Health and Healing.* Boston: Houghton Mifflin. (Revised and updated from 1983.)

– 1995. *Spontaneous Healing.* New York: Fawcett Columbine.

Wendell, S. 1993. Feminism, Disability and Transcendence of the Body. *Canadian Woman Studies* 12(4): 116–22.

Zi, N. 1986. *The Art of Breathing.* New York: Bantam Books.

11

Not So Strange Bedfellows: Indigenous Knowledge, Literature Studies, and African Development

HANDEL KASHOPE WRIGHT

Certain Afrocentric[1] advances in the fields of development studies and literature studies can, in combination, create a discursive environment in which it is
possible for literature studies to contribute significantly to the development
process in Africa. While development praxis began as a purely economics
based field, virtually every contemporary school of thought on the matter
would incorporate a human element in its conception of development and
would regard education as an integral tool in fostering development. However,
literature is probably one of the last fields of study that comes to mind when one
considers disciplines that could contribute to the development process. Given
that literature has been perceived as and indeed has operated as an élitist,
insular, aesthetics-driven discipline, while development discourse has been
perceived as and has operated as a purely utilitarian, economics-based discipline, the notion that the two might have much to do with each other appears
nothing short of ludicrous at first blush. I hope to illustrate nonetheless that
recent Afrocentric reconceptions of the nature, aims, and functions of both
literature studies and development suggest not only that these two fields are
compatible but also that literature studies can contribute substantially to both
development studies and the development process in Africa.

What Has Literature Got to Do with It?

This chapter is both inspired by and based on Chinua Achebe's 1988 essay,
'What Has Literature Got to Do With It?'[2] In it he illustrates that literature can
make a contribution to the discourse and process of development in Africa. The
title indicates his acute awareness that literature studies and development are
not traditionally associated with each other.[3] In bringing the two together,
Achebe is engaging in an exercise in what could be called 'utilitarian litera-

ture.'[4] In other words, he illustrates how an Afrocentric version of the tradition-ally anti-utilitarian discourse of literature can be appropriated and made to serve the cause of a decidedly utilitarian development discourse.

After identifying development (or as he prefers, modernization) as the undisputed comprehensive goal of 'developing' countries, Achebe points out that what is in dispute is 'the quickest and safest route for the journey into modernization and what items should make up the traveller's rather limited baggage allowance' (Achebe, 1988: 106). To illustrate his stance that literature can contribute to development theory and practice, Achebe provides us with the following couplet:

> There! we have it on the best authority
> Theorists of development cannot agree! (1988: 109)

Here Achebe has chosen quite deliberately to make a point about develop-ment theory and praxis through poetry. Although the example is playful and rather perfunctory, it brings to the surface a point that underscores the entire essay, namely that literature (in this specific case, poetry) can be pressed into the service of discussions around development.

Conventional notions of development equate modernization with Westerni-zation. In contrast, Achebe is arguing that the maintenance and utilization of traditions in general, and 'orature' in particular, need not be in opposition to the processes of modernization.[5] When the processes of modernization, cosmopolitanization, and the creation of a modern identity (on the one hand), are made to confront the processes of traditionalization and the retrieval of a long-established, now-threatened traditional identity (on the other hand), a viable and productive paradox has been constucted. One needs the rootedness of the latter, he argues, to balance the venturism and uncertainty of the former.

However, Achebe does not perceive traditional culture as purely stagnant; nor does he view it as a restrictive force of conformity. In fact he employs a revised notion of traditional culture in illustrating how tradition can be more than a source of stability and can actually *promote* change. Taking up Igbo parables as literature,[6] Achebe illustrates that orature can not only explain the status quo of social values but also, in some cases, instigate revolutionary social change: 'Stories can combine in a most admirable manner the aesthetic quali-ties of a successful work of imagination with those homiletic virtues demanded of active definers and custodians of society's values. But we must not see the role of literature only in terms of providing latent support for things as they are, for it does also offer the kinetic energy necessary for social transition and change' (1988: 115).

Thus Achebe sees orature playing a dual role in relation to development. It serves as a stabilizing force by providing proven and reliable values and perspectives as Africans launch into the uncertain and destabilizing processes of modernization. Yet at the same time, orature serves as a *catalyst* for change, by pointing to the need for change, and indicating the directions in which society should be moving, and why.

Having reviewed Achebe's arguments, I now intend to build on his project of indicating how literature studies can make a contribution to the discourse and process of development. For example, Achebe operates with a revised definition of literature that incorporates African orature, and with a revised definition of development that extends beyond economic concerns to deal with the world views and spiritual, cultural, and sociopolitical well-being of African peoples. It is important to provide a context and history for these 'redefinitions' and for some of the stances he takes in order to illustrate not only that they do have precedents but also, and more importantly, that they are viable. My intention here is to undertake a more systematic approach that deals with six specific issues. The first two (the redefinition of literature and its function in society, and the redefinition of development) are background issues; the last four (African collectivity; self-reliance; democracy, social difference, and justice; and the development of orality and literacy) are issues that Achebe either does not include in his discussion or only touches on without any in-depth discussion.

(Re)defining Literature and Its Role in Society

We live in a time when the commonsense notion of what 'valid knowledge' is being strongly challenged. In particular, the dominance of patriarchal, Eurocentric knowledge is being challenged by the newly emerging discourses of identity politics (such as feminism and Afrocentrism), and by postmodernist, poststructuralist, and postcolonialist reconceptions of the world. It is a time, therefore, in which the traditional practices of both literature studies and development are under attack.

As far as literature studies is concerned, theory and criticism used to depend on literature for their existence and to be their servants; but they have since declared their independence and now seemingly shun literature as an old, distant, and irrelevant relative. This is a time when critics like Eagleton (1983) have actually called for the death of literature; Marrouchi (1991) has gone further and boldly declared, 'literature is dead, long live theory.' The virtually miasmic spread of indulgence in theorizing, apparently as an end in itself, and the related rapid proliferation of theories (especially in the West) has been described disparagingly by Christian (1990) as a Eurocentric 'race for theory.' Meanwhile, the new discourses of media studies and cultural studies threaten to make literature studies redundant in the West, and the economic and political crises in Africa and the consequent emphasis on technological and infrastructural development threaten to render it an ostentatious indulgence in African institutions. It is little wonder, therefore, that Kernan (1990) has warned that far from being the wishful thinking of a few madcap professors, the death of literature is in fact imminent and can only be stayed by a reconceptualization of literature and its role in society. What is clear from all of this is that literature as a field of study can no longer afford its traditional insularity, élitism, and exclusivity, nor its universalist, 'apolitical' aim to simply 'instruct through delight.'

Many African writers and critics from Soyinka (1976) to Nkosi (1981), Izevbaye (1971), and Onoge (1982) have insisted that African literature is political and utilitarian. As Izevbaye asserts: 'Many English-speaking African writers accept the notion that African art is functional ... and therefore the concept of art for art's sake should not be allowed to take root in African critical thought' (1971: 25). These writers and critics are concerned with what literature can contribute to addressing issues dealing with Africans' world views and gnosis, and issues of social, cultural, and political concern to Africans, whether on an individual, communal, regional, or continental level.

Unfortunately, this utilitarian orientation has not characterized what has emerged as the dominant approach to literature studies in Africa. African critics have too often developed their criticism individually, much like European critics, and the tendency in African classrooms has been to utilize Western approaches to literature and literature studies. As a result, all literature studies – including studies of African literature – are characterized by insularity, élitism, and hyperliteracy. If the study of literature is to survive and thrive in Africa, it will have to be decolonized and removed from the Eurocentric, 'apolitical' tradition.[7] Also, it will have to be reconceptualized to make it more relevant to the experiences, values, norms, and world views of Africans. Finally, it will have to become a means for interrogating, celebrating, and contributing to the development of African cultures and societies. In short, literature studies must become Afrocentric.

The project of constructing Afrocentric literature studies started in the 1920s with the work of the Negritude poets and critics, who included Cesaire, Damas, and Senghor. More recently, the work of Ngugi (e.g., wa Thiong'o, 1986) exemplifies the overt and sustained effort to decolonize and Africanize literature, criticism, and literature studies in Africa. The following are some of the characteristics of an evolving Afrocentric literary practice. First, it does not have the élitist aim to instruct through delight; rather, it embraces the more utilitarian aim of celebrating, interrogating, and transforming African culture in an Afrocentric project of possibility. Second, it rebels against the traditional

Eurocentric emphasis on aesthetics and suppression of utilitarian value; how-ever, it does not take up function as an exclusive end in itself by declaring, as Bennett (1990) does, that aesthetics is really useless knowledge. Rather, draw-ing on traditional African perceptions of art and performance, it recognizes that aesthetics and utilitarian value are closely if not inextricably linked, and steers a course between what sometimes becomes narrow African functionalist criti-cism on the one hand and traditional Eurocentric, 'apolitical' criticism on the other. Third, it replaces the Eurocentric preoccupation with the individual in the creation and appreciation of literature, with an Afrocentric notion of social and communal motivation, creativity, and appreciation. Fourth, it reverses the traditional Western hierarchization that assumes the superiority of written over oral forms and that conceives of drama (especially as performance) as a dubious genre of literature situated on the fringes of fiction and poetry. The call to recognize the central place of orature in African ceremonial and everyday life has been made by Aidoo (see Elder, 1987) and Okpewho (1992), among others.

(Re)definitions of Development

Before attempting to illustrate how such a revised notion of literature studies can contribute to the development process in Africa, it is necessary to identify and outline the concept of development being employed here, since there exists a bewildering plethora of definitions and approaches to development. As Black points out, development 'has no precise meaning, no generally accepted defini-tion ... Like other terms that have acquired a positive connotation, development is user-friendly: It means whatever one wants or needs it to mean' (1991: 1). Although Black is right about the ambiguity and adaptability of the term development, other theorists would disagree strongly with her description of the term as 'user-friendly' and would consider its malleability a negative characteristic – one which masks its nature as a dangerous ideology. Sachs (1992: 6), for example, describes development as 'a concept full of emptiness' and points out that 'development thus has no content but it does have a function: it allows any intervention to be sanctified in the name of a higher, evolutionary goal. Watch out!'

Some African development theorists would agree with Sachs. In fact, the term development has become quite controversial in contemporary Africa as elsewhere in the world, partly because it suggests the existence of something in some countries (i.e., the developed world) and a lack of that thing in others (i.e., developing or least developed countries). A hierarchy of advancement is thus created that comes uncomfortably close to suggesting a hierarchy among civilizations.

In the 1950s development was taken to be a purely economic concept, one that took per capita income as the chief indicator of level of development and gross domestic product as the conventional tool for measuring growth. As a field of study, development involved the economic analysis of the processes of modernization. In more recent times, the purely economics-based notion of development has come under considerable attack from some intellectuals. For example, Sachs has written what he calls a guide to the ruins of development. His play on the term *ruin* suggests both the ruin that narrow, economics-based conceptions of development have wrought on the 'Third World,' and that this concept is antiquated, dangerously narrow, and counterproductive and is or ought to be in ruins. Marxists like Sachs see the economics-based discourse of development as one that continues to be utilized in the exploitation of certain parts of the world. This process started through colonization and is now manifest in the unequal and exploitative relations existing between the North and the South – a status quo arising from the machinations of global capitalism and the 'world market.' From its purely economistic definition of poverty to its destruction of subsistence economies, from its hierarchical, imperialistic assumptions (Western modernization being a norm to be imposed on the rest of the world) to its failure to benefit rural populations even where it produces increases in gross domestic product, from its ever-changing focus to its declining significance in the 'new world order' in which the watchword of the only remaining superpower (and the North in general) is now 'security,' from its promotion of dependence on the part of developing countries to its destruction of self-sufficient, small-scale economies in the name of raw material production for the 'world market,' development has been decried as too malleable, contradictory, and paternalistic, and as counterproductive. As Sachs concludes: 'The idea of development was once a towering monument inspiring international enthusiasm. Today, the structure is falling apart and in danger of total collapse. But its imposing ruins still linger over everything and block the way out. The task, then, is to push the rubble aside and open up new ground' (1992: 6).

While they would share Sachs's criticisms of the discourse and process of development, progressive African development theorists seem less ready to accept his recommended solution – namely, a simple and complete abrogation of the term and a rejection of the practice of development. Dei, for example, points out: 'I do not think replacing development with another terminology is the answer, [rather] I do recognise that perhaps there is an urgent need to deconstruct what conventional development has come to mean and to reconstruct what contemporary development could more appropriately be for local peoples' (Dei, 1992a: 5).

Here Dei chooses to step inside/outside the discourse and praxis of development to insist on both a deconstruction and a reconstruction of development.[8]

Adedeji shares this position, and in the following critique of 'structural adjust-ment' (the currently popular model of development being applied in and imposed on Africa and the Third World in general), outlines in broad strokes what a reconceptualization of development might entail in terms of goals:

> Africa needs fundamental change and transformation, not just adjustment. The change and transformation required are not just narrow, economic and mechani-cal ones. They are the broader and fundamental changes that will bring about, over time, the new Africa of our vision where there is development and economic justice, not just growth; where there is democrcay and accountability not just despotism, authoritarianism and kleptocracy; and where the governed and their governments are moving hand-in-hand in the promotion of the common good, and where it is the will of the people rather than the wishes of one person or a group of persons, however powerful, that prevails. (1990: 37)

African Collectivity

As far as African collectivity is concerned, Africa already has organizations such as the Organization of African Unity, the Economic Community of West African States (ECOWAS), and the Intergovernmental Authority on Drought and Development (IGADD) in the horn of Africa. Shaw (1992) and Ramphal (quoted in Shaw, 1992), among others, strongly believe that despite some of the shortcomings and failures of some attempts, regional co-operation is vital to fostering development in Africa. As far as some of those shortcomings are concerned, I believe that attempts at creating collectivity are limited and limiting because they are too often restricted to economic collectivity. I feel strongly that adding and or taking seriously the sociocultural dimension to such organizations will enhance better understanding between the peoples involved (as opposed to only the governments), and will create a more comprehensive unity among Africans and enhance the possibilities for economic collectivity to succeed. Literature education as it is reconceptualized here could contribute substantially to this process by enabling students to study the societies and cultures of other African countries through works from those countries. The African literature sections of the West African 'O' and 'A' Level literature syllabuses (see WAEC, 1988) are an example of how the literature of African peoples can be disseminated all over Africa. What needs to be done is to emphasize the cultural aspects of such texts, as opposed to merely taking them up as literature and looking for 'universal' literary items such as character, style, and plot.

Furthermore, there is a need to share and compare elements of African orature between ethnic groups and across national and regional boundaries.

While the sharing of literature (in its traditional sense) would be restricted to situations of formal schooling, orature could be taken up in formal education and also used in community-based discussions. Although aspects of orature are often taken up informally in schools (specifically at the primary level), many African countries (e.g., Sierra Leone) do not include orature in their formal school curricula. Some countries, however, such as Kenya, do include orature, not merely as part of extracurricular activities, and not only at the primary level, but also at the secondary level. In fact the Kenyan secondary school syllabus includes oral literature as an aspect of literature studies at every level of secondary education, from form one to 'O' Level (Kenya Institute of Education, 1992; Ministry of Education, 1992). The following are sample extracts from the Kenyan Ministry of Education syllabus:

FORM I
5.0 LITERATURE ...
5.12 Oral Literature
Oral literature should help the learner to appreciate the cultural roots of his society and equip him with a critical and creative awareness of his dynamic environment. The learner should note that Oral Literature can be an effective tool in enhancing other writing skills e.g. narrative compositions.

The following are some of the genres of Oral Literature:

* oral narratives;
* poems (sung and recited);
* proverbs;
* riddles;
* tongue twisters;
* children's games.

5.13 Field work
In this course, fieldwork is an important activity in the learning of oral literature. The learner is expected to carry out field-work of a limited nature. He should collect oral narratives, poems, proverbs, riddles, songs, tongue twisters, children's games etc from the immediate social environment and present to his class for discussion. It should be noted that discussions at this level should be aimed at the learner's enjoyment and not for serious analysis. Oral literature materials collected should be stored in folders for future use. [p. 53]

FORM IV
19.12 Oral literature
The study of oral literature in form four as in form three should aim at developing the

learner's ability to analyse literary aspects such as narrative and dramatic techniques, creating of atmosphere, time, form and style. The oral literature material so far collected should be used in training the learner to acquire the techniques of transcription, translation and analysis of material.

During discussions on the collected materials, the learner should be encouraged to perform his materials in class. [p. 64]

The extracts indicate that oral literature as it conceptualized in the Kenyan curriculum already has in place several of the characteristics that indicate it has some potential to contribute to development studies and practice. However, the framework within which oral literature is taken up still appears to conceptualize literature as a superior form to which oral literature should aspire.[9] The schism that exists between indigenous educational systems and modern, Eurocentric education is a matter not only of educational concern but also of vital sociocultural and communal concern. Modern education has resulted in the displacement of traditional teachers, the loss or devaluation of traditional values, and the creation of a schism between older and younger generations. The following words from a Dinka chief, quoted in Deng, speak to all these issues:

> Educated youth have pushed us aside saying that there is nothing we know. Even if an elder talks of the important things of the country, they say, 'There is nothing you know.' How can there be nothing we know when we are their fathers? Did we not bear them ourselves? When we put them in school, we thought they would learn new things to add to what we, their elders, would pass on to them. We hoped they would listen to our words and then add to them the new words of learning. But now it is said that there is nothing we know. This has really saddened our hearts very much. (1978: 106–7)

What the Dinka elders had hoped for was a happy marriage of the distinct systems of education. Instead, Western-influenced schooling has rendered both them and traditional education redundant. Ngugi wa Thiong'o (1981) is one African literary and cultural figure who has called for traditional knowledge to be introduced into the Western-style educational system. What I am proposing here is a concrete measure that would make the two systems complementary and that would actually integrate elements of traditional education into formal schooling.

Several changes are necessary before oral literature as it is conceptualized here can be transformed into orature as an aspect of cultural studies and thereby contribute significantly to development studies and practice. Of particular importance is the element of performance: the requirement that students collect and perform orature will mean that orature is taken up not merely as text to be read (as in literature) but as text to be performed. This is an element that would make oral literature akin to orature as cultural studies. What needs to change are the aims of 'studying' orature and the means of introducing orature into the school setting.

In terms of the aims of orature, it is interesting to note that at present in the lower grades, the aim is to 'help the learner to appreciate the cultural roots of his society and equip him [sic] with a critical and creative awareness of his dynamic environment.' Students are merely supposed to 'enjoy themselves' and not study orature seriously. At the upper levels (form IV), however, the aim is to develop 'the learner's ability to analyse literary aspects such as narrative and dramatic techniques, creating of atmosphere, time, form and style.' It is at this level that students are meant to study orature seriously. These aims are reflective of a literary framework in which the overall aim is to get students to take up orature as literature: serious analysis is represented by elements of literary analysis, while nonserious analysis is represented by links between orature and community. A cultural studies approach would demand the exact opposite: the aim at the higher levels of schooling would be to examine orature for what it says about different community values in a country or in Africa in general – to make those stories and values part of the curriculum (to be learned as well as interrogated). It is aims such as this which are ultimately of the most importance and which are linked to sociocultural analysis and African collectivity. At the lower levels, students can be introduced to the performance criteria (which need not be the literary elements mentioned in the current curriculum). These elements are important for understanding the forms and should be the foundation on which more complex sociocultural and political analysis would later be based.

In terms of introducing orature into schools, the present curriculum demands that the students collect the stories, proverbs, and so on and introduce them into their school. The community is, of course, the source of these stories; thus, the present arrangement maintains the separation between school and community that colonial education introduced in Africa. It would be preferable to have the community members who are the experts in orature (students' parents and grandparents, elders in the community, storytellers, praise singers, drummers, chroniclers and so on) introduce such orature into the schools. It would also be wise to ensure that, in turn, the students perform in the community. Such performances would constitute reciprocity in terms of school/community relations, and ensure that in return for the community becoming an important part of school culture, the school becomes part of the community culture.

Introducing the community into the school and the school into the community would re-establish the links between school and community that once existed in indigenous education systems. It would resurrect both in the school setting and in the general community some of the content of indigenous education, and some of the reverence for the wisdom of elders and traditional performers that existed in traditional society. As far back as the 1960s, the poet Okot p'Bitek (1967) was advocating that oral historians be recruited as university professors and schoolteachers. To introduce the serious study of orature into the school system would be to implement (belatedly) his recommendation. The present curriculum recommends that students' stories be collected for future use, but it does not specify what this use will be. It would be preferable if performances of orature were given by community experts and were recorded (in audio but preferably in video) for distribution well beyond the borders of the ethnic group or even the country, so that they could be appreciated and utilized in other communities (in translation if necessary).[10]

The notion of African collectivity should also involve a retreat from Eurocentric preoccupations with the individual to recapture the strength and interdependency of traditional African communalism. Literature is notoriously individualistic, but African writers and critics have emphasized the social and communal rather than the individual writer and reader. Achebe (1964, 1975), for example, stresses the social role of the artist in African art; and Ashcroft and colleagues (1989: 125) point out that this insistence on the social role of the African artist, and corresponding rejection of the European preoccupation with individual experience, has been one of the most important and distinctive features in the assertion of a unique African aesthetics.

Thus, taking up Afrocentric literature studies seriously means promoting a concern for the individual as a social animal, and embracing and promoting notions of collectivity and communalism rather than individualism. This attitude of collectivism is a crucial element in communal involvement in development projects.

Finally, African collectivity involves a comprehensive notion of African identity. From Pan-Africanism to Negritude and most recently Afrocentrism, Africans both continental and diasporic have been actively promoting such a notion of global African *recueillement*.

Self-Reliance

As far as the issue of self-reliance is concerned, as far back as the 1960s Ali Mazrui (1967) and others were warning of the dangers of neodependency following the flag independence of African states. Almost three decades later, Mazrui still has cause to discuss the persistence of African countries' dependency on the former European colonizers and the new imperialists (the prime example being the United States). Mazrui goes to the heart of the role that universities have played in maintaining several forms of dependency, especially cultural dependency. African universities have often been expected to serve as important instruments of development in their societies. But what if those universities also constitute links in a chain of dependency? 'An institution can itself be dependent without necessarily spreading dependency over the wider society. But the university in Africa is not only sick itself – it is also a source of wider infection and societal contagion. That is why this paper is about cultural dependency, and not merely about academic dependency within the university structure on its own' (1992: 95).

Here Mazrui is making a point that has quite significant implications for how the university is perceived in development discourse. Education is usually seen as a crucial element of development, and the university as the principal means of spreading the highest and best form of knowledge; Mazrui turns this conception on its head by pointing to the university as an agent of neodependency and the primary means through which academic and cultural dependency is spread and perpetuated. The position he is taking here should serve at the very least as a caveat to the perception that modern formal education is inherently positive in terms of its relevance to individual, community and national development. Mazrui recommends three broad strategies for overturning African universities' promotion and perpetuation of dependency. The first is to 'domesticate' modernity – that is, to relate it more firmly to local cultural and economic needs. The second is to diversify modernity so that Africans extend their foreign references beyond the West to include other non-African civilizations. The third involves Africans counter-penetrating the Western academy and Western civilization with African cultural and knowledge production. He ends by strongly advocating independence and self-reliance as crucial for the decolonization of African education.

It is obvious that the goal of ending neodependency and engendering African self-reliance is yet to be achieved, in education or in any other sphere. In terms of resisting neodependency, it is the handful of African countries that deliberately chose not to become capitalist satellite states and de facto neocolonies of Western countries that have succeeded to varying degrees in creating and maintaining national self-reliance. Prominent among such countries are Guinea (under Ahmed Sheku Turey) and Tanzania (under Julius Nyerere). However, it should be remembered that for the struggle to achieve self-reliance, Amin (1990) proposes 'delinking,' not 'autarchy.' The Guinean revolution succeeded (albeit in a limited sense) partly because it was characterized by autarchy: Guinea severed virtually all ties with the outside world. Nyerere's (1968) more successful philosophy of *Ujamaa* involved self-reliance and African communalism but not necessarily autarchy. The lesson to be learned from these two examples is that African states should not attempt to be completely isolationist and self-sufficient, but rather should look first to themselves for development; and that they should construct their own terms for engaging the outside world.

Conventionally, development projects are initiated at the national level, and are reflective of international and national politics, and do not take into account the politics, needs, and perspectives of local peoples. Many such projects have either failed completely or have failed to benefit rural and poor people in Africa. Theorists such as Dei (1993), Porter, Allen, and Thompson (1991), and Deng (1986) have insisted that if development projects are to succeed, they must reflect the interests, concerns, and world views of local peoples, and the local population must be involved at every stage.

The Development of Orality and Literacy

The promotion of local languages that the study of Afrocentric literature entails would focus on the production of texts in local languages, the standardization of written forms of languages, and the development of written forms of languages where this has not yet been done. Also, it would promote student literacy in local languages. Beyond mechanical literacy – that is, learning the mechanics of reading and writing – Afrocentric literature studies would promote the ability to read critically (Willinsky, 1990). Thus, students would be encouraged to 'read the word and the world' (Freire and Macedo, 1987), and to interrogate not only texts but the world around them. In this way they would be able to begin to articulate their vision of how society can be improved.

It should be emphasized, however, that literacy is not in and of itself a panacea for all social problems. The alarmist talk of a crisis of literacy in Western countries such as Canada and the United States, in the face of the fact that millions of people live out very fruitful lives without being literate, is an indication of Western hyperliteracy. We must never forget that this sort of discourse undermines any attempt to take seriously the wealth of oral tradition we have in Africa and the use we should be making of orality in communication. Aidoo puts the case thus: 'I totally disagree with people who feel that oral literature is one stage in the development of man's artistic genius. To me it's an end in itself ... We cannot tell our stories maybe with the same expertise as our forefathers, but to me, all the art of speaking voice could be brought back so easily. We are not that far from our traditions' (quoted in Elder, 1987: 109).

Aidoo's statement conveys several important messages. First, she is expressing resistance to the Eurocentric perception that orature is a stage in the evolution of literature (and therefore inferior to written literature). Second, she is asserting the need to reclaim, practice, and cherish (and, I would add, critically interrogate) a traditional form that educated Africans, in their pursuit of Eurocentric forms, have started to lose touch with. Third, she is making a strong case for celebrating and utilizing orality as a medium of communication and artistic expression instead of overrelying on the hyperliteracy of Eurocentric genres. In Afrocentric literary practice, orature would thus be regarded as a legitimate aspect of literature; it would in fact become the crucial, pivotal genre. In promoting orality through Afrocentric literature studies, we would be avoiding the pitfalls of Western hyperliteracy and the stigmatizing of 'the illiterate' among us.

Conclusion

In this chapter I have attempted to show how literature as cultural studies can contribute significantly to the discourse and praxis of development. Achebe's 1988 essay, in which he juxtaposed literature and development, was the inspiration and starting point of this chapter. I have attempted to elaborate on his arguments and to broaden and strengthen them by introducing other points that support his basic thesis. It should be noted that if conventional conceptions of development and literature had been utilized by either Achebe or myself, the juxtaposition of the two would have been not only unproductive but untenable. If literature can contribute to development, it is only because both have been reconceptualized. As evident in the work of Porter and colleagues, reconceptualization can be and is being undertaken by development theorists. This illustrates clearly that local African performance in particular, and culture in general, can be utilized in a serious, systematic, productive analysis of development in Africa.

NOTES

1 While there is an established and even burgeoning discourse of Afrocentrism as a philosophical and academic field, my use of the term 'Afrocentric' is not intended to site Achebe's or my own work within that specific field. Rather, I use the term much more loosely throughout this chapter the way it has been employed by non-Afrocentrists like Greg Tate (1992) – that is, to signify any point or perspective that is either distinctly African or that centres Africa and Africans in its consideration.

2 This brief essay is included in a collection of Achebe's (1988) literary criticism, *Hopes and Impediments.*

3 This point was underscored for me when I presented a paper (Wright, 1995) on the same topic at the 1995 meeting of the Canadian Association for the Study of International Development (CASID). (This chapter is based on that presentation.)

One audience member told me she was initially quite taken aback by the juxtaposition of literature and development studies. She pointed out that she had taught literature for many years and presently works in development studies and it would never have occurred to her that any plausible let alone viable and productive link could be made between the two fields.

4 By *utilitarian literature* I refer to a literary criticism and literature studies discourse that ventures beyond a consideration of aesthetics as a distinct, self-sufficient discourse to a consideration of function/utility and overt politics. By *function/utility* I mean the primacy of the African writer's role as a sociopolitical commentator. By *overtly political aesthetics* I mean the bridging of the aesthetics/politics divide undertaken by critics like Mukherjee (1988) in her construction of what she calls 'an aesthetics of opposition.'

5 Although Achebe argues against a conceptualization of modernization as synonymous with Westernization, the example he uses to launch this argument (a quote from a Japanese professor) is curious since it reflects the very confluence of modernization and Westernization he is arguing against: 'My grandfather graduated from the University of Tokyo at the Beginning of the 1880s. His notebooks were full of English. My father graduated from the same university in 1920 and half of his notes were filled with English. When I graduated a generation later my notes were all in Japanese. So ... it took three generations for us to consume western civilization totally via the means of our own language' (Kinichiro Toba, quoted in Achebe, 1988: 110). Without the last sentence the quote could have been used effectively to endorse the argument that modernization in Japan was undertaken simultaneously with a process of rediscovery and strengthening of elements of traditional Japanese culture. Thus the example could have been said to give the lie to the notion that modernization and Westernization are synonymous or inextricably linked processes. However, the last sentence indicates that Toba considers Japan to have been engaged not merely in a process of modernization but in fact in a process of consuming Western civilization in the process of modernization.

6 Achebe does not make a case here for taking up traditional African stories and parables as literature. Rather, he takes them up as such in a matter-of-fact, taken-for-granted manner. This is in itself, in my opinion, a bold and strategic move involving the legitimation of traditional African stories as orature (or as Achebe prefers, oral literature).

7 I do not mean to suggest here that there is a single, definitive European literary tradition and that this tradition is apolitical. There is a growing politicized European tradition embracing, variously, feminism, Marxism, and queer politics, for example. Despite these developments, the old tradition, which insists that literature is 'apolitical,' remains hegemonic in European literary discourse and

indeed internationally. It is this received, hegemonic tradition that Africans need to eschew.

8 Sachs and Dei are not necessarily far apart in their positions. The difference between them is that while Sachs is ready to abrogate the term and practice of development. Dei, it would appear, cannot in practical terms endure the vacuum that would ensue and would therefore rather work to change the discourse and praxis of development from within.

9 My preference for the term *orature* rather than *oral literature* reflects my conviction that oral literature drags too much of the baggage of literature with it, such that it is in the end a form of literature. Orature on the other hand connotes for me a distinct form, one that necessitates a distinctly different approach and framework of appreciation and application.

10 This is not to say that students should not also be encouraged to perform orature in class, or that their performances cannot be recorded and later shared with others in the community and beyond.

REFERENCES

Achebe, C. 1964. 'The Role of the Writer in a New Nation.' *Nigeria Magazine* 81.
– 1975. *Morning Yet on Creation Day.* New York: Doubleday.
– 1988. 'What Has Literature Got to Do With It?' In *Hopes and Impediments: Selected Essays 1965–87,* Nairobi: Heinemann.
Adedeji, A. 1990. *The African Charter for Popular Participation in Development and Transformation.* Part 11. Arusha, Tanzania.
Amin, S. 1990. *Delinking: Toward a Polycentric World.* London: Zed Books.
– 1975. *Unequal Development: An Essay on the Social Formation of Peripheral Capitalism.* Sussex: Harvester Press.
Asante, S.B. 1991. *African Development: Adebayo Adedeji's Alternative Strategies.* London: Hans Zell.
Ashcroft, B., G. Griffiths, and H. Tiffin. 1989. *The Empire Writes Back: Theory and Practice in Post-Colonial Literatures.* New York: Routledge.
Bennett, T. 1990. *Outside Literature.* London: Routledge.
Black, J.K. 1991. *Development in Theory and Practice: Bridging the Gap.* Boulder: Westview Press.
Christian, B. 1990. 'The Race for Theory.' In Abdul Janmohamed and David Lloyd (eds.), *The Nature and Context of Minority Discourse.* Oxford: Oxford University Press.
Dei, G. 1993. Towards an African View of Development. *Focus Africa.* November–March, 17–19.

– 1992a. An Afrocentric Critique of Development Discourse. Unpublished paper. Toronto: Department of Sociology. OISE.

– 1992b. 'The Indigenous Responses of a Ghanian Rural Community to Seasonal Food Supply Cycles and the Socio-Economic Stresses of the 1980s.' In D.R.F. Taylor and F. Mackenzie (Eds.), *Development From Within: Survival in Rural Africa.* New York: Routledge and Kegan Paul.

– 1990. Indigenous Knowledge and Economic Production. *Ecology of Food and Nutrition* 24(1): 1–20.

Deng, F. 1986. 'Learning in Context: An African Perspective.' In Alan Thomas and Edward W. Plowman (Eds.), *Learning and Development: A Global Perspective.* Toronto: OISE Press.

Eagleton, T. 1983. *Literary Theory: An Introduction.* Minneapolis: University of Minnesota Press.

Elder, A. 1987. 'Ama Ata Aidoo and the Oral Tradition: A Paradox of Form and Substance.' In Eldred Durosimi Jones, Eustace Palmer, and Marjorie Jones (Eds.), *Women in African Literature Today.* Trenton: Africa World Press.

Freire, P., and D. Macedo. 1987. *Literacy: Reading the Word and the World.* New York: Bergin and Garvey.

Gibbs, J. 1980. *Critical Perspectives on Wole Soyinka.* London: Heinemann Educational Books.

Izevbaye, D.S. 1971. 'Criticism and Literature in Africa.' In Christopher Heywood (Ed.), *Perspectives on African Literature.* London: Heinemann.

Kenya Institute of Education. 1992. *Ministry of Education: Secondary Education Syllabus Volume Five.* Nairobi: Kenya Literature Bureau.

Kenyan Ministry of Education. 1992. *A Guide to English Teaching in Secondary Schools.* Nairobi: Ministry of Education.

Kernan, A. 1990. *The Death of Literature.* New Haven: Yale University Press.

Kipusi, N. 1992. Articulations of Development Discourse: An African Perspective. Unpublished paper, OISE, Ontario.

Marrouchi, B. 1991. Literature Is Dead, Long Live Theory. *Queen's Quarterly* 978 (4): 1–29.

Mazrui, A. 1992. Toward Diagnosing and Treating Cultural Dependency: The Case of the African University. *International Journal of Educational Development* 12(2): 95–111.

– 1967. *Towards a Pax-Africana: A Study of Ideology and Ambition.* London: Weidenfeld and Nicolson.

Mukherjee, A. 1988. *Towards an Aesthetics of Opposition: Essays on Literature, Criticism and Cultural Imperialism.* Stratford: Williams-Wallace.

Nkosi, L. 1981. *Tasks and Masks: Themes and Styles of African Literature.* Essex: Longman Group.

Nyerere, J. 1968. *Ujamaa: Essays on Socialism.* Nairobi: Oxford University Press.

Okpewho, I. 1992. *African Oral Literature: Backgrounds, Character, and Continuity.* Bloomington: Indiana University Press.

Onoge, O.F. 1982. 'The Crisis of Consciousness in Modern African Literature.' In George Gugelberger (Ed.), *Marxism and African literature.* Trenton: Africa World Press.

p. Bitek, okot (1967). *Song of Lawino.* London: Heineman.

Porter, D., B. Allen, and G. Thompson. (1991). *Development in Practice: Paved with Good Intentions.* London: Routledge.

Rodney, W. 1981. *How Europe Underdeveloped Africa.* Washington: Howard University Press.

Sachs, W. 1992. Development: A Guide to the Ruins. *New Internationalist.* June: 4–27.

Shaw, T. 1992. Prospects for 'New' Regionalisms in Africa in the 1990s: Case Study of IGADD. Paper presented at the conference of the Canadian Association for the Study of International Development, Prince Edward Island.

Simon, R. 1988. 'For a Pedagogy of Possibility.' In John Smyth (Ed.), *Critical Pedagogy Networker: A Publication on Critical Issues in Education.* Victoria: Deakin University Press.

Soyinka, W. 1976. *Myth, Literature and the African World.* Cambridge: Cambridge University Press.

Tate, G. 1992. *Flyboy in the Buttermilk: Essays on Contemporary America.* New York: Simon and Schuster.

Taylor, D. and F. Mackenzie. 1992. *Development From Within: Survival in Rural Africa,* New York: Routledge and Kegan Paul.

Taylor, P. 1989. 'DuBois, Garvey, Nkrumah, and Fanon on Development. In Simeon Waliaula Chulungu and Sada Niang (Eds.), *African Continuities / L'heritage Africain.* Toronto: Terebi Press.

Turok, B. 1987. *Africa: What Must be Done?* London: Zed Books.

wa Thiong'o, N. 1981. *Detained: A Writer's Prison Diary.* London: Heinmann Educational Books.

W.A.E.C. 1988. *Regulations and Syllabuses for the Joint Examinations for the School Certificate and the General Certificate of Education Ordinary level and for the School Certificate of Education Advanced level 1989–92.* Lagos: Academy Press.

Willinsky, J. 1990. *The New Literacy: Redefining Reading and Writing in the Schools.* New York: Routledge.

Wright, H.K. 1994. Educational Reform in Sierra Leone: The Case for Critical African Drama. *International Journal of Educational Development* 14(2): 177–93.

12

Breaking the Educational Silence: *For Seven Generations*, an Information Legacy of the Royal Commission on Aboriginal Peoples

BUDD L. HALL

One of the major aims of this Royal Commission will be public education. That means telling and teaching non-Aboriginal People what it is like to be Aboriginal in Canada.

Commissioner Mary Sillet, Inuvik, Northwest Territories

We have to remind people that Aboriginal People have an oral history which is part of the reason there isn't a balanced history.

Co-chair Georges Erasmus, Whitehorse, Yukon

The struggle for the survival and recovery of the words, images, and dreams of the original people of our threatened planet goes on in all parts of the world. In many parts of the world all traces of the first peoples have been obliterated. Their stories are no longer heard in the forests, the mountains, or the plains. One of the encouraging notes in these times is that in spite of all manner of historic and contemporary violence and aggression, both the stories and the peoples still exist in many parts of our world. It is given to those of us who work in university settings to create spaces theoretically, spiritually, culturally, and physically for these stories and these peoples. Universities play a powerful role in the legitimation of knowledge process in our societies. As teachers, researchers, and project organizers, we have an opportunity and a historic responsibility to shape our courses, our research, our reading lists, and our professional interventions in ways that will redress some of the distortions of the past. Scholars and academics who fail to resist ongoing Eurocentric and white supremacist knowledge agendas contribute to the continuation of the unjust claims to knowledge that swirl around us daily.

This chapter reports on the development of a new source of information on the lives of the aboriginal peoples of Canada: *For Seven Generations*, a CD-ROM created by the Royal Commission on Aboriginal Peoples. This new data base serves as an example of how traditional knowledge and modern technology can work together for others. It provides a practical tool for supporting the spirit of this book, which calls for indigenous knowledges to be included in the Western academies and Western schools. This chapter also describes the CD-ROM's structure, content, and technical features. The availability of this information, which is framed by aboriginal peoples in their own world view and words, is a historic breakthrough for academics, educators, and others who wish to learn, teach, share, or do research based on the direct and indirect words, voices, and ideas of aboriginal peoples. The chapter further suggests that the existence of this data base offers many new possibilities for teachers, curriculum developers, history book writers, adult educators, antiracist educators, and environmental educators, to name a few. The chapter closes with suggestions for how this material might be used for a national public education process linking study circles across Canada. The existence of this data base changes the landscape dramatically for all educators concerned with acquiring a deeper and more accurate understanding of the experiences and hopes of aboriginal peoples.

Background

For over 500 years, people of nonaboriginal descent have been living in what is called Canada. Year after year since the arrival of the Europeans on this continent, the nonaboriginal education system has been erasing the stories, the histories, the cultures, the languages, and the ways of knowing of aboriginal peoples. This project of silencing Canada's first peoples has reinforced the appropriation of land, the degradation of the environment, the creation of assimilationist residential schools, and the continuation of racist stereotypes about people of aboriginal descent. And through curriculum design, program planning, school reform, textbook adoption, language policies, limitations of language provision, and thousands of smaller ways, many nonaboriginal educators have participated knowingly or unknowingly in this educational silencing. The accumulated result of this systematic exclusion has been that information about aboriginal life has not been easily accessible to students, teachers, and adult educators. In particular, the perspectives of aboriginal peoples, expressed in their own voices without the mediation of Western culture, have been largely absent.

For Seven Generations is a unique set of information by and about aboriginal peoples and their lives from creation until 1995. It was created by the Royal Commission on Aboriginal Peoples as a direct product of its hearings, round tables, research projects, and deliberations. *For Seven Generations* contains thousands of pages of direct testimony from aboriginal women, men, young people, and elders on a searchable CD-ROM that can be read by any multimedia computer. This data base can be used by both formal and nonformal educators to help break the educational silence that envelops all of us, whatever our heritage. It is important for readers to know that I write this chapter as a white, male, middle-aged university professor. I believe it is our responsibility as nonaboriginal educators to educate ourselves about the nature of the educational silencing that has occurred and to create opportunities in our own locations to learn from and about aboriginal knowledges. All schools and all educational settings should make themselves aware of the full history and contemporary possibilities of the first peoples in this part of Turtle Island (the name used by some aboriginal peoples for the North American continent). It is from this perspective that a number of us at the Ontario Institute for Studies in Education accepted an invitation to help the commission prepare the Educational Guide that accompanies *For Seven Generations.*

The Royal Commission on Aboriginal Peoples

The Royal Commission on Aboriginal Peoples (RCAP) was established in August 1992 and released its final report in November 1996. RCAP had conducted an extensive inquiry into the history, current situations, and future prospects of Canada's aboriginal peoples. This involved broad consultations with thousands of aboriginal people, research by aboriginal and nonaboriginal researchers, and reflection by the members of the commission itself, leading to the final report and recommendations. RCAP was mandated to 'investigate the evolution of the relationship among Aboriginal Peoples (Indian, Inuit and Metis), the Canadian government and Canadian society as a whole.'[1] It was charged with proposing 'specific solutions, rooted in domestic and international experience, to the problems which have plagued those relationships and which confront Aboriginal Peoples today.'[2] Although there have been many inquiries and commissions on aboriginal affairs, RCAP was the first to have a majority of aboriginal commissioners. The chairpersons were Georges Erasmus, former national chief of the Assembly of First Nations, and René Dussault, Justice of the Quebec Court of Appeal. Other members were Paul Chartrand, professor, Department of Native Studies, University of Manitoba; Viola Robinson, former president of the Native Council of Canada; Mary Sillett, former president of the Inuit Women's Association of Canada and former vice-president of Inuit Tapirisat of Canada; Bertha Wilson, retired Justice of the

Supreme Court of Canada; and Peter Meekison, professor, Department of Political Science, University of Alberta.

The commission conducted public hearings in all parts of Canada, which generated a stack of transcripts three-and-a-half metres tall. Round table presentations, research findings, and other processes more than doubled this volume of information. Oral testimony was heard in languages including Inuktitut, Cree, Ojibwa, Chipewyan, English, and French. The commissioners wanted to hear what the aboriginal peoples themselves were saying. They wanted an accessible record that did not filter, edit, paraphrase, or restate the words of the people and organizations that came to the public consultation process.

The *For Seven Generations* CD-ROM[3]

The resulting data base is unequalled in its coverage of the experience of aboriginal people and the complex relationship between them and the rest of Canadian society. *For Seven Generations* was drawn from this information and is available for educational and research purposes on a searchable CD-ROM. Provided on the CD-ROM are oral presentations made by over 2,000 individuals and organizations; community studies, legal analyses, life histories, and scholarly papers brought together in over 200 research reports; summaries of 140 intervener submissions; transcripts and reports of five national round tables; a bibliography and overview of previous commissions and task forces on Canadian aboriginal affairs over the past twenty-five years; and fourteen topical briefing books drawing out policy issues from the varied submissions.[4] Educators thus have access to the actual testimony given before RCAP. *For Seven Generations* provides a means for aboriginal peoples to have their own words read by educators, secondary school students, literacy tutors, school administrators, and adult education study circles, and by aboriginal peoples themselves in their own communities. Here is the beginning of a new approach to history – one that gives pride of place to the oral traditions and present realities of aboriginal peoples as they themselves see and remember.

For Seven Generations uses a modified version of Folio Views search software. This software allows the entire data base to be searched from a multimedia computer in either Windows or Macintosh format. It was modified to take into account some of the unique requirements of the project. Three innovations in particular were created for *For Seven Generations*: the WordFinder; tagging for mode of Discourse; and intervener demographics. The WordFinder is a thesaurus of more than 600 entries that links words used by participants or interveners in the hearings with corresponding mainstream, bureaucratic, and legal terms. For example, the WordFinder reminds Euro-Canadians that the land the Europeans named 'North America' was known long before as 'Turtle Island.'

Other Features of *For Seven Generations*

For Seven Generations provides a full description of the commission and its mandate and terms of reference. It also includes biographies of the commissioners and the ethical guidelines the commission followed. It also contains a copy of the RCAP Final Report (a five-volume print report). Some of the most powerful material is found in the 'Public Consultations' section, which documents the testimony taken from the more than 2,000 interveners in four separate rounds of hearings. It was at the hundreds of open hearings that people were encouraged to 'speak from the heart' about the history of relations between aboriginal peoples, the Government of Canada, and Canadian society as a whole.

The transcripts and reports of the national round tables and special consultations cover a broad range of subjects: economics, education, health, values, justice, and many others. Each section has its own table of contents and list of speakers and has a full search capacity. The education round table contains separate sections on adult and lifelong education, cultural diversity, parent involvement in schools, and school/community partnerships.

The commissioners defined fifteen themes, around which they structured the final report. These fifteen themes were arts and heritage, culture, economic development, education, elders' perspective, governance, health, justice, land and resources, Métis, the North, treaties, urban aboriginal perspectives, aboriginal women, and aboriginal youth. RCAP's own policy analysts drew material together from the many sources, paying special attention to the interconnections between themes. The results of this research are available on the CD-ROM as 'Source Guides.' There are detailed briefing notes drawn from all RCAP data sources for all the fifteen themes.

Special mention needs to be made of the section titled 'Review of Past Government Commissions.' RCAP commissioned Carleton University to study past commissions and task forces on aboriginal issues. The analyses and findings of these past commissions are categorized and summarized on the CD-ROM. There are the equivalent of four print volumes of material just in this section alone. The themes of these commentaries include the following: governance, land and economy, sociocultural affairs, aboriginal women, urban issues, aboriginal youth, the North, British Columbia, the Prairies, Ontario,

Quebec, the Maritimes, and Newfoundland and Labrador. Each of these sections is in turn broken down into subsections: definitions, broad themes and issues, and concluding remarks.

Detailed instructions on using Folio Views are contained on the CD-ROM. Also, many useful suggestions on how to use the disk in educational settings are found in the 'Educational Guides' section. However, it is important for educators to know that there are other ways besides the WordFinder and the Source Guides to access material from the RCAP information collection.

The Word Search

Say, for example, the user clicks on the Query icon and types in the word he or she is looking for – 'creator,' perhaps. The screen will indicate how many times this word appears in the 'Hearings' transcripts. When the user clicks 'OK,' the computer will find and display the words of the first speaker, the name of that speaker, and the date and location of that speaker's presentation. Again from the Hearings transcripts, when the user applies the WordFinder function to the term 'spiritually,' a list of words related to this concept will be displayed, including *ancestors, creation stories, creator, elder*, and *Turtle Island*. These words can then be searched to find further information.

The Source Guides

The Source Guides offer a different approach to the data. Say, for example, you open up the Source Guides section of the data base. In the table of contents you see the theme 'Elders' Perspectives.' When you click from here into the Public Consultations infobase, the software will search the data base using a query developed by RCAP's on-staff researchers. You will have access to information on the spiritual nature of the teachings that was presented during the hearings. These are the creation stories of many aboriginal peoples as told to the RCAP commissioners.

Making Your Own Files

Students, teachers, adult educators, researchers, and others can create their own files of the precise information they want or need. The only limitation to what can be done this way is the searcher's own imagination. For example, you might want to compare aboriginal youth perspectives on economic development in several parts of Canada. Once you have identified testimony and opinion through the various search strategies, you can save this material to your own folder in a wide choice of word processing formats. Instructions on how to use this feature, and various options, are contained on the CD-ROM itself.

Potential Applications for Formal and Nonformal Education

School Settings

The opportunities opened up by the *For Seven Generations* CD-ROM are limited only by our imagination and time. The disk provides history teachers with access for the first time to information that can do much to correct the partial and Eurocentric histories that most students learn. For example, texts of treaties can be printed out from the disk to share with students. First-contact stories, creation stories, and wisdom from elders are all available for both students and teachers. The educational guidelines included on the CD-ROM provide further illustrations of how the data base can be incorporated into elementary and secondary education. Sociology courses and language and literature courses are two obvious places where aboriginal and non-aboriginal students and educators can make direct use of the data base.

Adult Education

If we think of adult education as that learning which adults do in all their contexts and settings, we begin to appreciate the potential of a broad, adult educational approach to transforming the relationship between aboriginal peoples and Canadian society as a whole. The *For Seven Generations* CD-ROM provides teachers, researchers, officials in education ministries, school boards, and many others with a powerful and unique tool for a variety of tasks. The provision of such a large and remarkable body of information reflecting such diverse aboriginal perspectives is by no means a solution to centuries of oppression and a continued climate of inaction, but it can be an important source of ideas and inspiration for all who want to make this country a better place. And for those among us who have a special interest in Native Studies, *For Seven Generations* is a gift like no other before. Its data base can be used in a wide variety of adult learning settings. It can be used by individuals learning or studying on their own, by tutors in one-on-one learning settings, in workshop settings, in long-term courses, in informal study groups, and in public education programs. The next sections of this chapter make a number of suggestions as to how the data base can be used.

Aboriginal Adult Education

As the commission itself noted during its hearings, the shortage of culturally appropriate and aboriginally centred adult education materials must be addressed. One of the most immediate and effective uses of the data base is as a resource for the aboriginal adult-education program, a wide variety of which are offered in every aboriginal community and in all urban centres throughout Canada. As Renée Abram of the Ontario Native Literacy Coalition said in the Round One hearings, 'Any program that is going to be successful in native terms has to be a program that relies on a cultural base.' The data base is a novel and stimulating resource for culturally relevant academic upgrading programs, for computer training, for research training of many types, for writer's workshops, for second-language teaching, and for healing circles.

Antiracism Education

Racism can mean direct discrimination against people in words or deeds, or it can mean indirect institutional or systematic racism. In the testimonies and reports in the data base, educators will find ways of understanding both forms of racism. Racist misconceptions are perpetuated when aboriginal history, culture, and knowledge are rendered invisible in the wider society. Are there parallels between the ways that aboriginal peoples and other vulnerable groups have been treated?

The data base contains thousands of references to all forms of racism. For example, a search of the data base for 'racism/discrimination' will produce 1,184 references (which the software refers to as 'hits'). There are a further 358 references to 'solution-recommendation/racism/discrimination.' Each reference tells the reader what was said, who said it, when it was said, and where it was said.

Many practical exercises can be developed around this data base. Examples:

1 Find how racism relates to other aspects of daily life in the words of aboriginal peoples.
2 Compare the experiences of aboriginal peoples in more isolated areas and reserves with those in urban settings.
3 For nonaboriginal learners/facilitators: How does our race and ancestral origins outside of Turtle Island offer us privileges that the aboriginal first peoples do not have?
4 From the various testimonies on racism, examine those which refer

specifically to the educational systems. How does racism work on a day-to-day basis in our schools, according to aboriginal testimony?

5 Who else besides aboriginal peoples experience racism, and what are the differences in the ways that race is experienced by others?

Environmental Education

Contemporary environmental adult education calls for broader and more holistic approaches to understanding the land. In the traditions and practices of aboriginal peoples, there are approaches to land use and holistic learning that can benefit the whole of society ... perhaps even the planet. For example, if we search for references that include the term 'Mother Earth' we will find much to ponder. Ethel Blondin, speaking in Fort Simpson, Northwest Territories, on 26 May 1992, said, 'What happens on Mother Earth is important for Aboriginal Peoples ... we know that it is all one network, it all works together.' In Waswanipi, Quebec, on 6 June 1992, Paul Gull noted that 'if our past is strong ... and it is taught, our people can tell the non-native people how to clean up this situation we are presently in.' A depth of understanding and sadness can be heard in the words of Chief Darrell Boissoneau of the Garden River First Nation: 'So we wish to continue after we now have examined the last 500 years of our relationship with these people who came to our lands and the destruction that they have put on Mother Earth and how much abuse that they have brought into our community' (11 June 1990). And Dave Courchene Jr. of the Mother Earth Spiritual Camp said: 'Indigenous People are increasingly being called upon to assist others in understanding spirituality. There is a huge emptiness within most individuals and within Western civilization ... There is no doubt by any individual in the world that a drastic transformation must be developed if humanity is to reverse the course of its own destruction' (30 October 1992).

Entrepreneurial Economic Development Education

There are many aboriginal business training courses and economic development programs across Canada. The RCAP data base offers considerable insight and information that is helpful whether you are designing a program, teaching in such a program, developing materials, doing research on culturally appropriate models, or simply interested as an adult learner. For example, from the 'Issues' and 'Solutions' sections of the data base you could choose the topics that most closely relate to the topics you are concerned with. There are 70 references in the solutions section that correspond to the search 'model/economics/employment.' There are 99 references linked to the search 'model/funding/Aboriginal business,' and 612 references linked to 'solution-model/employment.' A wide variety of issues can be explored using these and other sources of information. What are the implications of aboriginal cultural values for business and related economic projects? What are the implications of the following?

1 Nonaboriginal employers hiring aboriginal employees.
2 Aboriginal businesses hiring nonaboriginal employees.
3 Aboriginal businesses doing business with nonaboriginal businesses and financial institutions.
4 Nonaboriginal businesses adopting aboriginal cultural values.

A National Study Circle Program on the Establishment of a New Relationship between Canada's Aboriginal and Nonaboriginal Peoples?

Study circles – groups of adults learning autonomously as equals – are a long cherished form of adult learning. Their roots are in nonaboriginal adult education – specifically, in the Antigonish movement in Nova Scotia during the 1930s and 1940s and in the Farm Radio Forum experiences of the 1940s and 1950s. The circle is also a common metaphor in aboriginal teachings. One could well argue that the future of Canada as a nation depends on our ability to deal with two fundamental areas of public political life: the relationship between the English-speaking and French-speaking European peoples, and the relationship between the aboriginal peoples of Canada and the rest of Canadian society.

The RCAP report and the *For Seven Generations* data base provide us for the first time in our history with a comprehensive examination of the relationship between aboriginal and nonaboriginal peoples, as well as detailed suggestions for finding ways to move forward. These materials could easily be developed into study materials for groups all across Canada. Church groups, environmental groups, adult education organizations, community centres, friendship centres, literacy classes, local radio stations, and women's organizations might all find ways to participate in a national dialogue.

Each study group could be provided with guidelines on how best to work as a study circle. It could also acquire a copy of *For Seven Generations* as a source of direct information for any topic it wishes to explore. Groups might want to specialize and look at new ideas for schooling, for economic rebuilding in the North, for inclusive living in urban communities, for redefining who we are as Canadians, for recovering lost ceremonies and powers of healing, or for establishing new political relationships. Stan McKay said it this way in Round One of the hearings: 'There's something here about the spiritual connection to the earth that I think Canada has to deal with and the global community has to deal with. It's not a political question. It's not an ecological question. It's the question of our lives together as human beings.'

NOTES

I would like to acknowledge the efforts of Mary Brodhead and Karen Ginsberg of the RCAP staff, Rouleen Wignall, Gail Winter, and Joyce Scane of OISE/UT, and, most deeply, Marlene Brant Castellano, co-director of research for RCAP. All of them helped me understand the structure, potential, importance, and beauty of *For Seven Generations*. Special thanks to Marilyn Proctor for her help with the preparation of this chapter.

1 Order in Council 26, August 1991. For the full text of the RCAP terms of reference, see the *Royal Commission on Aboriginal Peoples, Report*, Volume 1, *Looking Forward, Looking Back*, Appendix A (Ottawa: Canada Communications Group, 1996).
2 RCAP. *Information Management at the Royal Commission on Aboriginal Peoples*. Ottawa: RCAP, October 1993 (p. 1).
3 The *For Seven Generations* CD-ROM is available from Libraxus Inc., 500–63 Sparks Street, Ottawa, Ontario, C1P 5A6, or on the Internet (www.libraxus.com).
4 The full text of intervener submissions and 700 briefs and letters submitted to RCAP have been deposited, along with other documents, at the National Archives of Canada.

PART IV

Indigenous Knowledges and Transforming Practices

Indigenous knowledges have been and still are transforming a variety of social practices in our societies, including medicine, health, peace education, and the idea of the university. For example, Ayurvedic medicine, which has its origins in South Asia, is now practised in all parts of the world. Ayurveda contributes to the development of complementary medicine by countering the fragmentation of knowledge and practice resulting from patriarchal and capitalistic dominant forces. Also, health ministries in some jurisdictions have begun to incorporate aboriginal elders' and indigenous knowledges to create new policies. In the process, dominant ideas and culture are being challenged.

In Sierra Leone, a country that has been torn apart by war and violence in the late twentieth century, African traditional perspectives on conflict resolution are shedding light on contemporary practices of peace research and peace education. Of particular interest is the holistic understanding of peace in traditional perspectives, which stresses the primacy of harmonious relations with both community and the Earth. Similarly, even the idea of the university itself is being challenged. Our attention is drawn to the importance of African peoples and peoples of the African diaspora recovering African knowledges and ways of knowing. For all African peoples and for the benefit of all cultures and societies, the object is not to place the ancient knowledges in a 'romantic' framework, but to reconnect the powerful and transformative capacities of traditional theory and practice with the problems of our times.

13

Ayurveda: Mother of Indigenous Health Knowledge

FARAH M. SHROFF

In India, as elsewhere, indigenous knowledges stem largely from spiritual or religious thought forms. Ayurvedic medical knowledge, one of the world's oldest documented systems of medicine, is no exception. Ayurveda arises from a world view in which the starting point is the universe (as compared to the cell, which is the starting point in Western medicine). The unity of all elements in the universe is embodied in the five-element theory (*punchamahabhutas*). Ideas about unity and connection stem from a body of indigenous knowledge that seeks to integrate mind, body, and spirit. It is through this three-part lens of mind/body/spirit that Ayurveda views the world. This chapter looks at the following: overview of Ayurvedic medicine, history, texts, aims and stages of life, *punchamahabhutas*, *tridosha* theory, and the ecological and mental health aspects of Ayurveda. Due to limited space and the emphasis of this book, I will not be discussing the medical, clinical, and disease treatment aspects of Ayurvedic medicine; my emphasis will be on the cultural, historical, and social aspects of one of the world's oldest documented forms of indigenous knowledge.

Ayurveda is practised in India and elsewhere by people whose qualifications vary wildly. Ayurveda, like other systems of medicine, thus has its share of charlatans. Some of these people claim to be practising Ayurveda but do not have significant training and may be mixing allopathic or other drugs with Ayurvedic remedies. In India, as in virtually all countries, the practice of Ayurveda is not standardized and no regulatory bodies exist to root out unworthy representations of Ayurveda.

In the modern world, in which capitalism, patriarchy, racism, and other forms of oppression have created fragmented and alienated societies, Ayurveda and other forms of holistic health care play a transformative role in the lives of many people. By teaching people about their mind/body constitutions (*tridosha* theory is explained later in this chapter) and the interconnectedness of human beings and the ecological world, and by offering easy-to-follow dietary guidelines, Ayurvedic practice has shown people how to trust their own cultural and personal wisdom.

Ayurveda encourages people to keep well through daily regimens. For example, people are encouraged to wake early, to observe the coating on their tongue so as to keep track of digestive tract concerns, and to scrape their tongue for cleanliness. Daily gargling with warm water is also recommended; this helps clean the mouth and also clears the throat of mucus. Early morning yoga and meditation are suggested, followed by a breakfast designed to meet the individual's nutritional needs. Some Ayurvedic experts have created weekly schedules, which suggest when during the day people should eat, what they should eat, how much they should sleep, when they should eliminate wastes, and how sexually active they should be, and so forth. While many such recommendations exist, Ayurvedic theory is not dogmatic about these things. For instance, when people eat food that is difficult for their particular constitution to digest, they may chew on fennel or cardamom to aid digestion.

My interest in Ayurvedic medicine stems from my work as a health activist. I was born in Kenya of parents born in India, and my activism arose from a trip I made to my parents' birthplace when I was fifteen. In India I realized that it was a sheer accident of birth that gave me economic, social, and educational privileges that neither of my working-class parents enjoyed (nor did most Indians). My feelings of connectedness to struggling people in India led me to become involved in social justice movements. I have worked in movements for peace, international development, and community health. Most recently I have focused on gender and antiracism issues.

Through my work as a researcher, trainer, and community health worker in many parts of the South and the North, I have become aware of the inadequacy of Western medicine as a solution to peoples' health problems. Western, 'reductionist' medicine was imposed on many nations by French, English, Spanish, and other colonial regimes. Once allopathic medicine was made the dominant form of health care all over the world, indigenous forms of health knowledge and health care were often displaced, or their practices were forced underground. This destruction of local health knowledge and health systems has devastated the health status of the majority of the peoples of the South and of the First Nations, largely because the colonial regimes also reduced their access to the social determinants of health: income, food, security, safe drinking water, sanitation, education, and so forth.

The social context of reductionist medicine and its therapeutic value have both come under question. My interest in doing more than merely critiquing reductionist medicine led me to consider revolutionary *and* healing paths in the struggle for health. The struggle to reclaim holistic health care involves decolonizing the mind, which is a political benefit; at the same time, it has the potential to offer valuable therapeutic contributions to health care. Ayurvedic medicine is considered the Mother of holistic health care and has accumulated an ample body of philosophical and medical knowledge. As an activist, I have tried to examine Ayurveda as critically as I have examined allopathy.

The material in this chapter comes partly from interviews I conducted in India with Ayurvedic practitioners and educators, partly from discussions with Ayurvedic experts in Canada, and partly from written sources.

An Overview of Ayurvedic Medicine

Ayurveda is a Sanskrit word: *ayus* or *ayur* means life, and *veda* means science or knowledge, further, 'uncreated knowledge' (secondarily it refers to the books called the Vedas). Knowledge has a two-fold meaning. 'The first [type of knowledge] is derived from the sense-organs and corroborated by varied evidence based upon the experiences of the sense-organs' (Nikilananda, 1963: 13). From this knowledge comes the physical sciences. The second type of knowledge is 'transcendent and is realized through the mental and spiritual discipline of yoga' (13). This latter type is the subject of the Vedas. Ayurveda is thus a science of life – a system of health and medicine that aims to help people live healthy lives. It provides knowledge of how to live naturally.

Most people in India have employed Ayurvedic health care for thousands of years. Despite several invasions of India, Ayurveda has survived, for a number of reasons. First, it is an effective system of health promotion, disease prevention, and treatment. Second, most *vaidyas* (Ayurvedic practitioners) are located in villages, where the majority of Indians live. Third, practitioners tend to be members of the local community, and thus share many of the cultural values of the people. While this varies from locale to locale, until recently most *vaidyas* were from the élite Brahmin caste and were in highly respected positions. Fourth, Ayurveda is rooted in the cosmology of the Indian people. Fifth, Ayurvedic consultations traditionally do not cost more than clients can reasonably afford, though there have always been exceptions to this, especially for virilization therapies. Finally, Ayurvedic treatments, when properly employed, do not usually produce harsh side effects. This system of medicine has been adapted to many parts of the world, including Tibet, Thailand, Indonesia, Indo-China, and Mongolia. Tibetans communicated it to the Mongols (Filliozat, 1964).

A Brief History of Ayurveda

The history of Ayurveda is lodged within Hindu culture, which is deeply influenced by religious and spiritual thought. Ayurvedic theory is thus based on a world view that is explicitly religious. This aspect of Ayurveda may deflect some people who are not interested in learning about religion and are seeking health information, but it need not: it is still possible to understand the health aspects of Ayurveda without an in-depth study of Hindu or Indian philosophy. Many people believe that Hinduism is not only a religion but a way of life. In this chapter I do not attempt to promote any religious beliefs. Rather, I seek to explain the philosophical world view of Ayurveda and its relevance to health and the human body/mind/spirit. I am not attempting to 'sell' Ayurvedic medicine to the unconvinced; rather, I hope to encourage readers to open their minds sufficiently to begin analyzing this nonallopathic system.

Ancient History

The preservation of health has been an instinctive need of (hu)mankind from the very beginning of creation. Ayurveda originated in Hindu religious texts, the Vedas. Ayurvedic foundations are thus systematized as one of the Upavedas and attached to Rgveda and Atharvaveda (Sharma, 1992). Like the other Vedic texts, Ayurvedic theory is believed to have originated with Hindu Gods and Goddesses and to have been transmitted to ancient seers and then to other humans.

Ayurveda is believed to be 5000–6000 years old (Bala, 1991; Karunakarun, 1993). Archaeological findings at Mohenjadaro in Sindh and at Harappa in Punjab (approximately 3000 years old) have uncovered a high level of social sanitation and hygiene as well as various therapeutic substances. There are two phases of Hindu medicine: the Vedic (1500 BCE) and the post-Vedic (600 BCE). (Some scholars contend there was a third phase, the pre-Vedic, or ancient, period. The pre-Vedic period covers the time before the emergence of the Vedas, and includes prehistory and protohistory, including the Indus Valley civilization; see Sharma, 1992.)

European Colonialism

The spice trade catalysed contact between the Indian and European systems of medicine. There had been a demand for spices in Europe since Roman times, and the cargoes of spices always contained a high proportion of substances that were used medicinally. In 1498 Portuguese colonizers arrived in India. By 1510 they were established on the west coast, with Goa as their capital. Among prominent members of the Portuguese community there was much praise for Indian physicians, who had acquired great prestige by their successful cures and were granted special privileges (Comba, 1987: 24). Despite this initial positive contact between Portuguese and Indian medicine, by the beginning of the seventeenth century Portuguese doctors were denouncing Indian doctors as faith healers. Colonial violence escalated, and in 1618 the municipal council of Goa decreed that no one could practise medicine or surgery without taking an exam prepared by the Chief Physician and Surgeon. The number of Hindu practitioners was limited to thirty, and 'medicine' was defined as European medicine (Arnold, 1993).

In the eighteenth century the British defeated the Portuguese and Dutch in battle; in 1762 the British East India Company defeated the French on land and became the world's most powerful trading company. This state-sponsored military violence ensured British domination of the Indian subcontinent, which made it possible for them to scorn all things Indian, including medicine. Until the 1820s, however, Indian people were employed as subordinate workers in the colonial medical sector. Demand for these 'native doctors' temporarily increased, and a school for teaching native doctors was founded in Bengal in 1822, with Ayurvedic classes commencing in 1827; some allopathic concepts were also taught. This 'experiment' ended in 1835 in compliance with more aggressive British policies to 'push out the native medicine of India and patronize the European system' (Gupta, 1976: 370). Thus, for the greater part of the nineteenth century most Europeans were contemptuous of Indian medicine and science. By 1833 the British East India Company had banned all Ayurvedic schools. An allopathic medical school was opened in Calcutta (Heyn, 1987). However, even Calcutta, 'second city of the British empire,' a colonial metropolis of one million people, could barely support one hundred practitioners of allopathic medicine. During this time, despite the oppressive colonial attitudes toward holistic indigenous medical systems, a number of Europeans praised the sophistication of the indigenous medical knowledge, especially in the areas of herbology, cesarean sections, inoculations, and plastic surgery – particularly rhinoplasty (nasal-area surgery) (Shankar, 1992).

By the turn of the twentieth century, allopathy was still not established among the Indian masses, and its practitioners had difficulty spreading the system beyond the major cities. Despite the patronage of the colonial state, and its own scientific claims and monopolistic aspirations, Western medicine had singularly failed to displace its indigenous rivals (Arnold, 1993: 3). Arnold cites three reasons for this situation. First, allopathic medicine remained too closely identified with the requirements of the colonial state and thus was remote from people's needs. Second, allopathy failed to make the transition from state medicine to a public health system. Third, the masses remained content with practitioners of Ayurveda and of other indigenous systems of medicine, as their services were accessible geographically and financially, particularly for village Indians. In addition, the fees charged by allopathic practitioners were prohibitively high for most Indians.

Between 1880 and 1914, 'health and medicine (as the West conceived them) crossed a cultural threshold in India and became an active ingredient in indigenous rhetoric and social practice' (Arnold, 1993: 241). The impact of allopathic medicine on indigenous health practices had been minimal up to this time, but colonization had slowly been working on the collective Indian psyche. The change in consciousness (of some Indians) was accompanied by more aggressive British policies toward health care.

Possibly the biggest impact of British colonialism on Ayurveda was the closing of the Ayurvedic universities at Benares and Taxila, which had been thriving when the British first arrived. By forcing these universities to close, the British arrested Ayurvedic research in India. The consequences are felt to this day: it is possible that many modern health problems, such as various cancers and acquired immune deficiency syndrome (AIDS), could be cured by Ayurvedic remedies, but this would require modern research conducted within a holistic paradigm.

The Twentieth Century

Darshan Shankar (1992) states that in order to understand the status of Ayurveda today, we must assess the impact of colonial rule, the pre-Independence policies of the Indian National Congress, and the post-Independence policies of the Indian state. His article, 'Indigenous Systems of Medicine – the State of the Art' thoroughly discusses these matters. After 1914, allopathic medicine took greater hold among the Indian élite, most of whom were urban based. According to Arnold (1993: 241), 'health and medicine were integral to an Indian drive for "improvement" and for a redefinition of "self" ... Terms and images plucked from the colonial language of medicine began to infiltrate the phraseology of Indian self expression, to become part of the ideological formulation of a new nationalist order.'

Among the majority of Indians, allopathy was both resented and desired. Allopathic medicine started to achieve a strong base in India in the middle of the twentieth century, with support from urban upper classes/castes, members of the extremely influential Indian armed forces, Anglo-Indians, Parsis, and other powerful members of Indian society. The colonized minds of India had become convinced that their oppressors were more advanced in virtually all arenas, including medicine. They had never known anything but British domination. Local élites funded the building of allopathic hospitals, partly to curry favour with the British and partly to display their own economic power. Allopathic medicine thus grew as a result of indigenous patronage and leadership.

Mahatma Gandhi vigorously opposed this colonized approach to medicine. He saw health as integral to the spiritual and physical quest for self-discipline and for *swaraj* (home rule) in its widest and most intimate sense. He believed that good health did not mean the services of a good doctor, but rather the ability to control bodily desires, to prevent disease, and to nurture one's spiritual well-being. Gandhi urged the Indian masses to realize that *'to study European medicine is to deepen our slavery'* (in Arnold, 1993: 282; my emphasis). Other forms of resistance were also expressed, with the seat of revolt in Bengal. Many nationalists made significant attempts to invoke a sense of pride in indigenous knowledge (Shankar, 1992). Shankar asserts that British colonialism virtually always had Indian opponents.

Texts

The most important Ayurvedic texts are *The Carakasamhita* and *The Sushrutasamhita*. Both *samhitas* were written on palm leaves. Sushruta was a surgeon, and his treatise deals mostly with surgical medicine. Caraka was a general physician, and his treatise is about general medicine. These texts are thousands of years old and are still considered the most authoritative original texts. Some critics (e.g., Filliozat, 1964) argue that these texts are not preserved in their original form and have been revised by several others. Like all historical documents, they may be flawed. More important than the accuracy of the content is the salience of the content, and it is this salience which is the subject of this chapter. Many other writings exist, from the perspective of both Indians and foreigners. Foreigners tend to write from their own perspective, and in some cases they document Ayurvedic concepts incorrectly. They often write for a European audience that knows virtually nothing about Ayurveda. Some of the writings thus try to 'Westernize' Ayurvedic concepts. The Indian-based writers often assume that the reader has an understanding of the basic Hindu concepts. Some of these writings offer caste, class, and sexist interpretations of Ayurveda. This is also true of the writings by outsiders.

So none of the sources are flawless. I have chosen to focus more on the writings of insiders, as I am trying to understand Ayurveda from an Indian perspective. Heyn (1987) notes that there are two types of current Ayurvedic literature: that which adheres strictly to the classical concepts, and that which determines the validity of Ayurvedic theory under the test of allopathic proof. Heyn (1987) argues that the former is more authentic and less diluted. Like Heyn, I have chosen to understand Ayurveda more from the perspective of the 'purists' so that the fundamental understandings are 'correct.' Note, however, that some of this theory has been written by non-Indians such as Birgit Heyn and Robert Svoboda.

The Aims of Ayurveda

Ayurveda has two basic aims (Dash and Junius, 1983): the first is to preserve the health of healthy people and to help them attain the four principle aims of life; the second is to treat illness and disease. Thus, the Ayurvedic definition of health: one whose *doshas*[3] are in balance, whose appetite is good, whose *dhatus*[4] are functioning normally, whose *malas*[5] are in balance, and whose physiology, mind, and senses are always full of bliss, is called a healthy person (Sushruta in Desai 1989: 56).

Additionally, health, according to Ayurvedic theory, is uninterrupted physical, mental, and spiritual happiness and fulfilment; a true balance of organs/ systems, psyche, and spirit; balanced and creative relationships with fellow creatures and nature as a whole, with family, friends, work, climate, ideals, and customs, with truth and ourselves (Dash and Junius, 1983), and with the universe and ourselves. According to the Caraka Samhita, well-being is a 'disease-free state' to be pursued for the attainment of 'virtue, wealth, and gratification' (Desai, 1989: 22). A person whose self, mind, and senses are harmonious and cheerful is healthy. In Sanskrit, *svastha* means healthy: *sva* means self and *stha* means established; thus 'established in self.' Self has three parts – body, mind, and spirit (Svoboda, 1989). To be healthy is thus to have mental, spiritual, and physical peace, along with social well-being (Naidoo, 1989).

On the physical level, health is the 'continued maintenance of the best possible working of the human body under normal, and sometimes even abnormal, environmental conditions' (Naidoo, 1989: 643). A healthy, peaceful person is totally satisfied with the physical body and experiences no strain or tension; because of this ease, he or she is partly not aware of the physical body and is able to move/live beyond the body. The mind is considered to be the 'spiritual silhouette' of the physical body (Nitya, 1994); the mind and body are intricately connected at these different levels.

The Four Aims of Life (*purusarthas*)

According to Hindu cosmovision, the four aims of life are *dharma* (virtue), *artha* (purpose or wealth), *kama* (pleasure), and *moksha* (the fourth part and supreme end of life; release or liberation from the cycle of rebirth). The ultimate goal of life is to reach the final stage of *moksha*, which is also known as *nirvana* (a Buddhist word), or *samadhi* (a yogic word), or other terms in various traditions. These aims are not rigidly enforced either in theory or in practice; they are general guidelines for living a fulfilling life. Also, there is no rigid distinction between the stages, and each of the first three stages are generally carried out at the same time; people ought to be learning, earning, and enjoying during each stage. Some theorists believe that it is possible to attain liberation by disciplined adherence to just one of these stages (Nitya, 1994).

The Four Stages of Life (*asramas*)

The pursuit of one of the four aims of life is recommended during each of the four stages of life: 'apprenticeship or student-hood' (*brahma-charya*) – the phase of general and religious education; 'householdership' (*garhasthya*) – the phase of life in the home, generally with family; 'forest dwelling' (*vanaprastha*) – the phase of retirement and the preparation for detachment from worldly processes; and 'renunciation' (*sannyasa*) – the time when all identity and possessions are given up in austere preparation for physical dissolution and spiritual liberation. In the lives of most Hindus, these stages serve as guidelines for the inevitable. Relatively few expect to reach the *sannyasin* stage, and even fewer realize *moksha* (liberation from the cycle of rebirth). For many modern Indians, these 'stages' are not viewed as rigid mileposts that must be attained. Clearly, this kind of lock-step linear progression does not reflect the diversity of lives in the Indian subcontinent or elsewhere. Some may choose not to procreate. And the forest retreat is not necessarily an option for many people, as deforestation has occurred at a great rate. In the modern age, these stages may thus be more metaphorical than literal. Ayurveda's aim is to assist people in living a healthy life, in the full diversity of lifestyles that exist.

Samsara (literally meaning 'making anew') is the stream of birth, initiation, marriage and family life, aging, death, and rebirth. Death is considered the opposite not of life but of birth. These two events mark the passage through the cycle of births. One of the goals of Hindu cremation ceremonies is to return the body to its original form, using fire as a purifying agent (Desai, 1982).

Punchamahabhutas

In Ayurveda, holism is embodied in the concept of *punchamahabhutas*. *Panca* in Sanskrit means 'five.' *Maha* means 'great.' *Bhutas* means 'elements or states,' in the ancient sense; they are sometimes known as proto-elements. (*Bhutas* are thus not to be confused with the elements as they appear in modern chemistry; within modern chemistry they would be considered compounds.) The *punchamahabhutas* are thus the five great 'elements.' This 'five-element theory' states that ether,[6] air, fire, water, and earth, the *punchamahabhutas*, are the foundation of existence. They are contained in all animate and inanimate entities. Energy and matter are considered interchangeable. Although the elements themselves and how they combine are different, Chinese five-element theory parallels this: '[E]verything on earth is dominated by one of these elements and their constant interplay, combined with those of *yin* and *yang*, explain all change and activity in nature' (Vogel, 1991: 180).

According to holistic principles, the smallest particle of the universe is the universe in miniature. The interaction between the universe and the individual takes place through the intake and output of matter. The universe is thus the macrocosm, and other entities – including human beings – are the microcosm. To illustrate this simple yet profound concept, the words of some of the world's spiritual teachers follow:

> It has been said in the Vedas, 'knowing one lump of clay we know the nature of all the clay that is in the universe.' Take up a little plant and study its life, and we know the universe as it is. If we know one grain of sand, we understand the secret of the whole universe. Applying this course of reasoning to phenomena, we find, in the first place, that everything is almost similar at the beginning and the end. The mountain comes from the sand, and goes back to the sand, the river comes out of vapour, and goes back to vapour; plant life comes from the seed, and goes back to the seed; human life comes out of human germs, and goes back to human germs. The universe with its stars and planets has come out of a nebulous state and must go back to it. (Swami Vivekananda, 1896/1989: 218)

The essence of punchamahabhuta principles lies in their spiritual import. Holistic principles state that there is a unity and oneness in the universe and that all is connected.

> All the spiritual teachers of humanity have told us the same thing, that the purpose of life on earth is to achieve union with our fundamental, enlightened nature ... to realize and embody our true being. (Sogyal Rinpoche, 1993: 127)

When one is in direct contact, do you know what happens? Space disappears, the space between two people disappears and therefore there is immense peace – and this is only possible when there is freedom, freedom from the making of images, from the myths, the ideologies, so that you are in direct contact. Then, when you are directly in contact with the actual, there is transformation. (Krishnamurthi, 1991: 108–9)

Tridosha Theory

Ayurvedic theory is posited on the notion that observing nature is the best way to learn about the human body (Sathaye, 1993). From the five *bhutas*, each of which is found in the human body, arise the *tridoshas*. From ether and air the *vata dosha* is created, from fire and water the *pitta dosha* is created, and from water and earth the *kapha dosha* is created. *Doshas* are resting states from which mind/body constitutions are created. They are the dynamic energy forces or inner principles within the living body that govern the entire organism. Ayurvedic theory states that all human bodies are not the same. There are seven basic *prakrtis*, or constitutions, arising from *vata*, *pitta*, and *kapha* and their combinations: *vata, pitta, kapha, vata-pitta, vata-kapha, pitta-kapha*, and *vata-pitta-kapha*. It is thus possible to be uni-*doshic*, bi-*doshic*, or tri-*doshic* (fully balanced, which is very rare).

Embedded in macrocosm/microcosm theory is the notion that there is a constant interaction between the internal and external environments or universes. The macrocosm is governed by cosmic forces, and the microcosm is governed by the principles of *vata*, *pitta*, and *kapha*: 'According to Ayurveda, the first requirement for healing oneself and others is a clear understanding of the three *dosha*. The concept of *vata-pitta-kapha* is unique to Ayurveda and it holds the potential for revolutionizing the healing systems of the West. However, the concept of the three principles and the Sanskrit words, *vata-pitta-kapha*, are very difficult to translate into Western terms' (Lad 1984: 29). *Tridosha* theory is not the same as Greek and Roman humoral theory although it is often mistaken as such (Nadkarni, 1976); these theories are similar in some ways, but it is too facile and somewhat Eurocentric to assume that Indian concepts have already been conceived by Europeans and that terms simply need to be translated into a European language.

Each *dosha* has three states: *vrddhi* (aggravation), *ksaya* (diminution), and *samya* (state of equilibrium) (Dash and Junius, 1983). *Tridosha* theory applies to food, plants, and other elements of the environment. For example, *vata* is found in the lower part of the human torso (below the navel, urinary, bladder, pelvic region, thighs, legs, and bones), *pitta* in the middle part (between the navel and chest, concentrated in the small intestine, stomach, sweat, lymph, and blood), and *kapha* in the upper part (thorax, head, neck, joints, and fat tissues). *Vata* dominates in old age and in the evenings. *Pitta* predominates in adulthood and during midday. Kapha dominates during youth and in the early morning. Easy-to-follow charts to assist people in determining their *doshas* exist in several books, including Lad (1984) and Morningstar and Desai (1990).

Ecological Aspects

According to the principles of *punchamahabhutas*, all life is connected. Living in harmony with other beings is thus essential. The Plant Kingdom, for example, provides oxygen, wood (for building, paper, and so on), fibres for cloth, green manure to keep the soil fertile, and myriad other beneficial factors. For learning purposes, Ayurvedic models are built to show the parallel growth patterns of various species, such as a human fetus and a tree seed. The stages of growth are considered the same: expansion, unidirectional growth, conversion, liquefaction, and new growth (Sathaye, 1993).

Most Earth-based peoples hold a deep respect for animals and plants. By observing animals and plants, *yogis* and *yoginis* (practitioners of yoga) developed many yogic *asanas* (postures). Furthermore, Ayurvedic pharmacology was enhanced through observation of those animals which recognized the medicinal qualities of plants – particularly birds, boars, eagles, falcons, goats, oxen, porcupines, serpents, and sheep (Karembelkar, 1961). The Earth's ecology is intricately woven into the very definition of Ayurveda. For that reason it is difficult to extract what is *not* ecological about Ayurveda. The term 'ecology,' is derived from *oikos*, meaning 'home'; this embraces the Ayurvedic concept of connectedness: the Earth is the home of all beings. The well-being of the Earth is the well-being of all her inhabitants, and the demise of the Earth is the demise of all her inhabitants. This is similar to the Ojibwe belief that the Earth is mother, the Sky is father, the Moon is grandmother, and the Sun is grandfather to all beings (Mishkogabwe 1992). All Ayurvedic medicines are derived directly from the Earth, though some are changed chemically. According to Sushruta: 'Weather and climate – winds, sunshine, moonshine, darkness, heat, cold, rain, day, night, fortnight, months, seasons and solstices – contribute to the accumulation, augmentation, pacification and diminution of bodily humors' (in Kunjalal, 1963: 35).

The ecological aspects of Ayurveda include the connection between seasonal changes and the activities of human beings. When seasons change, Earth-based cultures, similar to most animals, adjust to these changes. Some bears hibernate during winter; squirrels gather and store nuts before winter so that they eat well during the cold months; some birds migrate to warmer climes for winter months.

Ayurvedic definitions of health include true balance with society, with fellow creatures, and with nature as a whole. Family, friends, work, ideals and customs, spiritual life, and climate and ecology are encompassed by this definition. The health of individuals is dependent on at least seven factors (Datye, 1971): these include the ecosystem category of the land, such as jungle, desert, or lakeshore; seasons in the ecosystem; available food material; fresh local produce available, such as fruits and vegetables; the way of living and habits of the people, such as siestas (napping during the afternoon); the availability of medicinal substances; the useful animals, particularly for agricultural and transportation purposes.

Out of the awareness of the unity of all life, some Ayurvedic aspirants recite the following stanza daily:

May all be happy
May all be free from disabilities
May all look to the good of others
May none suffer from sorrow. (Dash and Junius, 1983: 57)

Mental Health Aspects of Ayurveda

Mind, soul and body – these three are like a tripod; the world is sustained by their combination. They constitute the substratum for everything.

Caraka, c500 BCE

In Indian science the mind is believed to control all bodily functions. A disciplined, finely tuned, and spiritually connected mind thus has a large and positive impact on the overall health of the individual. One of the original branches of Ayurveda was devoted to mental health, yet there is little literature in English on this subject. Thus I am able to present here only brief discussion of some Ayurvedic mental health constructs. Within Ayurvedic cosmology, there are not one but three words and conceptualizations for the mind: *buddi* or intellect, *ahamkara* or ego, and *manas* or thought bundles. These have separate functions but work together. The acts of *manas* are governed by the *atman*, or soul, since the latter is conscious (Comba, 1987).

Vaidya Vasant Lad (1984: 19) notes that the concept of normalcy, in the dominant European discourse, depends on the common behaviour of the majority of people, while in Ayurveda, each individual is evaluated carefully to ascertain individual temperament and functioning. He notes that acceptance, observation, and experience are valued in the East and that Eastern science teaches students to move beyond dualistic abstractions of subjectivity and objectivity. Even in some Western thought, however, there is widespread acceptance that it is difficult to consider mental health apart from physical health, as psychological and somatic factors interact to produce health (Albino, 1983). The World Health Organization's definition of health, which is enshrined in its constitution – that health is a state of complete physical, mental, and social well-being and is not merely the absence of disease or infirmity – also underscores the international recognition of these concepts.

According to Ayurvedic theory, mental nature is more subtle than physical nature. Sometimes the body and mind are different types, one compensating for the other – for example, a *vata* mind in a *kapha* body. The categories of mental faculties are divided into three types, linked to *triguna* theory. *Triguna* theory conceptualizes three mental states. *Sattva* is derived from *sat*, 'truth or reality'; thus *sattva* is clarity, divine nature, unification of the head and heart, the basic clear quality of the mind. *Sattva* balances the other *gunas*. *Rajas* is agitation, stain, or smoke; it is the mind anxious with desire, wilfulness, anger, manipulativeness, and ego; *rajasic* behaviour is linked with seeking power, stimulation, and entertainment. *Rajas* also produces energy, vitality, and motion. The social world today is largely dominated by *rajasic* forces. *Tamas* is heaviness, inertia, or lethargy, sleep and inattention, lack of mental activity, insensitivity; *tamas* also provides stability and allows fixed forms to take shape in the physical body. *Tamas* can also be active; reactionary forces and bigotry may be *tamasic* because they refuse to change (Svoboda, 1995).

Lad (1984: 40–1) describes the deleterious effects of repressed emotions. He contends that toxins are created by emotional factors. He cites the example of repressed anger, which changes the flora of the gallbladder, bile duct, and small intestine and aggravates *pitta*; in turn, this causes inflamed patches on the mucus membranes of the stomach and small intestine. He also describes the problems created by fear and anxiety, which alter the flora of the large intestine; this leads to bloating of the large intestine, causing pain. He asserts that this pain is often confused with heart or liver dysfunction. He concludes: 'Because of the ill-effects of repression, it is recommended that neither the emotions nor any bodily urge, such as coughing, sneezing and passing gas, should be repressed ... Ayurveda recommends that emotions be observed with detachment and then allowed to dissipate. When emotions are repressed, that repression will cause disturbances in the mind and eventually in the functioning of the body' (41).

Given that the expression of emotions is discouraged in many cultures and that therefore many people repress their emotions, Ayurveda offers both mental and physical solutions to mental health imbalances. The mental healing options include the use of mantras, which are 'special seed syllables like *om* which reflect the cosmic creative vibration' (Lad and Frawley, 1986: 94). Lad and Frawley (94–5) explain how the physical and mental levels of healing are always related, as plants also have effects on the mind, and mantras also change physiology; both body and mind work with *prana*, from different places, within and without.

Summary

This chapter has discussed the historical and cultural elements of an ancient system of indigenous medical knowledge, Ayurveda. Ayurvedic medicine has its roots in peaceful, spiritual concepts that connect it to a larger philosophy and way of life. Seventy per cent of contemporary Indians continue to access it for their health care needs (Heyn, 1987), and most Indians are familiar with Ayurvedic concepts as part of their cultural upbringing. Hundreds of years of English colonialism were incapable of breaking people's health culture.

NOTES

I would like to thank members of the Ayurvedic community who have been invaluable in helping me learn about Ayurveda. I am very grateful to Vaidya Nalini Karunakarun, Vaidya P.M.S. Ravindranath, Ayurvedic expert and organizer Darshan Shankar, Dean B.V. Sathaye, and many others whose kindness and encouragement mean a lot to me. Vaidyas Thricovil Sukumaran and Robert Svoboda read an earlier version of this chapter. *Shukriar!* to all of you.

1 Other systems of holistic medicine have also thrived in India. These include siddha and unani medicine. Ayurveda is more widely practised than these forms.
2 The concept of the colonized mind has been theorized by Franz Fanon (1963) in *The Wretched of the Earth – The Handbook for the Black Revolution That Is Changing the World* (New York: Grove), by Malcolm X (1965) in *Malcolm X Speaks* (New York: Merit Publishers), and by Betty Shabazz and other anti-imperialist scholars.
3 *Doshas* are the three basic mind/body 'elements': air/ether, fire, and water/earth.
4 *Dhatus* are the seven basic and vital tissues/constructing elements.
5 *Malas* are waste products.

6 Ether may be difficult to understand for those not trained in Indian science. Ether is
space, emptiness, vacuousness, distance. In the subatomic sense, it is the 'nothingness' in which electrons rotate around the protons/neutrons. In modern chemistry it
is widely accepted that matter is composed mainly of *nothing*. This is the ancient
Indian concept of *akash*: that nothingness which is a part of all matter. *Akash* is not
endowed with action. It is of the largest dimension possible and the common
receptacle of all conjunct things in the universe. It is shapeless (see Comba, 1987).
Within quantum mechanics, *akash* is equivalent to the 'field.'

REFERENCES

Abadhuta, Srismat Swami Nitya Padananda. 1963. *The Philosophy of Union with the
Supreme.* India: Mahanirvan Math.
Albino, J. 1983. 'Health Psychology and Primary Prevention: Natural Allies.' In R.D.
Felner et al. (eds.), *Preventive Psychology.* New York: Pergamon.
Arnold, D. 1993. *Colonizing the Body – State Medicine and Epidemic Disease in
Nineteenth Century India.* California: University of California Press.
Bala, P. 1991. *Imperialism and Medicine in Bengal: A Sociohistorical Perspective.*
New Delhi: Sage.
Caraka. (c 500 BCE). *Agnivesa's Caraka Samhita.* Translated and discussed (1976)
by Ram Karan Sharma and Bhagwan Dash. Varanasi: Chowkhamba Sanskrit Series
Office.
Chopra, D. 1989. *Quantum Healing: Exploring the Frontiers of Mind/Body Medicine.*
New York: Bantam.
– 1991. *Perfect Health: the Complete Mind/Body Guide.* New York: Harmony
Books.
Comba, A. 1987. 'Caraka samhita, sarirasthana I and vaisesika philosophy.' In G.J.
and W.D. Muelenbeld (Eds.), *Studies in Indian Medical History.* The Netherlands:
Egbert Forsten.
Dash, B., and M. Junius. 1983. *A Handbook of Ayurveda,* New Delhi: Concept
Publishing.
Datye, M.P. 1971. *A Glance at Ayurveda the Indian Medical Science.* Mysore: P.M.
Datye.
Desai, P.N. 1989. *Health and Medicine in the Hindu Tradition: Continuity and
Cohesion.* New York: Crossroad.
Devaraj, T.L. 1992. *Ayurveda for Healthy Living.* New Delhi: UBS Publishers'
Distributors.
Doyal, L., with I. Pennell. 1979. *Political Economy of Health.* London: Pluto Press.
Filliozat, J. 1964. *The Classical Doctrine of Indian Medicine: Its Origins and Its*

Greek Parallels. New Delhi: Munshiram Manoharla Oriental Booksellers and
Publishers.

Frawley, D. 1989. *Ayurvedic Healing: A Comprehensive Guide.* New York: Passage
Press.

Gandhi, M.K. 1927. *The Story of My Experiments with Truth: An Autobiography.*
Ahmedabad: Navajivan Publishing.

George, Chief Dan. 1989. *My Spirit Soars.* Vancouver: Hancock House.

Grant-Cummings, J. 1994. Personal communications. Women's rights leader,
Toronto, Ontario.

Gupta, B. 1976. 'Indigenous Medicine in Nineteenth and Twentieth Century Bengal.'
In C. Leslie, (Ed.), *Asian Medical Systems.* University of California Press.

Heyn, B. 1987. *Ayurvedic Medicine – the Gentle Strength of Indian Healing.* New
Delhi: Indus.

Iyengar, B.K.S. 1989. *The Tree of Yoga.* Boston: Shambala.

Johari, H. 1994. *The Healing Cuisine: India's Art of Ayurvedic Cooking.* New York:
Healing Arts Press.

Karambelkar, V.W. 1961. *The Atharaveda and the Ayurveda.* India: Ku Usha
Karambelkar Nagpur.

Karunakaran, N. 1993. Personal communications. Ayurvedic practitioner, Hindu
Colony, Dadar, Bombay, India.

Kozak, L. 1995. *Allergies and Food: Your Health.* British Columbia Naturopathic
Association 1(1).

Krishnamurthi, J. 1991. *On Freedom.* San Francisco: Harper.

Kunjalal, K. 1963. An English translation of the *Sushruta Samhita.* Varanasi:
Chowkhamba Sanskrit Series Office.

Kuvalayananda and Vinekar. 1992. 'Yoga.' In M. Levy et al., *Life and Health:
Targeting Wellness.* New York: McGraw-Hill.

Lad, V. 1984. *Ayurveda, The Science of Self-Healing: A Practical Guide.* Boston:
Lotus Press.

Lad, V., and D. Frawley. 1986. *The Yoga of Herbs – an Ayurvedic Guide to Herbal
Medicine.* Boston: Lotus Press.

Lalonde, M. 1974. *A New Perspective on the Health of Canadians: A Working
Document.* Ottawa: Queen's Printer.

Matsen, J. 1987. *Eating Alive: Prevention Thru Good Digestion.* Vancouver:
Crompton Books.

Mehta, Y. 1987. Personal Communications. Allopathic physician, Dadar Medical
Clinic, Bombay, India.

Mishkogabwe (or Paul Bourgeois). 1992. Personal communications. Guest lecture in
public health at the Ontario College of Naturopathic Medicine. Professor of Native
Studies, Trent University, Peterborough, Ontario.

Morningstar, A., with U. Desai. 1990. *The Ayurvedic Cookbook*. Boston: Lotus Press.

Mutatkar, R.K. 1994. Editorial: The social responsibility of social scientists. *Social Science and Medicine* 39(6): 755–6.

Nadkarni, K.M. 1976. *Dr K.M. Nadkarni's Indian Materia Medica: With Ayurvedic, Unani-Tibba, Siddha, Allopathic, Homeopathic, Naturopathic and Home Remedies, Appendices and Indexes*, 3rd rev. ed. Bombay: Popular Prakashan.

Naidoo, T. 1989. *Health and Health Care: A Hindu Perspective*. Medicine and the Law. 7: 643–47.

Nikilananda, Swami. 1963. *The Upanishads* (abridged). London. George Allen & Unwin.

Nitya. 1995. Personal communications. Yoga teacher, Swami Vishnu Yoga Centre, 464 Dupont St, Toronto, Ontario.

– 1994. Personal communications. Yoga teacher, Swami Vishnu Yoga Centre, 464 Dupont St, Toronto, Ontario.

Patterson, T.J.S. 1993. 'The Relationship of Indian and European Practitioners of Medicine from the 16th Century.' In G.D. Singhal and T.J.S. Patterson, *Synopsis of Ayurveda: Based on Susruta Samhita*. New York: Oxford University Press, 1993.

Ray, D. 1937. *The Principle of Tridosha in Ayurveda*. Calcutta. S.C. Banerjee.

Sathaye, B.V. 1993. Personal communications. Dean, Podar Ayurvedic Medical College, Wurli, Bombay, India.

Shankar, D. 1995. 'Descent of Ayurveda' – hand-drawn chart sent to the author upon request. Bombay: Foundation for the Revitalisation of Local Health Traditions.

– 1992. 'Indigenous Health Services – The State of the Art.' In *Voluntary Health Association of India: State of India's Health*. New Delhi: Tong Swasthya Bhawan.

Sharma, P.V. (Ed.). 1992. *History of Medicine in India: From Antiquity to 1000 AD*. New Dehli: Indian National Science Academy.

Sogyal, R. 1993. *The Tibetan Book of Living and Dying*. New York: HarperCollins.

Sukumaran, Surendra. 1995. Personal communications. Ayurvedic physician, 4428 SE Marine Drive, Burnaby, BC.

Svoboda, R. 1989. *Prakruti: Your Ayurvedic Constitution*. New York: GEOCOM.

– 1995. Personal communications.

Tiwari, M. 1995. *Ayurveda: A Life of Balance*. San Francisco: Healing Arts Press.

Tripathi, S. c1992. 'Ayurvedic Nutrition from the Academy of Ayurveda' [mimeograph]. Obtainable from 2258 Danforth Avenue, Toronto, Ontario M4C 1L3.

Udupa, K.N. 1990. Editorial: Origin and development of Ayurveda. *Annals of the National Academy of Indian Medicine* 2–5(1).

Vivekananda, Swami. 1991. *Karma Yoga: The Yoga of Action*. Calcutta: Dvaita Ashrama Publication Department.

Vogel, H.G. 1991. 'Similarities Between Various Systems of Traditional Medicine: Considerations for the Future of Ethnopharmacology.' *J Ethnopharm* 35: 179–90.

Vivekananda, Swami. 1946. *Jnana Yoga – the Yoga of Knowledge*. Calcutta: Advaita Ashrama.

Yesudian, S. 1975. *Self-Reliance Through Yoga – Words of Wisdom and Inspiration*. London: Allen and Unwin.

Yogananda, Swami Paramahansa. 1968. *Autobiography of a Yogi*. New York: Self-Realization Fellowship Publishers.

Zimmer, H. 1951. *Philosophies of India*. New York: Pantheon.

14

Partnership in Practice: Some Reflections on the Aboriginal Healing and Wellness Strategy

SUZANNE DUDZIAK

I first encountered the Aboriginal Healing Wellness Strategy (AHWS) as a graduate student in social work. As a nonaboriginal Canadian, I have been a supporter of the rights of aboriginal peoples for many years. During a year-long practicum with the Ontario Native Affairs Secretariat, I became very involved in assisting with the development of the AHWS. That involvement led me to investigate new approaches to policymaking that do not repeat the colonial dynamics of dominance and control. In this respect, I believe there is much to be learned from case studies of actual partnerships in terms of how understanding across cultures can occur and, thus, how colonial relations can be transformed into new cultures of policymaking that are more egalitarian, just, and emancipatory. In this case study, aboriginal knowledge and values disrupted conventional policymaking practices and helped to create new social relations.

The last twenty-five years in Canadian-Aboriginal relations can be characterized as a period of intense political negotiation in terms of policymaking. The mass rejection by aboriginal peoples of the federal government's policy of assimilation, which was articulated in the White Paper of 1969, forced a change of policy direction in favour of resolving outstanding grievances (Fleras and Elliott, 1992; Angus, 1990). While evidence abounds that political negotiation has failed to produce substantial social change in terms of the needs of aboriginal peoples in Canada (Smith, 1993; Weaver, 1992; Cassidy, 1991), it is important to note the 180-degree turn in public and policy discourse that has occurred in this period, away from assimilation toward notions of self-government. While 180 degrees does not make the circle complete, it does indicate that at the federal level, aboriginal demands are increasingly being recognized.

The old paradigm was preoccupied with law, formality, and control of aboriginal peoples; the new paradigm is 'more concerned with justice, adaptation, and workable inter-cultural relations' based on historical and moral obligations of the State (Weaver 1990: 15). This shift in thinking affects not only policy content but also how policy is developed. In particular, Weaver identifies joint policy formulation and joint management as two key factors making it possible that fundamental political change will occur in federal policymaking.

The increased involvement of provincial governments in federal–Aboriginal relations in the early 1980s has added a number of new players to the political negotiations. Since 1985 the trend in Ontario has been to favour varying forms of aboriginal inclusion in the development and implementation of policies that directly affect aboriginal interests. This trend, begun under the Liberals, was solidified when the NDP came to power in 1990. Early in its mandate, the NDP government formally recognized aboriginal peoples' inherent right to self-government and adopted a partnership approach to dealing with major social-policy issues affecting them.

It is in this context of shifting paradigms that much can be learned from actual policy practices concerning the possibility that Canada can move beyond a colonial ethos in its relations with aboriginal peoples. This chapter analyzes one case study in policymaking, the Aboriginal Healing and Wellness Strategy. The AHWS was designed and developed over four years (1990–94) during the Rae government's tenure. Following a brief overview of the AHWS and the conditions that facilitated its development, this chapter will focus on the intercultural dynamics of this joint policy practice. Given that this book focuses on indigenous knowledges, particular attention will be paid to how aboriginal knowledges and cultural norms shaped and defined this policy exercise, as viewed from the perspectives of the participants.

This chapter represents part of an initial reflection on the design and development phase of the AHWS.[1] Data were gathered through a collaborative research project conducted by the author and the Joint Steering Committee of the AHWS, which is currently responsible for implementing of the strategy.[2] A subcommittee of the Joint Steering Committee provided direction and guidance throughout the research process and also reviewed this chapter. However, it is important to note that the views expressed in this chapter by former and current members of the Joint Steering Committee do not necessarily reflect the views of the committee as a whole, and that the analysis presented here remains mine alone.

The Aboriginal Healing and Wellness Strategy

The AHWS combines two developmental processes: a strategy for dealing with issues of family violence in aboriginal communities, and an aboriginal-specific health policy for aboriginal peoples in Ontario.

The first initiative, the Aboriginal Family Healing Strategy, began to take shape in 1990 when ten provincial ministries started to work with eight aboriginal/First Nations organizations representing the vast majority of aboriginal people in Ontario. The goal was to combat violence in families and to heal communities. A comprehensive and wholistic[3] framework for dealing with these issues was designed and developed in a collaborative manner.

In 1991 the Ministry of Health and the same aboriginal organizations began developing an aboriginal-specific health policy for Ontario. The goal of this initiative was to identify gaps in the services provided to aboriginal peoples as well as barriers to full access to health care. The policy articulates a set of principles and three strategic directions aimed at improving standards of care and at providing culturally appropriate health services.[4] While the two initiatives were developed separately, they had many common features, for example, the same target populations and conceptual approaches. In 1994 the two efforts were integrated by the Ontario government into one strategy – the Aboriginal Healing and Wellness Strategy.

The AHWS emerged from the most comprehensive community-based consultation ever undertaken with aboriginal peoples in Ontario. This positive, ongoing example of partnership led to the development of over 250 community-based projects in the first three years of implementation.[5] The health component of the strategy represents the largest provincially funded aboriginal health initiative in Canada. The strategy was highlighted as a model for development by the Royal Commission on Aboriginal Peoples, which has advocated 'widespread adoption of the Ontario approach.'[6] This chapter focuses on one component of the AHWS, namely, aspects of the design and development of the Aboriginal Family Healing Initiative.

Setting the Stage for Partnership

In retrospect, several forces converged to facilitate the development of the Aboriginal Family Healing initiative. By the late 1980s domestic violence and violence against women had become recognized as social issues in the public domain. The Ontario Women's Directorate had embarked on a five-year public education campaign about wife assault. As part of this effort, some aboriginal organizations received a number of small grants to do education work on this issue in their communities.

In 1990, two reports were tabled by aboriginal organizations emphasizing the magnitude of the problem. A report by the Ontario Native Women's Association (ONWA), *Breaking Free*, was especially influential. It documented that 80 per cent of aboriginal women and children in Ontario were victims of family violence. While the issue of family violence was by no means unique to aboriginal communities, there was an increasing awareness in government that solutions to the problem demanded different responses in aboriginal communities.

In their official response to the ONWA report, the ministers responsible for Women's Issues and Native Affairs indicated that 'consultation with Aboriginal groups and communities is a critical element in the development of a cohesive and culturally appropriate strategy in responding to Aboriginal family violence.'[7] The Ontario Women's Directorate was mandated to form an aboriginal subcommittee, involving a number of ministries, to begin to respond to the report. In July 1991, seven aboriginal organizations met with representatives from the Ontario Women's Directorate and the Ontario Native Affairs Secretariat and from seven provincial ministries to explore the possibility of working together.

Conditions for Joint Partnership

At the first meeting, the aboriginal organizations set out a number of conditions that would have to be met before they would agree to engage in a joint process with the Ontario government. The conditions included these:

- The initiative must be aboriginal focused and directed, with government playing only an administrative role.
- The initiative must be action-oriented, long-term, and broad in scope, and allow for an examination of root causes and for communities to address healing in a wholistic way. The initiative must be understood as long-term and as extending beyond the life of the government in office.
- There must be an aboriginal co-chair, and the aboriginal organizations must have input into where the lead responsibility in government will lie.
- There must be time and resources for an aboriginal caucus meeting prior to joint meetings.
- During strategy development, responsiveness to immediate needs must not be jeopardized but enhanced.[8]

The implications of these conditions were also discussed. It was noted that 'implementing an Aboriginal focus will require basic change in Aboriginal-government relationships and that the differences in perspectives between the parties can best be dealt with openly as they surface.'[9] It was further emphasized that 'maintaining an Aboriginal focus may require basic change in the conventional process of developing policy.'[10]

There was also substantial discussion at that first meeting regarding the need to consult with aboriginal communities in order to develop a strategy and the funding and resources required to carry it out. It was agreed that the ministries involved would seek funding to augment what was then available for consultation. The ground rules established at this first meeting had far-reaching implications for the aboriginal and government caucuses involved and for how social policy relating to aboriginal peoples would be developed in Ontario over the next few years.

The Aboriginal Family Healing Strategy was never conceived of or constructed as part of the agenda for formal government-to-government negotiations; nonetheless, it benefited from the sympathetic political climate in government at that time. Civil servants were being encouraged to adopt new modes of interaction and to treat aboriginal peoples as partners in government initiatives affecting them. More formalized, co-operative approaches were being developed that included the negotiation of issues, not just consultation.[11]

Aboriginal demands converged with a more inclusive and egalitarian approach to policymaking in government to enable a partnership to go forward. What emerged was a new culture or way of doing business: a hybrid process in which two cultures interacted with each other. What resulted was different from what either alone would have developed without the other.

Aboriginal organizations sought to change the traditional power imbalance through practices such as establishing separate caucuses for the aboriginal organizations and the ministries. The appointment of co-chairs established the partners as equals. The use of consensus, which is consistent with aboriginal cultural practices, as the approach to decision-making helped establish a power-sharing ethic.

Yet these structural features tell only part of the story. For a new culture of policymaking to emerge, aboriginal cultural norms and values had to be incorporated. Aboriginal knowledge had to be acknowledged and understood and then integrated with that of the government. Euro-Canadian norms could no longer be assumed, yet no blueprint existed for working in a cross-cultural context. As one senior official in government explained it, everyone necessarily became engaged in a process of 'learning by doing': a process that was full of awkward, difficult, and exhilarating moments. A theme of teaching and learning emerges in the talk of the participants. This dynamic will be discussed in relation to three dimensions of the process: the meaning of consultation, the conceptual frameworks adopted by the strategy, and the values that informed the process.

Consultation

One of the first challenges confronting participants was finding a way to carry out an extensive consultation with aboriginal communities on the issue of family violence. For the government caucus, this involved relinquishing power and control over the consultation process and supporting the aboriginal organizations as they performed their own consultations. An aboriginal representative commented:

> I guess in the consultation phase the really critical happening was over a series of meetings getting the government to understand that their only participation in the consultation would in fact be funding it. You know, go find the money, come back, we'll consult, we'll give you the results. Other than that you ain't the law, you don't define the consultation, you don't participate in the consultation, you don't have any role except to be there. (interview, 9 May 1996)

The internal struggle to 'let go' was described by one government respondent:

> The fundamental difference, I guess, was that we were able to agree with the organizations that in this instance it was appropriate for the organizations to consult with the communities rather than the government to consult with the communities. Now, this was a significant ideological issue. This isn't a minor matter ... If we hadn't had the political support, the support of the deputies, it would have been very, very difficult to say, well, okay, what we're going to now do is put up $700,000 which we're going to give to eight organizations who are going to run their own consultations, based on their own designs and the way that they want to do it. They're not going to have stats that are all the same, they're not going to have the same questionnaires, they're not going to use the same approaches. What we're going to do is ask each organization to define what it is they're going to do, and agree that they're going to provide information that will at least match a set of our objectives within certain terms of reference to this, which we did. And, of course, it worked. (interview, 26 April 1996)

For the aboriginal caucus, the challenge was how to assume responsibility for what some termed 'opening Pandora's box.' They understood the magnitude of the issue of family violence and communicated the implications to the government. A ministry representative noted:

> There was going to be a lot of resistance in the communities and the aboriginal representatives were very aware that it would probably result in a whole lot of behavioural stuff emerging. They predicted that there would be a real increase in the number of disclosures of violence and abuse as a result of the consultation process itself. That all happened and it's true. So it was like on the aboriginal side there was a pretty good handle on what they were getting themselves into and the amount of

work that it was going to entail to go out to that number of communities. They even included going to a number of the correctional institutions and facilities as well. There was really a lot of effort made to make the process as inclusive as possible, to make as much outreach as possible here. (interview, 24 April 1996)

Once the consultations were completed, the aboriginal caucus called for a three-day retreat to share its findings among the aboriginal organizations and with the government ministries. Many participants observed that the retreat helped break down barriers between the two caucuses. Two aboriginal respondents observed:

That retreat really cemented the players. We'd go back to our own rooms in the evening and just sort of think in singular terms. We were housed, and I guess the way the lots were drawn, you know, there'd be perhaps an on-reserve with an off-reserve and a government technician, you know. We would be roomed together and therefore respect, understanding. (interview 1 May 1996)

I think it was the beginning of the creative process. It didn't hurt that we were all isolated out there either. Well, that's probably where the group came together and was more cohesive ... In the meetings we were always aboriginal caucus at one end of the circle, like one half, and government the other half. Very little mixing. Coffee breaks and smoke breaks. And [at the retreat] we eliminated some barriers, some big barriers. Like just the perception that you're government and I'm not going to get close enough to touch you or work with you. And I guess I do mean that in sort of a prejudiced kind of way ... There were people that maybe didn't think they could work as closely together with the mixed bag of people that were there. That also happened between the ministries as well. So relationships were formed between different people and some other ministries where they didn't have any contact and really didn't work together. So I think it happened. And the same thing happened with the Aboriginal caucus between on and off reserve. All of the barriers sort of dissolved and then there was an expectation to get barriers out of the way and let's get the work done. And a good idea is a good idea regardless of who's the author of the idea. (interview 9 May 1996)

Some government participants noted the importance of aboriginal cultural practices in breaking down barriers and building cohesiveness:

It was the first time that I had experienced, for instance, the greetings that happen after the ceremonies where people go around in the circle and hug each other. In terms of conflict resolution, I know it comes from the traditions of the aboriginal communities, but looking at it from the perspective of somebody who hadn't experienced it, all I could think of was: If we could only do this in other situations we'd get things done! Because it's real hard, you know, once you've engaged in that kind of physical contact, to not speak to somebody anymore. There were all kinds of things, the including of an elder and having the opening ceremonies put things in context for you. (interview, 23 April 1996)

All participants viewed the consultation as a major strength in the overall process. An aboriginal participant reflected:

What was good about it from another perspective was learning more about commonalities that other aboriginal communities had. In terms of a nationhood we may represent a different nation or a language group, but in terms of basic human needs and our values for family, for relationships, for preserving our heritage, these were all reinforced by the other aboriginal participants, and by the end of the process we realized that we had done our job as teachers because I think we had helped the government representatives understand where we were coming from, from a policy level. So when they started to also be really committed to the process I think that we had done the job that we were supposed to be doing, which is helping people understand it from our world and from our experiences. (interview, 6 June 1996)

Consultation as practised in this joint initiative went beyond the usual boundary of information gathering: it served as the foundation for developing an actual strategy. It became a vehicle for community development and part of the broader movement toward healing; in some instances, consultation is what *initiated* healing.

For the participants, the retreat that followed the consultation was a significant event in terms of developing a strategy; it was also personally transformative. For the aboriginal representatives the retreat involved an intense process of sharing the pain of many communities, and left them, in the words of one respondent, 'depressed but empowered' to act on the issues at hand. Inviting government participants into that process served to break down barriers on a human level. As one government respondent put it, 'I felt less like a total outsider, I think more of an insider involved' (interview, 14 May 1996).

Aboriginal Conceptual Frameworks

Much learning occurred also with respect to how to develop a culture-based appropriate framework for dealing with the multiple issues arising from the consultations. The participants struggled through numerous meetings to find ways to integrate all the needs identified by the communities. The Western tendency to subdivide, prioritize, and reduce problems was resisted by the aboriginal caucus. The aboriginal approaches, based on the ability to envision the parts in relation to the whole effectively broke the impasse. One aboriginal participant graphically described the process of letting go of 'words' and returning to 'circles':

> We decided we would do it a different way and then in the community needs group coming up with the healing framework was really significant. What happened there was we were struggling with words put to a vision and gave up, and just went with the vision and began to draw it in circles. Then everybody saw what was happening and everybody started pitching in ... And what developed was the framework and that vision is what became the focus of developing the rest of the document. It was all these stages and it still excites me. (interview, 9 May 1996)

In effect, the participants turned to the traditional teachings of the Medicine Wheel, a central paradigm in many aboriginal cultures. From the Medicine Wheel, an eight-phase continuum of care was constructed that embodied community needs, and the types of services and programs required for healing, in whole and comprehensive ways. It also addressed all age groups contained in the teachings of the Cycle of Life.

Several participants reflected on the importance of aboriginal knowledge in designing the strategy. An aboriginal participant remarked:

> I think the whole discussion on the cultural approach, the Medicine Wheel teachings, to me was integral to the whole success of the strategy. And when that became understood by the participants, I think it kind of solidified the whole relevance of the strategy because it was kind of made by Indians, made by Indians for Indians, and supported by government. So I think that, to me, was probably the highlight of the whole strategy. (interview, 28 May 1996)

A government participant observed:

> So within that concept of wholistic also there was the consideration of more than just the physical dimensions of the program, that there were other things that were important to wellness, to well-being, that have to do with the emotional and spiritual, physical and psychological. I will admit that when I got involved in the process, to me, spiritual wasn't really ... I really didn't understand it to any great extent, it was something that kind of slid into emotional and psychological.

Wholistic approaches to knowledge, which are intrinsic to aboriginal epistemologies, were of central importance to developing the strategy. Aboriginal conceptual frameworks were viewed as 'culturally appropriate' practice; they were also valued as inherently useful for understanding complex issues and for providing comprehensive approaches for dealing with those issues.

Centring Aboriginal Values

Aboriginal participants from various cultural locations emphasized the value of spirituality. One aboriginal participant, who assumed a teaching role, spoke to some of the difficulties and rewards involved. In the following excerpt, knowledge is constructed as encompassing the physical, mental, emotional, and spiritual. The value of the spiritual as a way of life grounds this whole:

> I may be wrong, but I tend to think that it was the cultural and traditional values and beliefs of the native people that kind of put it together, and it was that alone that needed a lot of convincing to the ministries, the majority of whom are non-native and very bureaucratic and very difficult to see the spiritual aspect of native people and the healing process. It was very difficult for them to understand or to believe that our culture and our traditions are very strong in our lives. And I think that the turning point was convincing them of that ... I guess it was a dual role, teaching and also learning too at the same time, politically, and how hard it is for somebody with a different religion or different way of life that they've been raised with ... It was difficult trying to teach some things that were totally new to some people, they've never heard it before, how we look at things, how we parent, the birthing, how we raise children ... Even some of our own people, it was sort of difficult sometimes to help them understand the traditional ways of the Creator, creation stories. And the ministry reps too, it was hard at times ... We did pick up those that were truly picking up this spiritual, physical, mental, emotional, and spiritual aspect. For us, the number one is spiritual. If you don't have that then you're really down, if you don't have the spiritual in your life. Then we sensed that there were those from the ministries who were eager, we could feel it, and I think that what really energized us to keep us going was some of these people who were genuinely wanting to see this succeed and that's what kept us going. So it wasn't all bad guys, you know. I mean we had good guys [laughter]. (interview, 1 May 1996)

As a number of participants observed, the presence of elders and traditional practices facilitated the transfer of knowledge through a dynamic of teaching and learning in the whole group. One aboriginal respondent noted how essential this was to the whole process:

Some of the other things that helped, at least much more in Family Healing than in Aboriginal Health Policy – because we did not do it as much in Aboriginal Health Policy – was using traditional people and elders. I think that for many of the aboriginal organizations, that helped us to focus and remember the bigger picture, in terms of creation and spirit and all of those things. It helped us to remember to be good to each other and to be kind. Sometimes that did not always happen but at least there was some sense of recognition and respect for the fact that there were cultural people or traditions and reminders of spirit in the room ... I think there was a lot of teaching and a lot of value in sharing that with the government representatives who are nonaboriginal, who may have never been exposed to that before. At some times there was frustration in that education process, but I think that the end result, the fact that there is an Aboriginal Healing and Wellness Strategy, speaks volumes to the learning that went on and the sharing that went on. (interview, 12 April 1996)

While it is behaviour, not values, that we actually observe in practice, it is also evident that value systems have consequences for the functioning of organizations and for the individuals who participate in them (Chapman, McCaskill, and Newhouse, 1991).

Conclusions

This initial reflection, taken from one case study, suggests strongly that alternative approaches to policymaking that do not replicate colonial practices are indeed possible. Assuming that the political will exists in governments, more just and equitable approaches to policy development will mean, in Weaver's terms, developing 'workable cross-cultural relations.' At this early stage in the transition between old and new paradigms, nonaboriginal people are necessarily positioned as learners in relation to aboriginal teachers. It is this rebalancing, grounded in the sharing of power, resources, and knowledge, that enables relationship building and facilitates respect across differences.

This case study points to several significant implications for future joint initiatives and for further research. The first concerns the importance of the policy development phase itself: more attention must be paid to the process of developing policy as distinct from policy analysis (which is the usual emphasis). The willingness to engage in a collective process of 'learning by doing' challenges the conventional wisdom embedded in predetermined planning modes – modes that effectively exclude aboriginal perspectives and practices. A process-oriented approach creates space for aboriginal world views, conceptual thinking, and cultural practices; in turn, this facilitates sharing of the knowledge required to develop culturally appropriate solutions.

A second implication concerns the challenge to dominant ways of conceptualizing issues. Bicultural approaches to policy development that integrate aboriginal perspectives often lead to the reconceptualization of issues and the creation of new knowledge. If social change is to occur, such approaches should inform the core out of which policy is developed.

A further implication that can be drawn from this case study concerns the relevance of consultation. An inclusive policy-development approach considers consultation as an essential ingredient for designing strategies that are more effective, responsive, and accountable to the people and interests they are meant to serve. Whether viewed as following the aboriginal path or simply as good community development practice, meaningful consultation allows for the conventional practice of gathering necessary information and perspectives; it can also serve to mobilize those affected by a given social issue.

Bicultural partnerships anticipate the incorporation of aboriginal knowledge, values, cultural norms, and ways of relating in the developmental process. It is only by engaging in authentically bicultural partnerships – admittedly not an easy task – that governments can claim to support aboriginal self-determination.

NOTES

1 I wish to thank the Joint Steering Committee of the Aboriginal Healing and Wellness Strategy for making this study possible. I also wish to acknowledge the support of the Social Sciences and Humanities Research Council of Canada. See also *Working Together*, a more detailed report based on the data. I have also undertaken a second analysis of the data for a doctoral dissertation.

2 Of the 37 respondents interviewed, 28 had been direct participants, 7 held leadership positions either in aboriginal organizations or in the Ontario government, and 2 were elders who had been involved for varying amounts of time. The respondents comprise representatives from the eight aboriginal organizations involved and from nine out of ten of the ministries that participated.

3 'Wholistic' is not misspelled in the text; it reflects a decision of the Aboriginal Family Healing Joint Steering Committee to emphasize the 'whole' rather than the 'hole.'

4 *New Directions: Aboriginal Health Policy for Ontario*. 1994. Ministry of Health.

5 For further information contact the AHWS Project Office, 880 Bay St., 2nd Floor, Toronto, Ontario M7A 2B6, (416) 326–6905.

6 Final Report of the Royal Commission on Aboriginal Peoples, Vol. 3, pp. 287–9, 251.
7 *A Response to the Ontario Native Women's Association Report and Brief on Aboriginal Family Violence*, 1990. By Ian Scott, Minister Responsible for Native Affairs and Mavis Wilson, Minister Responsible for Women's Issues. June.
8 Summarized from the Minutes, Meeting to Discuss Development of an Aboriginal Family Violence Strategy. Westbury Hotel, Toronto, 9 July 1991.
9 Ibid., p. 13
10 Ibid.
11 Statement of Political Relationship, SPR Guidelines: Questions and Answers. Prepared by the Ontario Native Affairs Secretariat. August 1992.

REFERENCES

Aboriginal Family Healing Joint Steering Committee. 1993. *For Generations to Come: The Time Is Now*. A Strategy for Aboriginal Family Healing: A Final Report. Toronto. September.
Angus, Murray. 1990. *'... and the last shall be first': Native Policy in an Era of Cutbacks*. Ottawa: The Aboriginal Rights Coalition (Project North).
Cassidy, Frank (ed.). 1991. *Aboriginal Self-Determination: Proceedings of a Conference Held September 30 – October 3, 1990, 1–16, 252–82*. Halifax: Institute for Research on Public Policy.
Chapman, Ian, Don McCaskill, and David Newhouse. 1991. Management in Contemporary Aboriginal Organizations. *Canadian Journal of Native Studies* 10(2): 333–49.
Dudziak, Suzanne. 1996. *Working Together: Reflections on the Design and Development of the Aboriginal Healing and Wellness Strategy*. In conjunction with the Joint Steering Committee of the Aboriginal Healing and Wellness Strategy. December. Toronto.
Fleras, Augie, and Jean Leonard Elliott. 1992. *The Nations Within: Aboriginal Relations in Canada, the United States, and New Zealand, 8–116*. Don Mills, Ont: Oxford University Press.
Ontario Ministry of Health. 1994. *New Directions: Aboriginal Health Policy for Ontario*.
Ontario Native Women's Association. 1989. *Breaking Free: A Proposal for Change to Aboriginal Family Violence*. Thunder Bay. December.
Smith, Dan. 1993. *The Seventh Fire: The Struggle for Aboriginal Government*. Toronto: Key Porter.

Weaver, Sally M. 1990. A New Paradigm in Canadian Indian Policy for the 1990s. In *Canadian Ethnic Studies* 22(3): 8–18.

– 1992. Self-Government for Indians 1980–1990: Political Transformation or Symbolic Gestures. In J. Burnet, D. Jauteau, E. Padolsky, A. Raspovich, and A. Sirois (Eds.), 109–41. *UNESCO Conference Proceedings on Migration and the Transformation of Cultures in Canada.*

15

Peace Research and African Development: An Indigenous African Perspective

THOMAS MARK TURAY

'One tree does not make a forest'

(Sierra Leonean proverb)

I am a Sierra Leonean doctoral student studying at a Canadian university. For the past three years, my research has focused on engaging indigenous Africans to articulate their understandings of peace and conflict, with the goal of empowering ourselves to rediscover and share globally our indigenous skills at nurturing cultures of peace. My colonial education taught me to disconnect my being from my 'Africanness' and to regard my cultural heritage as inferior to that of other civilizations. The loss of my heritage created in me a state of 'peacelessness.' In response, I approach the above-mentioned topic with the desire and commitment to rediscover, reclaim, and regenerate positive indigenous African alternatives of living in peace with social and human environments. This chapter examines the concept of peace, from both theoretical and practical perspectives, and discusses the implications for African development from an indigenous African perspective. My focus is on West Africa, with particular reference to Sierra Leone, although I also draw from relevant experiences in other parts of Africa when appropriate.

Issues of peace and social justice are fundamental to the improvement of the quality of African people's lives and to the sustainability of the nonhuman environment. Peace research is integral to the goal of achieving 'living peace,' by which I mean sustainable social and ecological balance. Because Western approaches to peace have proven themselves unequal to the task of ensuring peaceful coexistence in African environments, it is imperative that African scholars and social activists examine indigenous African initiatives for living peace. The time has come for the marginalized voices of Africa to critically examine the root causes of their 'peacelessness' and to explore nonviolent alternatives for resolving their ethnic and regional conflicts. It is by hearing these voices out that effective methods of peace making will emerge.

I begin this chapter by briefly examining central concepts such as peace, structural violence, peace research, nonviolence, conflict, and conflict resolution. I also explore indigenous nonviolent African alternatives to resolving conflicts. By indigenous African alternatives, I mean 'local [African] knowledge[s] [and skills], derived from interactions between people and their environment' (Kroma, 1995: 13). These alternatives are grounded in local peoples' experiences, histories, and aspirations and in the realities of their environment. Indigenous knowledge forms take into account the roles that women play in social organization, traditional legal systems, and intrafamily arbitration; in African spirituality and traditional symbols; and in songs, proverbs, stories, and parables. The creation of a culture of peace is fundamental to indigenous African knowledge systems.

Conceptualizing the Issues

What Is Peace?

Peace means different things to different people. There are two conceptions of peace: 'positive peace' and 'negative peace' (Tandon, 1989; Brock-Utne, 1987). Negative peace refers to the absence of war or violent conflict (Assefa, 1993; Kekkonen, 1981; Brock-Utne, 1985; Galtung, 1975). In contrast, 'positive peace' is not necessarily the absence of war/conflict but rather a state of mind (O'Connel, 1984; Brock-Utne, 1987; Galtung, 1975). In an attempt to provide a more comprehensive definition of peace, Galtung argues that such a definition must include economic welfare, ecological balance, and the absence of war.

For the most part, Eurocentric/North American conceptualizations of peace focus on the negative aspects (Kisembo, 1993). As a result, global armed conflicts receive more international media attention than less overtly violent situations. It is common to hear about peace talks between rebel leaders and governments in war-torn African countries such as Rwanda, Liberia, Sierra Leone, the Democratic Republic of Congo, Angola, and Sudan, and about peace talks in 'trouble spots' such as Israel, Bosnia, and Ireland. All these examples emphasize the negative conception of peace, which has dominated over the centuries. But 'the absence of overt violence in any given society or community must not be seen as the presence of peace because both in the so-called developed and developing world, varying degrees of "structural violence" do exist.' Stedman (1991: 369) articulates this view further:

Therefore, peace is understood to exist among people when they are able to meet their basic needs; make informed political, religious/spiritual, socio-economic and cultural decisions regarding their very existence and the sustainability of their society (including their non-human environment). Among West African ethnic groups, for example, the Limba, Kono, Kissi, Themne and Mende in Sierra Leone, peace exists among the people when they are living in a harmonious relationship with God and among themselves, with their families, neighbors, ancestors and non-human environment. It follows that peace cannot exist without social justice, particularly the equitable distribution of power and wealth among the people in a given society and between the countries in the South and North.

What then should constitute an African-centred definition of peace? In my view, such a definition must include the following: the absence of war, the absence of internal and external exploitation of both human and nonhuman resources, gender equality, and respect for human rights (which include political and religious/spiritual freedoms and the right to education, health, and food security). In the indigenous sense, peace is a state of personal and social harmony. It also means respect for oneself and others, kindness, love, honesty, sensitivity, and the power to live one's dreams. An African-centred definition of peace must also speak to the issues of ecological balance and power equity between the North and the South. Assefa (1993: 4–5) sums this up when he defines peace as 'a philosophy, and in fact a paradigm, with its own values and precepts, which provide a framework to discern, understand, analyze, and regulate all human relations in order to create an integrated, holistic, and humane social order.'

What Is Structural Violence?

It is disheartening to note that '[structural violence] ... is responsible today for the death of approximately 15 million children per year (40,000 per day) in the world' (Handa, 1992: 24). I agree with Handa (70) that 'in the world today, [one of the] worst form[s] of violence is the violence of poverty, the structural violence, that is, the violence as a result of social structures which create, maintain, and tolerate mass poverty.' According to Assefa:

> Structural violence has been defined as social and personal violence arising from unjust, repressive, and oppressive national and international political and social structures. According to this view, a system that generates repression, abject poverty, malnutrition, and starvation for some members of a society while other

members enjoy opulence and unbridled power inflicts covert violence with the ability to destroy life as much as overt violence, except that it does it in more subtle ways. (1993: 3)

In Africa external and internal factors are in play that perpetuate structural violence; they are the major factors contributing to Africa's lack of sustained development. Relative peace will not be achieved by Africans until the dynamics of structural violence are critically re-examined, and until the root causes of that violence are analyzed. The ultimate goal of this effort must be to transform unjust structures.

What Is Conflict?

Conflict is another concept with both positive and negative meanings. From a negative point of view, conflict is construed to be destructive and unproductive and must therefore be eliminated. On the other hand, 'conflict, it may be noted, performs many important social functions' (Dahrendorf, 1972: 62). In fact, Himes (1980: 28) argues that 'conflict [is] universal and natural in human society [and] functionally speaking, contribute[s] to the organization, unification, change, and progress of human society.' Thus, conflict of itself is not necessarily evil; rather, it is an inevitable ingredient of human experience (Pelton, 1974; Zartman, 1991).

Stedman (1991: 367) argues that 'conflict in Africa arises from problems basic to all populations: the tugs and pulls of different identities, the differential distribution of resources and access to power, and competing definitions of what is right, fair, and just.' The critical issue here is not how humankind can eliminate conflict but how it will be waged (Pelton, 1974). The emphasis is on how a conflict is dealt with by opposing parties. Bozeman (1976: 3) states that 'conflict is valued not so much as an end in itself but rather as a process that serves to clarify issues in dispute and narrow areas of concentration so as to induce some measure of ultimate conciliation or accord.'

Assefa (1993: 5–6) elaborates on a comprehensive program for peace that allows for the reconceptualizing of peace in positive terms and for a focus on the process by which conflicts are to be resolved:

1 One cannot resolve conflicts and make peace unless the root causes of the conflicts are identified and dealt with ... [In other words], lasting peace between conflicting parties is possible only when deeper needs are accommodated and satisfied.

2 It is not possible to resolve conflicts and attain peace unless attention is given to the justice and fairness of the process as well as the outcome of the settlement.
3 People's deeper needs are not totally incompatible. Parties in a conflict can discover commonality of interests and objectives which can lead to mutually acceptable solutions to their problems.
4 Conflict resolution and therefore peacemaking involves a restructuring of relationships ...

Most African leaders today tend to avoid dealing with socioeconomic and political crises in a participative and democratic manner. Civil demonstrations for basic needs and democratic governance often meet with a violent response. A problem-solving approach which posits that conflict is not something that has to be won, but rather something that has to be *solved*, is the most democratic and sustainable way of handling conflicts. In this approach, each person considers both his or her own and the other person's feelings and needs, and all those involved work together to solve the problem. As I will illustrate later, the role in conflict transformation of traditional African symbols, proverbs, stories, and songs – the traditional approaches to dealing with social/community conflicts – is based on the problem-solving or win/win (as opposed to win/lose) approach.

For example, among the Themne ethnic group in Sierra Leone, elders mediating a conflict often use proverbs such as 'Ma n'k ka th'ntha k'sonkor, a sar n'yi do ratha' (in English: 'There is no smoke without fire') when appealing to the disputants to critically identify and analyze the root causes of their conflict; they urge the disputants to listen to each other carefully and to see things from the other's perspective. Indigenous African approaches to conflict transformation need to be studied and interrogated with a view to identifying useful lessons that can be applied to the building of peace in contemporary Africa.

African Alternatives to Living Peace

The current regional and national armed conflicts in Africa, the Middle East and Far East, and the 'unproclaimed' nuclear build-up by the industrialized states, and human rights abuses, and gender and racial inequalities, and global health and environmental degradation, all make 'peace' one of the most neglected basic human and earth rights.

Africa remains the most 'peaceless' continent on this planet. The African Association for Literacy and Adult Education (1994: 1) supports this view: 'Today, more than at any other time in her history, the African continent is locked in the most extensive, most intensive and most ferocious, yet senseless and escalating wars of mutual annihilation ... The African peoples are right now the only race caught up in sustained wars for their own self-destruction.'

But armed conflicts are not the only cause of Africa's 'peacelessness': foreign domination contributes heavily. Djibril Diallo (cited in Prendergast, 1996: 28) articulates this point further:

> Africa's problem – Africa's biggest problem – is too many people going around the continent with solutions to problems they don't understand. Many of these solutions are half-baked. Tremendous resources have gone to supporting these external problem-solvers. About US$4 billion a year goes into technical assistance to Africa, mostly to salaries of the estimated 100,000 expatriate advisers working in Africa.

It is immoral and against the African people's basic democratic rights for the West to continue to serve as the 'think tank' and 'problem solver' for Africa. Africans must play a central role in identifying and solving their own problems.

Africans, like other peoples, deserve the right to enjoy the fullness of creation. If Africans are to meet the challenges of the twenty-first century, they must deal with their current 'peacelessness' from an African-centred perspective.

It is not the aim of this paper to romanticize African-centred approaches to conflict resolution and management. I agree with Dei (1994: 16) that 'we can have a simultaneous celebration and a serious interrogation of African cultures, cultural values, and norms.' However, as part of my political project I want to concentrate on the need to research the positive aspects of African approaches to living peace, since, as Tedla (1995) argues, there is abundant literature on the negative aspects of the African people. I call on 'Africans everywhere [to] begin to appreciate the variety and richness of their past histories, cultures and traditions' (Dei, 1994: 9).

The Role of African Women in the Sustenance of Peace

In Africa, as in most other countries in the world, 'women's voices and visions are pushed aside, shunted off to the margins of existence – i.e. marginalized' (Evangelista, 1997: 1). Yet women contribute the bulk of the domestic labour for food production and processing, child rearing and caring, and home management. Evangelista (2) also highlights the plight of women and their children:

> It is much more obvious to people in other countries, especially to poor people,

that perhaps the heaviest burdens of war fall on women and children. Women are tasked with continuing their households, running their families as economic units, sometimes with men away, in hiding, fighting or dead. At the same time all the other economic supports may fail – there may be no crops, no markets, no business, no lights or water – but people must still be fed, the sick cared for, etc.

The role of African women in nurturing cultures of peace needs to be documented, valued, and disseminated globally. Brock-Utne (1987: 35) has argued that 'women have a different upbringing than men, are a more peaceful sex, and more capable than men of solving conflicts in a nonviolent manner.'

In light of this view, I argue that Africa's peace-building initiatives must integrate African feminist perspectives on the meaning of peace and on non-violent alternatives for preventing, resolving, and managing violent conflicts. Conflict resolution and management must begin within the family. This is because 'the home is the center or heart of traditional learning [and] it is here that the child begins and ends his/her journey to becoming a true person' (Tedla, 1995: 152). It is important to note that women play a central role in this learning process and that therefore it is essential to interrogate the distribution of power and economic resources within the family. Brock-Utne supports this point of view, arguing (1987: 139) that it is necessary to look into the following:

1 how economic resources are distributed within the family and with what consequences.
2 which family members have acquired greater decision-making power over others.
3 who within the family makes how much contribution to family income.
4 what the labour contribution of each family member is.
5 whether the labour contribution of each family member is commensurate with the benefits he or she derives from membership in it.

The lack of recognition of the labour inputs of each member of the family – particularly the women and children – is a potential source of conflict within the family. Peace studies must investigate the traditional roles of the women and validate their contributions both to their families and to society as a whole. 'Since women and elders are the custodians of African cultural values, to leave them out is tantamount to destroying African culture' (Tedla, 1995: 198). Against this background, Brock-Utne (1987) calls for a broadening of peace research to encompass the issue of personal violence against women.

Gberie (1997) provides a very typical example of the ability of women to mediate between warring factions and to resolve conflicts through nonviolent alternatives. Members of the Sierra Leone Women's Movement for Peace were among the first peace activists to initiate peace dialogues with the rebels of the Revolutionary United Front (a rebel group that had been waging war against the Sierra Leone government and its people since 1991). Through their mass 'peaceful demonstrations,' they convinced the military government to organize democratic elections in 1996. A number of women in the eastern part of the country met their deaths when they organized peace marches to rebel strongholds in an effort to negotiate with the rebels to end their war against their own people. Such actions exemplify the commitment of these African women to peace-building and nonviolence.

African women's initiatives are often quite innovative. In Sierra Leone, the wives (including widows) of soldiers taught their children how to run small-scale enterprises, such as soap and bread making, vegetable farming, and petty trading, as a means to augment the meager salaries of their spouses. Such indigenous 'business education' enabled the children to learn bargaining/negotiation skills, which are critical to resolving day-to-day conflicts. In-depth studies on how such creative initiatives contribute to living peace need to be undertaken by African peace scholars.

A number of indigenous women's approaches to living peace could be investigated by African scholars interested in peace studies. A few examples are briefly described below.

In Sierra Leone, the Bondo society is the most significant nonformal educational institution for the women of most ethnic groups (the main exception being the Creole ethnic group). This traditional institution plays a vital role in transmitting the society's cultural heritage – its values, beliefs, customs, spirituality, norms, and so on. This institution is responsible for preparing young girls for womanhood – for instructing them in their roles and responsibilities in nurturing children, safeguarding the environment, producing food, and developing their community in general. Local women with long expertise in traditional African science and art teach the young female 'initiates' the art of living. During their initiation period in the 'Bondo bush,' these initiates learn that 'diversity is the principle of women's work and knowledge.'

In the 1990s some Western and African feminist, health, and human rights activists, with the support of the United Nations and the international media, have argued strongly against the existence of such institutions because the 'initiates' have to undergo female circumcision. For example, they have labelled female circumcision 'genital mutilation' and have pressured African leaders to ban this practice. However, the role of this traditional institution in improving the quality of life of women must be interrogated by the women and children themselves, so that they can make informed decisions about the relevance of this practice to their lives. Can a balance be found? For example, can female circumcision be separated from the other educational aspects?

There are several indigenous male societies for some of the ethnic groups in Sierra Leone. These include the *poro* (predominantly for boys of the Mende, Themne, Sherbro, and Kissi groups), the *gbagbani* (for the Limba), and the *rabai* (for the Loko). These societies perform roles similar to those of the Bondo societies. These indigenous educational institutions play a significant role in educating and training young boys in various aspects of African art, science, spirituality, and culture. In these societies, during the period of initiation, youths learn about war and peace and about how to survive generally.

These societies have been labelled superstitious, primitive, and barbaric by the Western media. However, I was initiated into the *gbagbani* society and I was never closer to mother nature or more connected to my African roots than when I was going through my nonformal education and training as an initiate.

The central question is this: What lessons about peaceful living among women between men and women, and between human and nonhuman environments do these indigenous institutions teach us?

The Role of Traditional Legal Systems

In Africa's recent history, armed conflicts have generally been resolved by military intervention, often at the bidding of the West. These military interventions have sometimes had the unexpected consequence of forging governments with considerable military might. Such governments are firmly rooted in Western traditions of governance. However, sustained peace cannot be achieved in Africa unless it is based on the historical, cultural, spiritual, socioeconomic and political experiences of the African people. Africa's people need to rediscover the wisdom of their traditional legal systems, which have sustained their communities for many centuries.

Tedla (1995: 111), therefore, states that 'a crucial lesson to be learned from the [North] is that it does not abandon its heritage [but rather] it selectively borrows ideas and technologies from everywhere and places them within its own cultural and conceptual framework.' According to Richardson (1963, cited in Bozeman, 1976: 234), the good news is that 'African scholars are now intensifying research into the customary law of their respective countries, that judges and law officers are increasingly conscious of the social advantages offered by flexible native traditions of litigation and that governments are determined to create national legal systems with a decidedly African character.'

Intrafamily Arbitration

In most of rural Africa today, so-called Western civilization has had little impact or influence, and indigenous arbitration methods continue to play a major role in resolving or containing intrafamily conflicts. Bozeman (1976: 237) explains the significance of this:

> [African arbitration proceedings] are rooted in the demands of intrafamily rela-
> tions, in the context of which it is taken for granted that the family head knows the
> parties as well as the issue in contention and can be expected, if necessary – with
> the assistance of the elders or other members of the household – to settle quarrels,
> discipline those who misbehave and restore harmony in the group by exerting
> persuasion rather than imposing a verdict in strict accordance to customary law.

For example, among the three major ethnic groups in Sierra Leone, the Limba, the Themne, and the Mende, the paramount chiefs, village headwomen/ men, councils of elders, and leaders of secret societies play a vital role in mediating and negotiating disputes within and between families, between villages, and among social groups. Similarly, Bozeman (1976: 237) notes that among the Bunyoro in East Africa, 'impartial arbiters include: a village head-man [sic], village elders, a council of neighbors,' while among the Ashanti in Ghana they include a panel of stool-holders.

So there are different approaches to conflict resolution and management. Eurocentric approaches focus on ensuring justice based on written objective norms; African approaches focus on conciliation (Bozeman, 1976). Further-more, 'African approaches to arbitral settlement ... ought to be accepted by scholars and practitioners on their own merits – all the more so, one may add, since they represent the African genius for reaching compromise and accom-modation' (238).

Another indigenous African approach to conflict resolution relates to settling disputes among spouses, particularly those related to divorce. Among most ethnic groups in Sierra Leone, it is the customary practice for marriages to be negotiated and approved by the families of both spouses. The parents and relatives from both sides negotiate with each other to determine the conditions under which a marriage will be arranged. This negotiation process can take several months or several years. On the day of the traditional marriage, the two families meet and exchange gifts and share words of wisdom from the ancestors. A typical dowry includes some money, needles and a roll of white thread, cola nuts, a white piece of cloth, a mat, a bag of salt, and a calabash, which are given by the bridegroom's parents and relatives to the bride's parents and relatives. Each of these items has its own symbolic significance; together they are meant to remind the new couple to be caring, forgiving, tolerant, loving, understanding, and patient with each other, especially during moments of conflict and when times are difficult. The involvement and commitment of both families makes it extremely difficult for the couple to divorce. This is because it requires both partners to convince all their parents and relatives that a divorce is warranted. Because of the strong family bonds that both families sustain and nurture day in and day out, many potentially serious conflicts are de-escalated at a very early stage through mediation and the exchange of visits and gifts.

There are many exceptions to the above example. Sometimes intrafamily disputes become abusive and violent. Many a time the wife and the children are the victims. In such cases the spouse and her parents and relatives can seek legal arbitration. Among most ethnic groups in Sierra Leone, local courts tend to favour the husband, because typically these courts are run by conservative male elders. The fairness of these local courts, and their relevance to contemporary African society, needs to be interrogated.

The Role of Indigenous African Mediators

Olusegun Obasanjo, president of Nigeria and now chairman of the African Leadership Forum, suggests that 'a corps of [African] mediators be developed to anticipate and defuse potential conflicts' (Prendergast, 1996: 89). Such a corps of mediators must utilize the wisdom and expertise of elder stateswomen and men who command high respect, trust, and credibility nationally, regionally, and internationally. 'Other members of civil society [such as] elders and chiefs, merchants, women, indigenous NGOs, youth groups, unions, and others all have roles to play in mediating conflicts' (Prendergast, 1996: 89). This is important because, as Zartman (1991: 311) argues, 'mediators tend to function best when they come from the parties' region, although regional identity is open to definition by the parties themselves.' It is high time Africans transformed their 'peacelessness' into a culture of hope and security. They must design, build, and sustain their own 'peaceful' bridges into the future.

The Role of African Spirituality in Peace-Building

African-centred knowledge systems recognize the key place of spirituality in

African peoples' ways of life. According to Dei (1994: 13), 'the African world view is centered around an intimate understanding and appreciation of the relationship between humans, society, and nature.' This refutes Christian and Islamic teachings, which for a long time perceived African forms of worship as superstitious and paganistic. This attitude is changing as Western development 'experts' begin to recognize that development cannot be sustained without a spiritual/religious blessing. As Ryan (1995:49) explains:

> Religion also parallels the process of development in the developing countries through a growing awareness that to be enduring both religious teachings and development strategies need to be integrated within local peoples' cultures, not simply layered on top of local cultural practices or substituted for them. In Africa, for example, theologians and development researchers are presently exploring how to integrate the deep reverence for ancestors and the world of spirits into their Gospel teachings and their development initiatives, respectively. It is, indeed, high time that professionals admit that both Christianity and development processes have been overly Westernized, and have often been blind to significant positive values already existing in local cultures and beliefs.

'To Africans, [therefore,] spirituality permeates all aspects of life [and] since this is a sacred world, reverence for life dictates that everyone act right by each other' (Tedla, 1995: 214). Spirituality plays a central role in transforming improper social behaviour among individuals in society. For example, among the Themne and Limba ethnic groups in Sierra Leone, it is believed that socially unacceptable behaviour (e.g., stealing, rape) by an individual will be punished by illness, bad luck, or some other mishap.

It is important to recognize the role that spirituality plays in promoting peace and harmony among individuals and communities. Among many ethnic groups in West Africa there are beliefs that help protect the environment. For example, the Limba, Themne, Mende, Kuranko, and Loko of Sierra Leone believe that certain big trees host ancestral spirits. These trees are protected by the community, and it is a crime to destroy them by any means. Western civilization often dismisses such beliefs as superstitions, but beliefs such as these are relevant to the need to sustain the environment.

The Role of Traditional Symbols, Proverbs, Stories, Folklore, and Songs

In traditional African societies, symbols, proverbs, stories, folklore, and songs play a significant role in sustaining peace and transforming conflicts. Their relevance and effectiveness in 'the structural transformation of [African societies]' (Dahrendorf, 1972: 62) needs to be explored. The following examples illustrate some of these cultural norms. From time immemorial, humankind has used symbols as means of communication and social control. Among the Limba in Sierra Leone, for example, the *ragbele* (a bundle of oil palm fronds wrapped with wild ferns) is an important symbol used in settling land disputes. When two parties dispute over the ownership, control, or use of a particular parcel of land, the members of the *gbangbani* secret society (an exclusively male society) intervene by placing the *ragbele* at a strategic place on the disputed land for all disputants to see. This ritual gesture is a means of suspending the right of ownership and use of the disputed parcel by any of the disputants until the conflict is resolved through mediation and reconciliation. Similarly, among the Themne ethnic group in Sierra Leone, members of the male-dominated *poro* secret society erect a *poro* (a pole with raffia palm fronds tied around its tip) on the disputed parcel until the disputants reach a consensus (through the arbitration of the elders of the *poro* society and other local authorities).

The cola nut is another symbol used to communicate with the ancestors. In many African societies it performs myriad functions. For example, during traditional marriages in Sierra Leone, most ethnic groups (e.g., Limba, Mende, Themne, Loko, Fullah, Susu, Mandingo, Kono) use cola nuts as part of the dowry. These nuts are also exchanged as gifts by both sets of parents and relatives to symbolize peace and harmony among them. Chinua Achebe notes in *Things Fall Apart* (1958) that Nigerians, for example, believe that 'he [or she] who brings cola, brings life.' The exchange of the cola nut, as a sign of peaceful living and reconciliation among disputants, is very common among the diverse ethnic groups of West Africa. Among most ethnic groups in Sierra Leone (e.g., the Themne and Limba), items such as knives, needles, and razor blades are not sold or loaned at night in rural areas/villages. This is a way of preventing them from being used violently.

It is essential that Africans rediscover the significance and relevance of traditional symbols as means for reducing conflicts. 'We need to reach back into our past and take with us all that works and is positive' (Tedla, 1995: 1).

Proverbs, Stories/Folklore and Songs

According to Boadu (1985: 83), 'oral art embraces all the activities that depend on the spoken word for transmitting important messages to collectivity and, more important, for maintaining societal continuity from one generation to another.' In most of rural Africa, especially where formal education has had the least impact, oral art remains the most important means for transmitting traditional knowledge and skills from one generation to the next. Proverbs, stories, folklore, and songs, for example, are part and parcel of most of Africans' way of life. However, Boadu (1985) observes that oral art is one of the African traditional institutions that have fallen victim to modern technology. Any initiatives aimed at contributing to the mediation and transformation of African conflicts must acknowledge the importance and unique contributions of traditional methods of oral transmission.

Implications of Peace Research and Advocacy in African Development

Peace research and advocacy has a variety of political and socioeconomic implications for sustainable development in Africa. For example, an inquiry into the causes of civil wars in Africa has national as well as international political implications. It is obvious that the industrialized nations through their multinational corporations are implicated in any inquiry into this process; as are the corrupt and despotic African leaders the continent has produced since independence. Citing the Horn of Africa, Prendergast (1996: 16) provides some useful insights: 'Many commentators trace the region's conflicts to tribal or religious differences. In fact, the socio-economic roots of modern-day violence lie to a large degree in the policies of the region's former British and Italian colonial administration, and the monarchy that ruled Ethiopia until the downfall of Emperor Haile Selassie of Ethiopia in 1974.'

The mass production of weapons of unthinkable destruction by the industrialized countries is another case in point. Thus, Prendergast (17) argues: 'Local mediation [in Africa] has traditionally been a means of resolving disputes over access to resources. With the advent of extremely destructive modern weapons and their easy accessibility, local disputes often escalate into civil wars, which are cynically exploited by outside interests.'

Broad-based and context-specific approaches to peace studies can be empowering, as they enable participants to articulate their lived experiences of 'peacelessness' and to take action to transform social injustices. In addition, peace research challenges the legitimacy of dominant groups' control of knowledge production. It also critiques the imbalances in how power and wealth are distributed among members of a particular society and between the countries of the South and the North. However, this process of social transformation challenges the status quo, and in so doing can lead to a backlash and further oppression.

Peace studies need to critically examine gender and power relations and challenge patriarchal structures in order to provide a space for women's inner voices. Such an approach has both socioeconomic and political implications, in that peace research can create opportunities for women and other oppressed groups to determine their own future destinies and to fight for the means to realize their fullest potential. Against this background, Ihejirika (1997: 106) comments: 'In order to create the appropriate conditions for this type of change to occur, enormous resources would be required for effective local capacity building. African peace educators cannot achieve this alone. A much wider and deeper collaboration between foreign and local resources needs to be established.'

Such collaboration must be built on mutual respect and trust, and on equal power relationships. It should be perceived as an opportunity for the North and the South to learn from each other's historical and cultural experiences. It would require the North to abandon its economic, political, cultural, educational, and religious dominance and to change its racist attitudes and policies toward the South. It would also require countries in the South, particularly African countries, to establish more democratic institutions, improve their human rights records, maintain political accountability and transparency, and ensure judicious management of their human and nonhuman resources. Unfortunately, the constant military coups in some African countries make it almost impossible to realize such democratic values. I therefore contend that Africa's political leadership must show more integrity and loyalty, as well as a stronger commitment to improve the quality of life of its peoples.

Conclusion

Indigenous African peace research initiatives 'must [therefore] speak to the social, spiritual, cultural, economic, [environmental], [gender], political and cosmological aspects of society' (Dei, 1993: 19). Such initiatives must be grounded in the positive historical realities of Africa's peoples. 'One area which served as an important educational vehicle for youth in traditional Africa and still does, is the area of oral literature' (Boateng, 1996: 111). Peace research should examine and evaluate the role that cultural symbols and oral traditions play in nurturing harmony among people and between people and their nonhuman environment.

'As African peoples struggle today to reproduce their lives and livelihoods, they must recover, reclaim and reconstitute aspects of their indigenous traditions and collective historical past' (Dei, 1994: 9). African peace researchers must seize this challenge by pursuing participatory peace studies that will empower indigenous African populations to become their own peacemakers and peacekeepers.

It has been argued that peace research in Africa has many political and socioeconomic implications. However, the growing 'popular desire for democratization in Africa' (Ihejirika, 1997) cannot be realized without a critical analysis of the root causes of the 'peacelessness' that is eroding the fabric of contemporary Africa. I conclude by calling for peace research to be an integral part of the process of rejuvenating the African continent.

REFERENCES

Achebe, C. 1958. *Things Fall Apart.* London: Heinemann.
African Association for Literacy and Adult Education, 1996. *The 1996 Programme of Activities: Peace Education, Human and Peoples Rights Programmes.* Nairobi: AALAE.
Assefa, H. 1993. *Peace and Reconciliation as a Paradigm: A Philosophy of Peace and Its Implications on Conflict, Governance and Economic Growth in Africa.* Nairobi: Nairobi Peace Initiative.
Boadu, S.O. 1985. 'African Oral Artistry and the New Social Order.' In M.K. Asante and A.W. Asante (Eds.), *African Culture: The Rhythms of Unity.* Toronto: Africa World Press.
Boateng, F. 1996. 'African Traditional Education: A Tool For International Communication.' In Asante, M.K. and K.W. Asante (Eds.), *African Culture: The Rhythms of Unity* (3rd ed.). Toronto: Africa World Press.
Bozeman, A.B. 1976. *Conflict in Africa: Concepts and Realities.* New Jersey: Princeton University Press.
Brock-Utne, B. 1987. *Educating for Peace: A Feminist Perspective.* (2nd ed.). New York: Pergamon Press.
Colorado School Mediation Project. 1994. *Alternative to Violence: A Two-Part Program on Conflict Resolution, Negotiation & Mediation.* Niles (IL): United Learning.
Dahrendorf, R. (1972). 'Authority Structure and Class Conflict.' In J. Lopreato and L.E. Hazelrigg (Eds.), *Class, Conflict, and Mobility: Theories and Studies of Class Structure.* San Francisco: Chandler Publishing.
De Bono, E. 1985. *Conflicts: A Way Better to Resolve Them.* Great Britain: European Music Ltd.
Dei, S.G. 1994. Afrocentricity: A Cornerstone of Pedagogy. *Anthropology & Education Quarterly* 25(1): 3–28.
– 1993. Towards an African View of Development. *Focus Africa* November–March: 17–19.
Evangelista, S. 1997. Women in Peacemaking: Inner Voices and Outer Positions. *Canadian Journal of Peace Studies* 29(1): 1–24.
Galtung, J. 1975. *Peace, Research, Education, Action: Essays in Peace Research.* Volume I. Copenhagen: Christian Ejlers.

Gberie, L. 1997. Available E-mail: gber0419@machl.wlu.ca. Paper on Women ...

Handa, M. L. 1992. *Manifesto for a Peaceful World: Beyond Capitalism and Socialism – The Cosmic Way Paradigm* (2nd ed.). Toronto: Cosmic Way Publications.

Himes, J.S. 1980. *Conflict and Conflict Management.* Athens: University of Georgia Press.

Ihejirika, S. I. 1997. The Challenges for Peace Education in Post-Cold War Africa. *Canadian Journal of Peace Studies* 29(1): 100–12.

Kekkonen, Helena. 1981. *Peace Education.* Helsinki: Finnish Adult Education Association.

Kisembo, P. 1993. *A Popular Version of Yash Tandon's Militarism and Peace Education in Africa.* Nairobi: African Association for Literacy and Adult Education.

Kroma, S. 1995. Popularizing Science Education in Developing Countries Through Indigenous Knowledge. *Indigenous and Development Monitor* 3(3): 13–15.

Mies, M., and V. Shiva. 1993. *Ecofeminism.* Halifax: Fernwood Publications.

O'Connel, J. 1989. 'Meanings, Strategies and Structures: Another Look at Non-Violent Force and Violence.' In A.R. Hinde and D.A. Parry, 1989, *Education for Peace.* Nottingham: Spokesman.

Pelton, L.H. 1974. *The Psychology of Nonviolence.* New York: Pergamon Press.

Prendergast, J. 1996. *Crisis and Hope in Africa.* Toronto: Inter-Church Group Center of Concern.

Report of the Voice of Women Roundtable: Culture of Peace. 1997. Toronto. January.

Ryan, W.F. 1995. *Culture, Spirituality, and Economic Development: Opening a Dialogue.* Ottawa: IDRC.

Stedman, S.J. 1991. 'Conflict and Conflict Resolution in Africa: A Conceptual Framework.' In F.M. Deng and I.W. Zartman, (Eds.), *Conflict Resolution in Africa.* Washington: The Brookings Institution.

Tandon, Y. 1989. *Militarism and Peace Education in Africa: A Guide and Manual for Peace Education and Action in Africa.* Nairobi: African Association for Literacy and Adult Education.

Tedla, E. 1995. *Sankofa: African Thought and Education.* New York: Peter Lang.

Zartman, I.W. 1991. 'Conflict Reduction: Prevention, Management, and Resolution.' In F.M. Deng and I.W. Zartman (Eds.), *Conflict Resolution in Africa.* Washington: The Brookings Institution.

16

Mpambo,[1] the African Multiversity: A Philosophy to Rekindle the African Spirit

PAUL WANGOOLA[2]

In the Beginning

For millennia, African communities were guided and driven by a world view and value system at the centre of which was a closely intertwined trinity of forces, values, and considerations. The trinity consisted of spirituality, development, and politics, with spirituality forming the base and controlling and informing everything that happened in the realm of development and politics.

In the African world view, social life was dominated by spirituality, following which there was some development and a little politics. At the centre of African spirituality was the unshakable belief that humans were but a weak link in the vast chain of nature, which encompassed the many animals, plants, birds, insects, and worms, and indeed inanimate things such as stones and rocks. The world was not for conquering, but for living within adorant harmony and reverence. According to African spirituality, *being* is the perpetual flow of energy among animate and inanimate things and between all of these and the gods.

African spirituality has these essential notions:

- Harmony.
- The sanctity of nature.
- Humans are part of rather that apart from nature and are the most vulnerable link in the vast chain of nature. The Earth is not for them to conquer and subdue, but their mother to live with in harmony and reverence.
- Human beings are not here in transit to elsewhere – for example, to heaven or hell. The Earth is the only abode in perpetuity for the living, for the dead, and for those yet unborn. For this reason human beings have a perpetual and active interest in the well-being of the Earth.

- God is revealed simultaneously to all peoples of the world.
- Collective identities include collective self-reliance and the brotherhood/sisterhood of humans, animals, plants, insects, and so on.

People sustain themselves through and draw their strength from the free, friendly, collaborative, and reciprocal flow of energy among themselves, their family, their clan, and their community; the dead and the yet unborn; the animals (domestic and wild), plants, rocks, and so on; and ultimately the gods. You do not kill any animal except in self-defence, or to provide food for immediate sustenance, or as sacrifice. Even then at these times you carry out a ceremony to apologize to the animal family and the gods and to ask for their understanding.

The African system of totems illustrates clearly the close relationship between humans, animals, and plants. For example, members of a clan whose totem is the buffalo do not eat this animal, nor do they sit on its skin or wear buffalo leather or do any harm to the beast. The clan members consider the buffalo their brother or sister. They believe also that the buffalo reciprocates this relationship and thus does not trample the food crops of its brothers and sisters. In many African communities (before commoditization), the cleansing ceremony carried out for someone who killed a human being, even if by accident, was the same as the one carried out for killing the big cats: the lion and leopard.

The notion of kinship with animals and plants was so deeply ingrained among the people that I remember as a little boy growing up on the plains of Busoga, Uganda, being troubled for days when I accidentally killed an ant. We suppose that the drive toward good-neighbourliness with fellow humans and animals alike stemmed from the theological teaching that the Earth is our only abode. As there was no heaven or hell to escape to, we were all destined to be together in perpetuity. Good-neighbourliness was extended to the Earth, in that the soil was treated as a deposit account from which the depositors (people) drew for consumption only part of the accumulated interest, without ever touching the principal.

Post-Industrial Revolution Europe Meets Africa

Such was Africa's world view and development paradigm at the turn of the last century, when she came face-to-face with a Europe bent at colonizing her. When they could not hold or turn the tide, the African wise women and men decided on a tactical retreat: to send the second or third best sons and daughters to study the ways of the colonizer, and that way gather information and intelligence to inform subsequent battles against the occupying force. Children were sent to school not to abandon the African ways of life, but rather to better equip themselves and their communities to defend the African heritage and sovereignty. But many of the youths assigned espionage tasks ended up following the colonizer. Over time these same people assumed leadership positions. As a result, Africa's conquest gathered momentum and depth; increasingly, the continent was sucked into the Western world outlook and the modernization development paradigm.

The modernization development paradigm, whether of the capitalist or socialist variety, tended to regard comfort, well-being, and material and capital acquisition as the central goals of life. Thus poverty was perceived to be the central enemy, and development its antidote. Democracy (politics) was supposed to provide an enabling environment, without which poverty could not be rolled back by development. In all this, spirituality was assigned quite clearly a secondary or even tertiary role.

Thus, in the trinity of spirituality, development, and politics, *politics* rather than spirituality formed the base. Everyday life came to be dominated by politics; this allowed for a little indigenous development as well as some spirituality.

The Struggle for Independence

Across the African continent, colonialism applied a variety of methods to subdue the African peoples. These included:

- Brute force.
- Granting corruptive advantages and privileges – for example, land and jobs – to a select few.
- Undermining African values, ceremonies, festivals, and so on through the churches and schools, and through legislation and local administration.
- Persecuting, suppressing, and exterminating priests of African religions and their institutions.
- Breaking up African institutional governance.
- Disrupting of African commerce, industry, and technology.
- Imposing capitalist production relations and confiscating lands, thereby forcing Africans to work as farm, mine, and factory labourers. Thousands were employed as blue-collar workers in the government and the private sector.

The colonizer's methods fragmented the African peoples along the following lines: the workers; the petty bourgeoisie and intellectuals; the traders; the leaders of the various indigenous establishments (for example, the chiefs, healers, priests, midwives, musicians, and artists); and by far the largest group, the peasants.

These class and social interests first spontaneously and later deliberately tried to organize themselves to press for their specific interests; but they quickly realized that under colonialism, social progress was not possible. This realization led to the different sectors forging a united front that was opposed to colonialism. The nationalist movement was thereby created. The unity of African nationalism was strengthened by the fact that the colonial economy had not completely divorced the people from the land that nourished their world view and values. The overwhelming majority of African people, including the leaders of the various social and political movements, were still tied to the land and to this world view.

The first generation of African leaders who resisted colonization (Samori Toure, Shaka Zulu, Kabalega, and their ilk) wanted to preserve a form of sovereignty based on African values and governance; however, those who followed them focused on the colonial state. It was argued that once the colonial state was captured and run by the Africans, a few reforms would be enough to turn it into an instrument that would serve the interests of Africa's peoples. Unfortunately, these leaders also came to embrace the modernization development paradigm.

Facing the Future with Hope and Confidence

For Africa, the 1960s were a time of high hopes – for democracy, national unity, national sovereignty, social progress, pan-African unity, and solidarity with Third World peoples. The instrument with which the African leaders (and to some extent peoples) expected to achieve their objectives was basically the modernization development paradigm, which embraced either capitalism or socialism or a 'creative blend' of the two. Four basic notions informed the modernization development paradigm:

- Development involved becoming like someone else – which until recently meant catching up with the West (via capitalism) or the East (via socialism). In both options, the African world view was increasingly looked upon by the 'international community' and African leaders as a 'backward impediment' that had to be done away with in order to pave the way for 'modernization.'
- In matters of 'modernization' and 'progress' there was only one knowledge, *Western* knowledge. Other knowledges were branded as inferior or pure

ignorance. Thus, African medicine became witchcraft; African religions, animism; agricultural science, subsistence agriculture; and so on.

- To achieve development, leadership had to be in the hands of carefully deculturalized Africans supervised by experts from the North, who were able to achieve a complete rupture with communal cultures.
- Foreign aid was essential to development. By the mid-1980s it did not matter which approach a country had opted for or was caught up in: Africa had been brought virtually to its knees by a series of mutually reinforcing crises and disasters including poverty, debt, instability, internal strife, interstate wars, civil wars, wars of liberation, leaderlessness, drought, famine, and floods. The situation was so dire that the United Nations in 1986 convened a special session of its General Assembly on what it termed 'the critical social and economic situation in Africa.'

Questioning Old Assumptions, Searching for New Solutions

Around the time of the special session of the UN General Assembly, a number of African leaders of civil society organizations (CSOs) examined what had gone wrong. A major handicap in this inquiry was that African leaders of CSOs had no real forum for systematically inquiring into substantive African issues. But events moved fast. In the 1980s and 1990s the Soviet Union and Soviet Bloc began their rapid though fairly peaceful disintegration. This event brought with it many epochal developments, questions, challenges, and uncertainties for Africa. It became urgent that Africa systematically analyze the new situation in order to plan its survival in the emerging new world order.

In 1991, with the support of the Canadian International Development Agency (CIDA), the African Association for Literacy and Adult Education (AALAE), the Centre for Community Studies and Development (CENOSAD), and the Organization of Rural Associations for Progress (ORAP) co-sponsored an African forum where participants could reflect on the African condition. This gathering brought together leaders of African NGOs and CSOs and development activists of different social backgrounds and political persuasions. They considered the nature of the post–Cold War era; and analyzed what future the emerging world order held in store for Africa, as well as the future that Africa's peoples held for their continent – a future that lay in the lap of African civil society. At the meeting it was concluded that the way forward for Africa's peoples lay in popular self-reliance founded on bottom-up initiatives for creating a new economy centred on communities, and that the creation and renewal of popular knowledge would be critical to this effort. This reflection initiated several follow-up forums and initiatives.

The first forum requested that I co-ordinate follow-up action. To push forward the outcomes of that first forum, a second forum convened in 1993 focused on 'Gender, Culture, and the African Family.' This forum concluded that for African peoples to regain the initiative, it would be essential for them to endogenously develop and institute an educational system centred around the community. After 1993 the leaders continued to consult by mail and around other events. In 1994 a task force was established to continue the systematic study and analysis that had begun in 1991.

The Findings

The process outlined above resulted in the following being judged the main reasons or 'disconnects' to explain Africa's predicament.

Disconnect No. 1

For millennia, African communities were held together by a trinity of closely intertwined forces. As mentioned in the introduction to this chapter, this trinity consisted of *spirituality*, *development*, and *politics*, with *spirituality* forming the base. In this world outlook, the purpose of life was harmony and balance with all existence: with the living and the dead, with nature, and with the gods. People were part of nature; the Earth was not for conquest and subjugation but for living with in harmony.

Under the Western development paradigm, Africa was increasingly sucked into modernization development models in which the acquisition of capital and material goods was the purpose of life, and other people and the planet itself were to be exploited to that end. Humans were in transit to heaven or hell, after which they would have no need for the Earth.

In Africa, the modernization development paradigm was translated into a trinity where there was little 'development' (as defined by modernization theory) and where spirituality, respect for nature, and living in harmony with the environment were relegated to secondary importance, with politics as the real force. It is not surprising that modern politics in Africa, having been divorced from nature, has been unstable and unreliable. The African general public views politics to be nothing but *pokopoko*, an art of conmanship.[3]

Disconnect No. 2

The second disconnect was (as also mentioned earlier) the conception that 'development,' and 'progress' meant 'becoming like someone else.'[4] Africa's history, culture, religion, clothes, food, architecture, names, music, and so on were 'backward impediments' to be systematically erased to pave the way for 'modernization.' In the colonial scheme, leadership was placed in the hands of carefully deculturalized Africans working in close concert with experts from the North – sometimes under their supervision. The resulting rupture with the communal cultures was considered vital to development, as was foreign aid.

Thus for Africa, the concept of 'development' as a process meant that 'progress' did not start from people's lives but from the 'experts' and others they wished to be like. It did not seek to make people better by starting from who they were historically and culturally; rather it set out to demean and erode their heritage. The result was the removal of initiative and leadership from the people and the creation of a frightening dependency in all human endeavours.

Disconnect No. 3

Before modernization, community power was exercised by wise women and men. People were considered wise when they became so knowledgeable and skilled in one or more aspects of social endeavour that they were recognized as compelling experts. However, just as the sun at dawn does not announce its rise, the birds do that, the wise do not announce themselves or campaign to be wise people – the community confers this title over time. Yet to be wise is not merely to be expert – it also means that the individual's outlook, understanding, opinions, and so on are not coloured or compromised by the partisan interests of only the familyor the clan; rather, that person's thoughts, intentions, and deeds are driven by the good of the community, and not only for today but also in perpetuity. In this context, community means the living, the unborn, the dead, and nature as a whole. The wise do not charge for their wise counsel, as they engage in productive activities for their livelihood. A wise person also encourages and works for the peaceful resolution of differences between and among people. The wise bring people together for these purposes.

As a result of the sometimes brutal and sometimes subtle and sustained attacks against African communal cultures, many African peoples and their leaders have succumbed to individualism and consumerism. Today it is common for modern African leaders to pursue individual, short-term interests at the expense of the common good. As well, a growing number of African leaders, at various levels, are proud not to be fluent in their own people's language and not to eat or drink their food or dress like them.

All of this has weakened both ordinary people and their leaders. The people are weaker because they lack good leaders, while the leaders are denied the support and strength of the community.

Disconnect No. 4

Most African communities have lost their old forums for systematically consolidating their knowledge base and for generating new knowledge. Those who do not generate their own knowledge, or fail to keep abreast of developments in their own areas of specialization, in time become unable to grasp and apply the knowledge and skills generated by others.

Just as no company can survive in this competitive world without an R&D program, African communities cannot hope to survive without building endogenous processes for creating, improving and advancing knowledge on the basis of their existing knowledge.

Strategic Challenges to African Civil Society

The above disconnects, alone or in mutually reinforcing combinations, have weakened Africa's civil society at many levels. For example, about fifty years ago the Gikuyu people of Kenya were able to organize the Mau Mau uprising against white occupation basically because they were united, as children of the soil, by a common world outlook. They had a common God (Ngai), common aspirations, and acknowledged leadership. A village could therefore assemble, speak with one voice, and make momentous decisions of life and death. Today the same village would find it virtually impossible to re-enact such a scenario. Communities have become strongly factionalized, and much competition and rivalry and animosity have been introduced. For example, families have been uprooted from their land and dispossessed and scattered. Communities are divided by Christianity and Islam. It is normal, for example, for a village of 3,000 people to have ten Christian denominations, all at each other's throats. Individual families are split along religious and denominational lines, and political factions are in disagreement. As well, there are people whose livelihood is linked to the soil and those who are divorced from it, people who are culturally diluted and those who are still culturally rooted, and so on.

Mpambo, the African Multiversity: A Strategic Response by African Communities

To respond to the strategic challenges and questions of our time, African communities need a long-term vision and a plan of action. The goal should be to put people and the Earth once again at the centre so that on the basis of their social capital built up over thousands of years, communities will be able to exercise their sovereignty and again become self-organizing and self-directing. The entry point for all this is the ancient tradition whereby community power and authority are exercised by the wise men and women. The idea here is to set up some appropriate institutional space for communities to sow, cultivate, and harvest knowledge and wisdom under the leadership of the wise. This space will be a centre for reflection, higher learning, and training to heal and strengthen civil society. This institutional space will be called Mpambo, the African Multiversity. It will be a centre for all wise people who want to improve their knowledge in matters that are at the frontiers of knowledge in their respective areas of specialization. Here they will be able to reflect on, study, and investigate their specialties at a high level of sophistication, and meet regularly with their peers. These wise women and men will be senior community 'professors' dedicated to consolidating and advancing the African knowledge base for the purpose of solving contemporary problems. In the main they will be mother-tongue philosophers who do not speak or think in 'hard currency' languages. Mpambo Multiversity will be a community knowledge bank from which the community and others can draw on the basis of need.

Mpambo, the African Multiversity, is premised on the idea that knowledge and skills are concrete, as well as specific to particular ecological, cultural, and historical settings. Since several ecological/cultural regions do exist, it follows that there are as many ecological/cultural knowledges. Just as biodiversity is essential to secure the vitality of each species and of nature as a whole, a broad spectrum of eco-cultural knowledges will secure the vitality of each knowledge as well as the vitality and dynamism of human knowledge as a whole. For this to happen, each community needs to deepen its own knowledge base. Having done so, each community will appreciate other communities' knowledges, and understand its own limitations, and thus learn from others while contributing to others' knowledge.

A *multi*versity differs from a *uni*versity insofar as it recognizes that the existence of alternative knowledges is important to human knowledge as a whole. Yet another important reason to establish an African Multiversity is that the problems facing humankind today cannot be resolved by modern scientific knowledge alone, or by indigenous knowledge alone. More durable solutions will be found in new synthesis between indigenous knowledges and modern scientific knowledge. The need for a new synthesis between these two is highlighted by the current acceptance that the problems we face today are such that neither the public sector (government), nor the private sector (business), nor civil society alone has comprehensive and durable solutions. It is through imaginative collaboration between these three sectors that societies will be able to conceptualize and organize sustainable solutions.

To be an effective centre for articulating of a new knowledge synthesis, Mpambo will welcome and work with scholars in the modern scientific sector who are wise in the sense that they too are committed to the search for a new synthesis. The guiding principle behind Mpambo is that being rooted in their own knowledge bases, people can engage in dialogue, synthesis, articulation, partnership, collaboration, the building of synergies, and cross-fertilization; all of this across sectors, knowledges, cultures, and civilizations.

The Philosophical Foundations, Principles, and Attributes of Mpambo

1 Mpambo is a world outlook, a philosophy, a spirit, a process, an institution, and a movement. It is a search for an endogenous African pedagogy rooted in African indigenous pedagogy. It is a popular search for education rooted in Africa's history, culture, values, and world outlook. It utilizes the continent's human and natural resources for the political, economic, social, cultural, philosophical, scientific, and technological advancement of Africa's peoples. It is the search for the African Renaissance.

2 Mpambo is a philosophy. We believe in ourselves and in what we have, and this is the starting point for moving forward.

3 Mpambo is founded on the unity-in-diversity of Africa's peoples. Its activities therefore are locally executed to achieve pan-African objectives and purposes.

4 Mpambo is an education-cum-development ideology that utilizes people's heritage and creative energies to promote their own development. It is therefore founded on the ethic of voluntary service and sacrifice.

5 Mpambo promotes people-initiated, people-centred, and people-led development. It is a centre for articulating and refining indigenous and endogenous ideas for development. Each individual constitutes a basis for mobilizing and harnessing endogenous energies. Mpambo thus is a popular movement – a forum for individuals, groups, institutions, and other parties interested in promoting African thought and development.

6 Mpambo is replicable and sustainable wherever Africans are. It is thus capable of generating energies and synergies on the continent and globally.

7 Mpambo is a living symbol of the true African spirit, identity, and consciousness, and of the commitment to diversity in nature and in social life.

8 Mpambo is liberative but peaceful.

9 Mpambo is pluralist and is open to all knowledges, but it is rooted in African thought and knowledge. It is the basis for reaching out to and interfacing with other peoples and their knowledges.

10 Mpambo's future shall be ensured through intergenerational harmony and systematic succession.

Some Aspects of African Values, Philosophy, and Outlook

- In the beginning there was chaos (matter) and, later on, God.
- The interests of the individual are subordinate to the community.
- Time is an elastic resource to be managed by women and men; they are masters of time.
- God is simultaneously revealed to all peoples of the world.
- Many Gods are better than one.
- Humans are part of nature. The Earth is not for them to conquer but to live in in adoration, harmony, and reverence.
- The devil cannot be destroyed. We have to perpetually negotiate with him for coexistence.
- The Earth is a place of abode of the dead, the living, and the yet unborn.
- Avoid war at all costs. If you must fight, fight to render the enemy harmless but not to destroy or annihilate him.
- The purpose of a fight is to establish who is stronger. For that reason, unequals do not fight, and the stronger never attacks the weaker. The strongest never fight. They train others to become as strong.
- The African works to live. She/he does not live to work.

Broad Objectives

Mpambo has four broad objectives:

- To liberate and rekindle the African spirit, and to promote popular endogenous initiatives rooted in the African knowledge base so as to enhance people's sovereignty.
- To provide an appropriate space for those most gifted in indigenous knowledge and skills to advance and deepen that knowledge and those skills, and to articulate a new synthesis between African indigenous knowledges and other knowledges.
- To halt the erosion of African collective identities.
- To connect with peoples outside Africa, and with their thought and knowledges.

The Scientific Basis for the Multiversity

Scientific research is currently preoccupied with preserving indigenous seeds and plants, and in fact all biodiversity. Many genetic and seed banks have been set up, and many of these are testimony to indigenous scientific research. If to face the future with more confidence we need seed and genetic banks, it is quite clear that we would further enhance our confidence if we maintained live indigenous knowledge banks as well.

Fields of Activity

Mpambo will focus on generating, organizing, and imparting socially relevant knowledge and skills.

Reflection and Research

Mpambo will help the wise strengthen their contacts, endeavours, and advances. It will facilitate individual and joint initiatives at the highest levels of learning as well as interactions among those dedicated to creating an inventory of advanced research to widen the frontiers of an indigenous African knowledge base. For an individual to participate at this level, proof of competence in the field of interest will need to be proven based on peer and community recognition. Those who want to learn with such researchers will be invited to be their assistants after demonstrating a minimum amount of knowledge, competence, and interest in the relevant field.

The researchers will disseminate the outcomes of their endeavours through print and nonprint media, seminars, conferences, public lectures, and the like.

Education and Training

Mpambo will not have teachers or professors in the sense of persons who teach what they do not practice. Instead, Mpambo will have tutors who can successfully perform the activities associated with their area of specialization and who have demonstrated their willingness and ability to share what they know. They will offer personal tutorship to their students in specific fields, which will have been socially determined. Requirements for students will include the following: interest; initial competence (i.e., a set of aptitudes and skills demonstrated in theory and practice); and community support. Formal schooling will not be a prerequisite for enrolment.

Mpambo's program will focus on the following thematic areas: spirituality; leadership; community governance; collaborative partnerships with the state, the private sector, and civil society; conflict, management; roles and responsibilities in families and communities; agricultural science; health; games and sports; and music, dance, and drama.

Dissemination and Networking

Dissemination and networking will be achieved through print, nonprint, and electronic media, through public and special lectures, through seminars and courses, and through exchanges, secondments, partnerships, and joint initiatives.

Conclusion

It is proposed to have the first campus of Mpambo in Jinja, Uganda, at the source of the Nile; and the second one in Bulawayo, Matebeleland, in Zimbabwe. It will take a great deal of consultation and planning on the ground to translate the idea of Mpambo, the African Multiversity, into a practical reality. The greatest challenge will be to mobilize resources and support among communities across the African continent, to ensure that development funding does not drain the life and vibrancy from this initiative.

NOTES

1 After the harvest the mother selects the best seeds for careful and safe keeping for planting the next season. Thereafter permission is given to eat the rest. In the Lusoga language of Uganda, *mpambo* means the best of the seeds that are kept away for propagation.

2 Paul Wangoola is the Nabyama of Mpambo, the African Multiversity. *Nabyama* means the one who is entrusted with all the community's strategic secrets, for use for the progress and advancement of the community – one who can never divulge the secrets of the community to strangers and enemies.

3 *Pokopoko* in Lusoga-Luganda means the practice by Africans of the white man's politics; the art of talking a lot without content, empty talk, unreliable, big public promises to secure public support without any intention of keeping any of them; sweet talk, art of conmanship.

4 Development as the process of becoming like someone else was such an integral part of the modernization theory that today even the former Soviet Bloc aspires to be like the United States of America!

Contributors

Sandra S. Awang is a writer and teacher. She is engaged in popularizing issues related to food and water security, intellectual property rights, genetic engineering, biodiversity, and biodemocracy.

Marlene Brant Castellano is a member of the Mohawk Nation, Wolf Clan, and Professor Emeritus of Trent University, Peterborough, Ontario. She served as chair of Trent's Department of Native Studies and was a leader in establishing Native Studies as an academic discipline in Canada. Her work has won honours from academic institutions, government agencies, and the aboriginal community. From 1992 to 1995 she was co-director of research for the Royal Commission on Aboriginal Peoples. She resides on Tyendinaga Mohawk Territory with her husband Vincent.

Joseph Couture, a Cree Métis, holds Canadian and American academic degrees. He specializes in educational psychology with an orientation to Native Americans, and clinical psychology with a focus on culturally formed cognitive and identity development and native rehabilitation. He has worked widely in Native Canadian human/cultural development and service delivery. His recent publications have focused on native adult dysfunctional behaviour, multicultural competence, and cross-cultural assessment.

George J. Sefa Dei is a professor and associate chair in the Department of Sociology and Equity, Ontario Institute of Studies in Education of the University of Toronto. He has published widely and is engaged in community activities on issues of antiracism in education. He is also director of the Centre for Integrative Anti-Racism Studies at OISE/UT.

Suzanne Dudziak is a professor of social work at St Thomas University in Fredericton, New Brunswick. With colleagues at the University of Toronto, she is a co-principal investigator of a long-term study evaluating the impact of services sponsored by the Aboriginal Healing and Wellness Strategy. Her background includes extensive work in the fields of community development and social policy.

Patience Elabor-Idemudia is an associate professor of sociology at the University of Saskatchewan. A social activist, she works on social justice, poverty, gender equity, and economic restructuring issues, and immigrant women's experiences in Canada. Her publications include 'Immigrant Women and Employment in Canada: A Situational Analysis' (1996) in L. Clippingdale (Ed.), *Feminist Voices*, and 'The Impact of Structural Adjustment Programs on Women and Their Households in Bendel and Ogun States in Nigeria' (1991) in C. Gladwin (Ed.), *Structural Adjustment and African Women Farmers*.

Budd L. Hall teaches in and heads the Department of Adult Education at OISE/UT. He is prominent in the development of participatory research, which emphasizes the role played by indigenous knowledges and other locally controlled knowledge processes. His research interests include environmental education, global civil society, and the political economy of adult education. A co-editor of *Voices for Change: Participatory Research in Canada and the United States* and author of numerous articles, he worked with the Royal Commission on Aboriginal Peoples in the preparation of the educational guide *For Seven Generations: An Information Legacy*, a CD-ROM (1996).

Leilani Holmes is a professor of Sociology and Cross-Cultural Studies at Grossmont College, San Diego, California. She is a student of *hula kahiko* (ancient hula) and has been active in Hawaiian organizations in Southern California. She has also served on Asian/Pacific Islander Advisory Councils to local and state superintendents of education in California.

Elizabeth McIsaac does community research and advocacy around immigrant and refugee issues. She has done research on antiracism education at OISE/UT and co-authored *Reconstructing Dropout: A Critical Ethnography of the Dynamics of Black Students' Disengagement from School* (1997) with George Dei, Josephine Mazzeca, and Jasmin Zine. She also contributed to the Lake Harbour Archival Photo Collection, a project of the Canadian Heritage Rivers Secretariat (1994).

Njoki Nathani Wane, an assistant professor in the Department of Sociology and Equity Studies at OISE/UT, teaches antiracist education, Black feminist studies, and pre-service education. She is interested in women's issues, and was an active member of the Maasai Women's Group in Kenya promoting indigenous knowledge as a complement to contemporary ways of life in the modern era.

Roxana Ng immigrated to Canada with her family in 1970. Since the mid-1970s she has worked to promote immigrant women as a field of specialization in feminist and immigration scholarship. She writes extensively on sexism, racism, nationalism, and community/state relations, as well as feminist and antiracist teaching. Her publications include *The Politics of Community Services: Immigrant Women, Class, and State* (1988, 1996), and *Anti-racism, Feminism, and Critical Approaches to Education* (1995). She is an associate professor in the adult education department at OISE/UT.

Dorothy Goldin Rosenberg, an education and film consultant on issues of equality, social and environmental justice, peace, and health, has worked with the National Film Board, school boards, and policy groups. She was editor of *Les femmes s'en melent: Making a World of Difference: A Directory of Women in Canada Specializing in Global Issues*, recipient of the Commemorative Medal for the 125th Anniversary of the Confederation of Canada, the Canadian Auto Workers (CAW) Award for Cancer Prevention, and the United Nations Environmental Program Award (UNEP) for Environmental Stewardship. She teaches the OISE/UT Transformative Learning Centre course on environmental health, transformative learning, and policy change. She was principal research consultant and associate producer of the film *Exposure: Environmental Links to Breast Cancer*, and wrote the companion guide *Taking Action for a Healthy Future*.

Vandana Shiva is a physicist, philosopher of science, and feminist. She is the director of the Research Foundation for Science, Technology, and Natural Resource Policy in India and author of *Staying Alive: Women, Ecology, and Development* (1988); *The Violence of the Green Revolution* (1990); *Monocultures of the Mind* (1990); with Maria Mies, *Ecofeminism* (1993), and numerous other publications.

Farah M. Shroff works in the area of social justice and health. An an activist, educator, reseacher, and planner, she has worked in many parts of the world. She edited and contributed to *The New Midwifery: Reflections of Renaissance* *and Regulation.* Her current research focuses on holistic health. She holds an academic appointment at the University of British Columbia, does evaluation research on community health programs, did a regular television spotlight on holistic health issues, and is involved in various social justice issues.

Thomas Mark Turay of Sierre Leone, West Africa, a doctoral candidate in Adult Education at OISE/UT, is former director of Caritas Makeni (Diocesan Catholic Development Office), and managing director (on study leave) of the Centre for Development and Peace Education (CD-PEACE), Sierra Leone. With international and indigenous NGOs in Africa, he has worked on the design, implementation, and evaluation of community development projects. His research interests include peace education and indigenous knowledge technology. He is married and has three daughters.

Paul Wangoola, former secretary general of the African Association for Literacy and Adult Education, is currently the Nabyama of Mpambo, the African multivarsity based in Uganda. He has authored and co-authored several articles and books on a variety of themes, including the political economy of education, civil society, African indigenous knowledge systems, participatory development, multisectoral development partnerships, and North/South development co-operation.

Handel Kashope Wright is associate professor of education at the University of Tennessee, Knoxville, where he teaches cultural studies and urban/ multicultural and antiracist education. He has published widely on African education, educational change in Sierra Leone, African cultural studies, curriculum theory, and the relationship between education and cultural studies.

Printed in the United States
4780